I Never Intended to Be Brave

A Woman's Bicycle Journey Through Southern Africa

by Heather Andersen

MAG MILE BOOKS

WINDY CITY PUBLISHERS   CHICAGO

I Never Intended to Be Brave

Windy City Publishers
2118 S. Plum Grove Rd., #349
Rolling Meadows, IL 60008
www.windycitypublishers.com

Published in the United States of America
10 9 8 7 6 5 4 3 2 1

First Edition: October 2011

Library of Congress Control Number: 2011904847

ISBN: 978-1-935766-15-5

Cover Photo: Heather's Bike Crossing the Zambezi River from Bovu Island, Zambia
Cover and Interior Photographs by Heather Andersen
Cover Design by Heather Andersen
Cover Production by Don Warner, DoubleD Graphics

All maps are courtesy of the State Department and the CIA.
Quote on Page 103: Reproduced with permission from Botswana, ed. 1, Paul Greenway © 2001 Lonely Planet

giving2green
The giving2green symbol on the back cover indicates that the user has committed to giving monies to the many organizations dedicated to the fight against global warming, decreasing greenhouse gas emissions, saving our rainforests and wetlands, and fighting water and air pollution.

Windy City Publishers
Chicago

For Mom and Dad
for "raising me to be a strong, independent woman,"
even if this trip isn't what you had in mind

For Richard
for your support of my taking this trip

To the people of southern Africa
Khotso. Pula. Nala.
Peace. Rain. Prosperity.

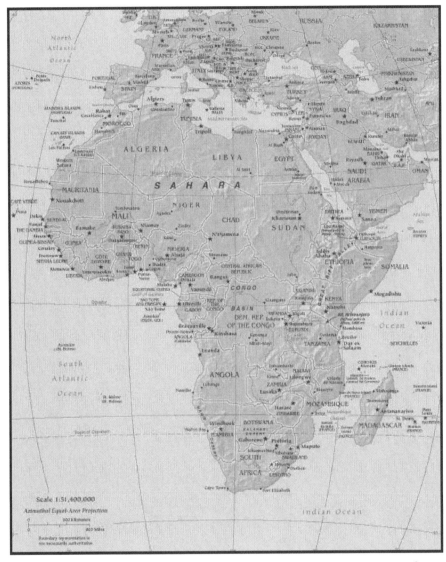

Africa

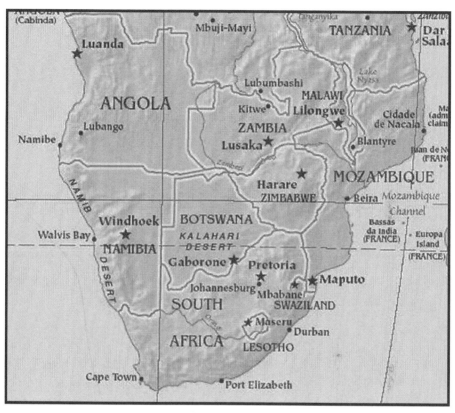

Southern Africa

Contents

Some names have been changed to protect people's privacy.
All characters, events, and places are real as I experienced and remember them;
there are no composites.

All the historical information was true at the time of this trip,
in 2003-4. Some regimes changed prior to publication.

For metric conversions, see the Appendix.

PART ONE

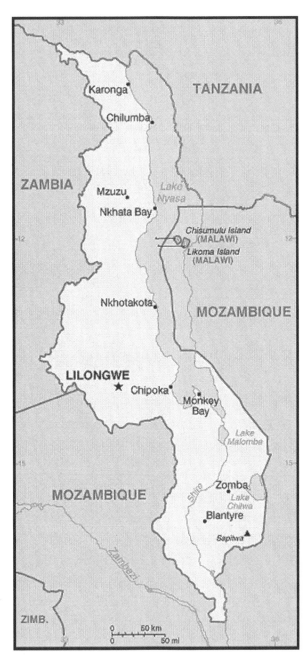

Malawi

Note: Lake Nyasa is now more commonly known as Lake Malawi, and it's referred to as such in the text

chapter one

An Ominous Start

"I want to meet Paul," says Elias again as we get off the plane in Blantyre, Malawi.

"Okay, but I haven't even met him yet," I reply.

I only just met Elias, who is returning home from a military training in South Africa, sitting next to him on the plane. With a ready smile, he wanted to know what was bringing me to his country, the "warm heart of Africa," a phrase I will hear repeated many times over the next few weeks. I explained that I was beginning a three-month bicycle journey here.

"Alone?" he asked.

No. I told him my story: I'd tried to put together a small group through a cycling organization but had found only one person to join me—and would be meeting this person, Paul, for the first time when we landed in Blantyre.

He raised his eyebrows.

African men and women don't travel together unless they are related, and Elias seemed unable to grasp that things were different in other cultures. He was educated and spoke English well. He understood all my words individually, but the concept of traveling with someone I'd met only through email, which he vaguely knew about but had never used, was just too foreign a concept. Throughout the flight, I asked Elias questions about Malawi and asked for his help pronouncing a few basic words of Chewa, the most commonly spoken language in the country. But he kept returning the conversation to my mysterious riding partner and asking me where Paul was. I kept telling him I wasn't sure but he should be on this plane with us.

As we get off the plane, Paul and I are able to identify each other by our carry-on luggage: panniers, or saddlebags, that clip onto a bicycle's rack. He looks like the bad photo on his web site—dark, brown, layered hair with a bit of wave, silver-rimmed rectangular glasses, medium build—but, with hunched shoulders, seems tense, unlike the easygoing guy I'd imagined from our emails. As I walk toward him, I wonder what he's really like? How well do I know him? We introduce ourselves and get in the "foreign passports" line to officially enter Malawi.

At times over the past several months, as I corresponded with people who were interested in joining me, I wondered if this trip was really going to happen. Now I have my answer. Here I am in Malawi, planning to spend the next three months cycling through Malawi, Zambia, Botswana, and Namibia with someone I'm just meeting. Elias' unspoken question, "Why are you traveling with him?" is one I will come to ask myself.

I've just finished my U.S. Peace Corps volunteer service in the tiny southern African country of Lesotho but I'm not ready to return to the U.S. I feel a strong need to see more of southern Africa, a region I was originally drawn to for its mix of culture, wildlife, and scenery. I don't want to return to the U.S. and start characterizing all of Africa as Lesotho. I do want to see more of the continent and understand the differences among the countries.

Contrary to the portrayal of Africa in the media as a war-torn, insect- and disease-infested, poverty-stricken monolith, it's an incredibly diverse continent, with terrain ranging from desert to mountains to rainforest to farmland. Like Europe, there are some similarities from country to country but also vast cultural differences across the continent. In my two years in Africa, I've met Kenya's Masai who still subsist largely on milk and blood, watched Basotho horsemen wearing blankets as coats ride by in Lesotho, sweltered bicycling across the equator in Uganda, been snowed on both in Lesotho and atop Mt. Kilimanjaro, watched a leopard hunt, seen cheetahs lounging under a tree, and met some of the warmest people I've ever known.

Paul is an American from the Chicago area taking a year off work to travel primarily by bicycle. He has already cycled in New Zealand and England on his own, is curious about Africa and wants a cycling partner for this portion of his trip. When we first agreed to do this trip together, we thought it was going to be as a group of three. Then our third person, a woman who'd emailed me that she was definitely committed to the trip, disappeared from contact. I have no idea whether she flaked out or died or what, but it's just Paul and me. We have been corresponding by email for about six months and seem to have similar interests and travel styles.

As we stand in the immigration line in the airport, Elias comes over to introduce himself to Paul. He reiterates an invitation he made to me on the plane to call him when we get to Zomba, where he is stationed, and he will show us around. After meeting Paul, Elias moves over to the more quickly moving "Malawi passports" line.

"Do you want to put the bikes together and ride to Doogles?" I say to Paul after we clear customs. By email, we decided to stay at Doogles, a backpackers' hostel with a camping area, so we'd have a meeting point in case either of us was delayed.

"You mean you want to bike now? From the airport?" He sounds surprised.

"Sure, it's what I usually do on a bike tour. But you've traveled farther than I have to get here. We can find a taxi big enough for our bike boxes if you prefer." As usual for airplane travel, our bikes are partially disassembled in cardboard boxes.

He does, so we find a taxi, or rather one finds us, as several taxi drivers approach us, offering their services. "You need taxi?"

After setting up our tents at Doogles, we sit at thick, wooden tables in their open-air restaurant, order dinner, and talk about the trip. Paul asks me a lot of questions about Africa, including whether I've been sick.

"Not seriously. I had a bad cough during Peace Corps training, a cold or flu-like thing once, and my stomach has been queasy at times, but no awful debilitating illnesses."

"I'm going to eat whatever you eat," he says with a smile but a serious tone.

"Okay, but I'm a vegetarian, so that's what you're committing to." I smile, too.

"Well, maybe I won't eat only whatever you eat."

Two days later, we are on the road.

"How far is it to town?" asks Paul.

"Which town?" replies Herman, whom we've just met.

If I believed in omens, I'd have to say this seems like a bad one. Only a few hours into a three-month bicycle journey, we are already lost—and not simply lost but lost with the sun setting and a broken bicycle.

After taking the obligatory beginning-of-a-long-journey photos, we cycled out of Blantyre, early in the afternoon, staying on the main road south. We were surprised when the road turned from asphalt to dirt. I suspected we might have missed a turn. This road didn't look or feel like a main road—the dirt and lack of traffic made me dubious, but Paul insisted it was. He had asked a local cyclist if we were on the road to Thloyo, and the cyclist had responded, "yes." In Africa, however, yes is frequently the right answer to give a foreigner. Tell him what he wants to hear, the thinking goes—don't be the one to disappoint him.

If yes had been the honest answer, though, we should be only a few kilometers from Thloyo, a sizeable enough dot on our map to be able to count on finding accommodation, when we stop by the side of the road because Paul's rear wheel isn't spinning as freely as it should.

While he's working on his bike, a short but stout, bearded, white South African in a small white truck stops to ask if we are okay. Herman introduces himself and we learn from him that we are definitely not on the road to Thloyo. We are on a backroad to Mulanje. We accidentally left the main road when it veered right and we stayed straight. This explains why the road we are on turned to dirt. We hadn't missed a sign; there wasn't one. If there had been, it should have read "Welcome to Africa, where logic does not always prevail."

Herman works at a road camp just off this road a few kilometers back. He tells us we're about thirty kilometers from a town in both directions on this road. Paul thinks he can eventually fix his bike but we're running out of daylight. I ask Herman if the road camp has anywhere we can spend the night.

"No," he quickly replies.

"What about somewhere we can set up our tents?"

"No, definitely not."

His abruptness shocks me. Africans are generally much more hospitable than this.

Camping along the side of the road without enough food or extra water is not an appealing option, especially for our first night on the road, but what choice do we have? No other people or villages are in sight, and no one else has passed since we stopped. Herman says maybe he could give us a lift to one of the towns but he has to check with his boss first. Paul thinks he might have to return to Blantyre to get a bike part anyway. Herman drives off to check, promising to return soon. Paul stares down at his bike in frustration, but I am more optimistic.

"As long as there are Africans running that camp, we'll have a place to stay and probably also dinner with them tonight," I say. I am confident that Africans' strong sense of hospitality would not allow them to leave us stranded here, despite Herman's initial outright rejection of the possibility of accommodation.

Even after putting on long pants and jackets, we both get chilled waiting for Herman's return. Journeys in Africa often involve intense heat. To avoid the worst of it, we are starting ours in mid-June, the beginning of winter in the southern hemisphere. When the sun was shining, we were comfortable cycling in T-shirts and shorts, but now with the sun and temperatures dropping, it's chilly. Luckily, we don't have to wait long.

Soon Herman's white truck approaches. He brings good news—we are invited to spend the night at the camp. It's not quite finished, he says, but you'll be warm tonight. And they even have a workshop where they'll help Paul fix his bike.

I offer to cycle to the camp, but they have security guards who won't let us in unless we arrive with Herman. We load both our bicycles into the back of his enclosed truck. They barely fit side-by-side with our gear packed around them.

Paul walks over to the front passenger door, turns towards me, and asks, "Are you comfortable waiting here?"

I understand that he is not. To most Westerners, this truck would be full, unable to take an additional passenger, and Herman offers to come back for me. But two years in Africa has changed my perspective. I tell him that's not necessary and squeeze myself into the back of the truck, reclining back across the tops of the bikes. If I try to sit up, I'll hit my head on the ceiling. It's not too uncomfortable—until the truck starts to move and every little bump starts to jostle me. I press my elbows and feet into opposite sides of the truck to keep from slipping and getting wedged between the bikes. The truck's back window has bars across it, and I wonder if prisoners have ever been transported in it.

When we arrive at the camp, I use my yoga-based flexibility to extricate myself from the back of the truck and look around. The camp is a fenced-in compound with a one-story white house near the center, a tin garage workshop that is about as big as the house off to the side, and faded yellow shipping containers converted into buildings near the outskirts. A sense of place is lacking. This isn't anyone's home, just a place to stay temporarily. Dead grass and gray clouds add to the barren feel.

Andries, another bearded South African with a slighter build and darker hair than Herman, introduces himself as the camp manager. He's most likely responsible for our invitation to the camp, and we thank him. Hierarchy is important here, and Herman probably told us we couldn't camp here because he didn't have the authority to give us permission.

"Do you have any food?" Andries asks.

"Some," we reply.

"If you'd like to join us for dinner, we eat at seven." He has someone show us around the camp—the main house, the workshop, and the container where we'll stay.

It's not unusual in Africa for shipping containers to be used as buildings after they are emptied. These intermodal containers are originally used to ship large loads of freight by cargo ship, train, or truck, and sometimes the freight costs of returning them empty are higher than replacement costs. I knew of one in Lesotho that had been used as a bicycle shop, but I'd never thought of one as a potential home. Yet it is a comfortable home for a night. It's heated and has two bedrooms and a bathroom with a hot shower—much more luxurious than our tents.

As we carry our bicycles up the three brick steps to our container, which rests on brick pedestals, Paul says, "I think they were considerate enough to give us one with two bedrooms because they don't know if we're a couple."

"You're probably right. White South Africans would wonder, because they do travel platonically with friends of the opposite sex. Others will assume we are," I reply.

When I told my Peace Corps friends about my plans for this trip, they almost invariably asked, "Who is this guy?" I explained that it isn't like that, there's nothing romantic or sexual between us. I hadn't even met him in person yet. The group I tried to put together for this trip, thinking that four or five people would be ideal, ended up as just the two of us, but it's not what we intended. I placed the ad in a cycling magazine looking for self-sufficient, compatible riding partners for an adventure trip. I wanted to have some company and didn't think I'd feel safe bicycle touring alone in the region. Paul answered for similar reasons. It wasn't a personals ad. This isn't a three-month blind date.

At seven we walk to the main house for dinner. It's Andries, Herman, and five Portuguese men, along with Paul and me. A cook serves us as we sit around a large wooden table that fills the dining room. We find out that the company that owns this camp is Portuguese and they have a contract to pave half the road that we've been cycling on since our missed turn. There is not enough money in the government's budget to pave all of it, so their contract is to pave only half. Maybe the rest will get done another year. They talk as if this is normal for doing business with the Malawi government. They are concerned that the money will run out early before their contract is up, so they are planning to finish early, to ensure they get paid. Andries talks about how they have built the whole camp since he arrived four months ago and about how the local people living there when he arrived had not taken care of their property.

"What happened to these people?" I ask.

"I don't know and I don't care," he immediately responds. Apartheid is no longer South Africa's government policy, but its sentiments live on in the hearts of many of the country's white citizens. Perhaps realizing by my silence that he has offended me, he adds, "We have provided the neighboring village with electricity and running water."

There's a lot of poking fun at each other and joking around at dinner—about the whiskey they are passing around and drinking and about how they built the camp. The most rotund of the Portuguese men keeps starting sentences with "Me speak." Not even allowing him to finish his sentences, Andries keeps interrupting and correcting him with "I speak."

After dinner, Paul and I walk back to our container.

"If I weren't worried about my bike, I'd love this," he says, "I thrive on these kinds of experiences."

"I know what you mean."

Experiences like these always reaffirm my choice to travel by bike. By traveling through an area at a human speed rather than zooming through enclosed in two tons of steel, I get to know it on a much deeper level, what it's really like rather than just how it appears through a window. Even problems such as wrong turns and broken bikes become opportunities to meet people and learn about their lives and cultures.

chapter two

The Men Don't Always Listen

Paul takes his rear hub apart and thoroughly cleans it in the morning. His wheel spins freely again, but he still thinks he might need to get a part sent ahead to avoid the problem recurring. It is time to road test his repair. Herman gives us some advice on places to stay along our projected route in Malawi, and we leave late in the morning.

Malawi is a long, skinny country, shaped like a crooked finger cradling a lake. Bordering Tanzania, Zambia, and Mozambique, it's approximately 900 kilometers long and only 80 to 150 kilometers wide. Malawi is the most densely populated of the four countries we'll be cycling through, and southern Malawi is the most densely populated part of the country. We have chosen to begin our journey here for the ease of finding food, water, and accommodation regularly at convenient cycling distances. At the other end of our planned journey is Namibia, one of the least-densely populated countries on the planet and where vast distances will be challenging.

Heading southeast, we continue along yesterday's dirt road, our only option out of the camp. It's the dry season, and the landscape is one of muted colors—shades of browns, soft greens, and some grays. The colors will be much lusher in the wet season, but the dirt roads will be mud roads then and no good for long-distance cycling. The flattish road goes gradually downhill more often than gradually uphill. It leads us through light brown grasses as tall as we are, shrubs with droopy, green, pointy leaves and some with maroon berries, and scrubby trees reaching for the still-cloudy sky lingering above us.

It's a smooth ride, easy to find a good line without too many ruts to cycle in. We catch glimpses of the bare granite and syenite faces of Mount Mulanje, whose peaks loom up to 3000 meters above sea level, though we cannot see the tallest among them from here.

The people along the way greet us by simply waving. This is a nice change from Lesotho, where protocol seemed to be stare at the white cyclist and ask for something, usually money or sweets. The men are generally dressed in Western clothing, commonly long pants and button-down shirts or T-shirts. The women tend to wear more traditional and brightly colored clothing, dresses or long skirts and fuller blouses in patterned fabrics. They aren't concerned about trying to look thin. Traditionally, being called fat is a compliment. Fat equals wealth. If you're fat, you've got plenty of food.

During Peace Corps training, some of my fellow volunteers gained weight and hated it when their host families, saying they'd been too thin and hadn't looked healthy, rejoiced that they were fattening up. By American standards, they'd been healthy and some not even particularly thin. None had thought they'd gain weight living in a poor African country.

After about thirty kilometers, Paul and I reach the main tar road that leads into the town of Mulanje. We stop in town for lunch at a takeaway stand with some outdoor seating. I order rice and beans, which is listed on the menu board.

"They are finished," says the man working at the stand.

"Then I'll have *nsima* with vegetables," I say with a slight frown, thinking about *nsima* and knowing that vegetables probably means cabbage.

"What's *nsima*?" says Paul to me.

I explain that *nsima* is the staple food of southern Africa. It goes by different names in different countries but is essentially the same everywhere. Made of corn meal stirred into boiling water, *nsima* congeals into a lumpy mass resembling mashed potatoes. It doesn't have much flavor itself and tends to take on the flavor of whatever it is served with—sauces, vegetables, meats. The poorest people sometimes can't afford anything to go with it and eat it plain.

"I'm not real fond of it," I say. "I'll eat it when there aren't any other options, but I prefer rice or potatoes. But at least it's filling—this is a plus on a bike trip."

"I guess I may as well try it now," says Paul. He turns to the man and orders *nsima* with chicken.

Over lunch, Paul and I decide to go on to Likabula, the gateway for hikes on Mount Mulanje. The man who runs the takeaway stand tells us that there is a road directly from Mulanje to Likabula and we don't have to backtrack on the highway at all. He has someone walk Paul to the road, so we'll know where it is when we're ready to leave.

I'm riding a mountain bike with knobby tires and no suspension, and Paul is riding a touring bike. Knobby tires give me better traction on the unpaved roads but also slow me down, as does the more upright riding position of a mountain bike. We each have both front and rear panniers to carry our gear—sleeping bags, a small camping stove, water filters, tools, spare bike parts, clothes, first aid kits, extra water when necessary, and food. We bungee our tents and sleeping pads across the top of our rear racks and panniers.

I first toured with all my gear packed on my bike like this sixteen years ago with a group of teenagers in Maine. I was only looking for a fun way to spend part of a summer. Instead I found a life-long passion that has led me along a bike path to Africa and this trip.

Each of the next couple summers, I took a bike touring vacation—one year in Alaska and the next from Seattle to San Francisco. Then I spent my junior year of college in Germany, saw the potential of using bikes for transportation, and started to dream. A couple years later, an internship with a national organization of bicyclists back in the States led me to a career in bike advocacy. By the time I applied to the Peace Corps, cycling was a lifestyle for me—work, vacation, transportation, and recreation. Before I accepted the offer from the Peace Corps, I called and asked to make sure I could bring my bike. They said yes, so I said yes.

The road to Likabula is dirt. It's rough at times and we bump along, but mostly it's a decent hard-packed dirt road. Cycling on dirt roads sometimes means a lot of bouncing over rocks or ruts. There are a few steep hills, and my legs get tired. By the end of the tour, today's ride will seem short, but now I'm not used to riding more than twenty kilometers per day. I've done enough bike touring that my legs remember what it's like. But it'll take at least a few days until muscle memory kicks in and my legs realize that this is a tour, not just a weekend ride. Since Paul has been touring in New Zealand and England recently, he's in much better shape starting out.

As we ride along, heading northeast now, the locals get more aggressive and start asking for money. We're getting close to a tourist area and they're probably used to tourists giving handouts. South African tourists frequently throw sweets out of their vehicles to the begging kids. I think "money" is the first and only English word some of the kids who don't go to school learn.

As we cycle past gently sloping tea fields, a local teenager sidles alongside us on his bike. "My name is Douglass. I am a guide. Ask for me."

Repeating this sentence many times, he rides with us, mostly next to Paul. At the turnoff into the forest reserve at the base of the mountain, where we want to spend the night, we pick up another tagalong, James, who is also a guide. Our first stop, with Douglass and James accompanying us, is the forest lodge where we hope to camp. But we find that we cannot: there is no toilet and shower available because someone staying in an indoor room is using the ones normally available to campers. We could lodge in their rooms but since this is more expensive than we anticipated, our prospective guides lead us along the dusky path to the nearby mission. A two-bedroom chalet doesn't cost much more than camping, so we choose it for the amenities: beds, a furnished living room, and private bathroom and kitchen. We pay 500 *kwacha* (less than $6 U.S.) each for the chalet. It's functional rather than fancy. This isn't a Swiss mountain chalet. Nonetheless, I'm disappointed to discover that the shower is cold water only. We'll soon learn that this is the norm for showers in Malawi. At least we have electricity and comfortable chairs. We cook spaghetti for dinner, and I write in my journal before going to bed.

In the morning, the weather is clear, so we decide to go for a day hike on the mountain and stay at the chalet for another night. We haven't talked about whom to choose as our guide when slender James, wearing a brown and white T-shirt, tan shorts, and a gray baseball cap, knocks on our door at eight. Guides are required by the Forestry Department, a common practice in Africa. At times not being able to hike on my own feels restrictive, but the trails are generally marked very poorly, if at all, and it'd be easy to get lost. Plus, requiring guides brings tourist dollars into the local economy. When the community benefits economically from nature-related tourism, the local people tend to value nature and support its preservation. But if they are not benefiting economically, they are much less likely to preserve it. Paul and I knew we needed a guide, but we hadn't talked about whether we wanted to go with James or Douglass or find someone else, which judging from our experience last night, would not have been difficult.

We ask James to wait outside while we talk.

"I don't trust him, or any guide," says Paul. "How do we know if he's giving us a fair price or trying to rip us off?"

I look over at the door, sensing James waiting outside. It's true that guides do sometimes try to rip people off, generally at least, I don't know about here. But I do trust James. He strikes me as honest.

"I want to check with the forest station about the right price for a guide,"

Paul continues.

"What do you want to tell James?" I ask.

"Why don't you ask him to show you the hike he's proposing on those maps we walked by on our way in last night? I'll go to the forest station while you go with him."

"Okay," I hear myself answering. I do like to look at maps, but I feel Paul is putting me in a potentially awkward spot as a decoy for him to slip out unnoticed.

James and I walk up to the mission to look at the map of the trails. When we return, the chalet is locked. I knock. No one answers.

"Where is he?" asks James.

"I don't know," I shrug, feeling guilty. "He must've gone out for something."

When Paul returns looking sheepish, Douglass is with him. Now we have to make a choice and disappoint one of them.

Again we confer inside.

"What do you want to do?" he asks.

"I'd choose James. When I was talking with him yesterday, he struck me as knowledgeable. He knew about the kinds of trees we were walking past," I reply.

"Douglass didn't talk about anything."

"All I heard him saying was 'My name is Douglass. I am a guide. Ask for me.' It didn't inspire me."

Douglass lowers his head when we tell them we're going to go with James. He walks away towards the forest station. We agree with James on a full-day hike that involves going up a steep route and coming down an easier way.

We climb along a well-maintained, steep trail through montane forest and grassland with expansive views back down into the verdant valley behind us. As we hike, James tells us about some of the foliage, including cedar trees and purple-and-pink mother-in-law flowers. Several men going down the mountain are carrying square-cut trees on their heads. They balance them like huge logs, and we move off the path to let them pass.

"What are they doing with the trees?" asks Paul.

James explains that these men are uneducated. They buy one tree at a time from the government, carry it down the mountain, and then sell the wood at the market. With some of their profit, they buy another tree from the government and repeat this process. There is someone stationed on the mountain who checks to make sure that they have really paid for the trees they are taking.

I ask James about himself. "How old are you?"

"I am 20." Students here are taught to always answer their teachers in complete sentences, and this habit tends to carryover to any other conversations with adults.

"Are you in school?"

"Yes, I am in my second year of secondary school." Secondary school is the equivalent of high school.

"This is my eleventh year in school," he continues. He must have repeated some grades.

"Do you have any brothers or sisters?" I ask.

"I have a younger sister. She is in primary school." Primary school, which encompasses both elementary and middle school, is free, but secondary school is not. Many kids drop out of school after primary school because their families cannot afford the secondary school fees.

As we climb through a slight mist, the clouds gradually close in. We stop at a viewpoint at a cable car station, about 1000 meters higher than we started our hike. The cable cars are not running but when they are, they carry only logs, not people. The government uses them to transport any logs it takes down the mountain, but the men who purchase trees must carry their trees down.

"So far, I'm not impressed with the scenery," says Paul.

"Really?" I say, pondering his comment as I take a deep breath of the cedar-filled air. "I'm enjoying being in a forest."

He glances at me in surprise.

"Oh, you were just in New Zealand," I remember.

New Zealand is one of the most gorgeous countries I've ever been to. If I were choosing a place for a return bike tour based simply on scenery, its south island would be near the top of my list. If New Zealand is his standard, this is going to be a tough trip. Whereas I've been living in a deforested country, so am happy to simply be amongst trees.

As we sit for a few minutes, the clouds move in and completely cover the view of the valley. I'm drained from the steep hiking after two days of cycling. The clouds make our decision to turn around early easy. As we lose about half the altitude that we'd gained, the first hour hiking down is not the easy walk we were expecting. It's steep and slippery at times, muddy and rocky, and I wish I had a walking stick. After the trail flattens out, we take a break at the base of a waterfall cascading down a granite rock face.

James turns to me and asks, "Will you sponsor me for a used bicycle?"

I shake my head no and get up and walk away, thinking this is enough body language to clearly indicate a "no." But it isn't.

On our final descent, he asks again and says, "I am begging you."

"We are paying you to be our guide. Why don't you use this money to save for a bicycle?"

"I am begging you."

After two years in Africa, I've come to believe handouts don't really help people. They turn them into beggars, which does not help them. Kenya is a stark example. There, some parents keep their kids out of school and send them to hang out at tourist spots to ask for pens and money. Rather than getting an education and an opportunity to break the poverty cycle, they spend their childhoods learning only how to beg.

I'm disappointed by James' request. Many African cultures say go ahead and ask for money because asking can't hurt. The worst you can get is a "no" and maybe you'll get some money. But being on the other side and getting asked for money seemingly all the time gets tiring. It tips relationships out of balance and reminds me that to some people, I will always be considered a source of money simply because I am white. I end up wondering if our conversations have been about establishing friendships or just giving them an opening to ask for money. And I get frustrated that I can't just spend a relaxing day in nature without being asked for money.

After the hike, Paul and I walk into Likabula to get groceries for dinner. Most of the stores are wooden open-air stands that have already closed for the day, as it's after five o'clock on a Saturday afternoon. We scrounge up bread, tomatoes, and rice from a stand and a couple of shops so small there's only room for a few customers at a time. When we return to our chalet, the power is out, so we can't use the kitchen stove. Rural African utilities can be unreliable. After hearing the volunteers in Lesotho who had running water and electricity talk about how often they were out, I was glad to have only a latrine, which always worked, and a gas stove that ran off a propane cylinder. We consider cooking on our camping stove, but the power comes back while we are eating tomato sandwiches as an appetizer by candlelight. We cook the rice and eat it with cream of tomato soup sauce, which we bought in Mulanje the previous day.

It's too cold for a cold shower, so I heat some water in a cooking pot and bring it into the bathroom for a bucket bath. I use a bowl to pour warm water over myself, soap up, then rinse the soap off by pouring more warm water. This is one traditional way of bathing in Africa, where many people do not have running water. I've found I prefer a warm bucket bath to a cold shower.

The following morning, we depart at ten—our earliest biking start yet. I like to get earlier starts rather than doing the bulk of the riding in the midday sun, but somehow this doesn't seem to be happening. Paul emailed me that overall, he was flexible and had started riding any time between six and one in New Zealand. I emailed back that I like to get earlier starts because the sun gets hot here but I was willing to start later if this is what the group wanted. He didn't respond to my comment and I let it go, figuring departure time would be a group decision.

Early in the ride, my front rack starts rubbing against my front tire. I stop and discover that the bolts have come loose. Once I tighten them, it's better.

Yesterday's clouds have cleared, and we have great views of the boulder-like summit of Mount Mulanje rising above the horizon line off to our right, the south. We cycle about thirty kilometers to a small town called Phalombe and stop at the Slow But Sure Grocery with red Coca-Cola advertisements painted next to its odd name. The building's graying white paint is peeling. White pillars and a tin-roof overhang form a basic front porch, and burglar bars adorn the windows. Inside, the few aisles contain a mix of staples—corn meal, rice, beans, flour, sugar, bread—and snacks, mostly cookies and potato chips. A refrigerated case offers cold drinks. We buy groceries and sit on a wooden bench under the tin-roof overhang, eating bread with peanut butter to the music of a "give me" chorus. A few kids with clothes worn almost to shreds sit near us, and one consistently asks for things—food, money, our possessions.

"I guess all this attention gets tiring pretty quickly," says Paul.

"Yeah, it does."

I knew dealing with what I've come to consider the hassles of Africa—primarily all the attention that is based on the color of our skin, how a white person is treated—on this trip would be a challenge. I'm starting it already tired of them, tired enough that I'd considered returning to the U.S. at the end of my Peace Corps service. But I wasn't otherwise ready to return. I decided that wanting to see more of the region was more important.

We spend the afternoon cycling north on a fairly flat dirt road, with Mount Mulanje now behind us. Our views are of the more immediate landscape, as the road takes us through tiny villages of mud-dung houses with thatched roofs. There are people all along our route. Not crowds, but always someone, walking along the road, standing outside their house, or working in their fields. Southern Malawi is not the place for solitude.

There's a feeling I love about cycling that I can't capture here. A feeling of being so in sync with nature, able to just go, a connection with the universe that traveling under one's own power brings. I remember cycling the Denali Highway in Alaska with a heightened sense of awareness, looking for bears and moose but also with a feeling of oneness with the earth. I was a part of their territory, rather than zooming through as an observer apart from them. Here, like in so much of the developing world, I am too much of an anomaly to capture this feeling. I am the center of attention wherever I go. Being pointed at and barraged with requests for money and sweets—and even just the waves and shrieks of surprise and delight to see a white person, especially one on a bicycle, passing through their villages—prohibits this connection. Here I am too much the center of the universe. I can't just blend in and glide along in sync.

But instead I have access to what life in these countries is like on a whole different level. My bicycle takes me to villages never mentioned in guidebooks, some not even on maps. Along with the hordes of screaming children comes a knowledge and an understanding of life here, a connection to people rather than to the universe. When I allow myself to be open to it. When I am present and open to the blessing of each moment, rather than closed off because I am tired and sick of the attention that comes with being a white person in sub-Saharan Africa. These people didn't invite me into their countries. I chose to come here of my own free will, to get to know their countries.

Sometimes it is hard to remember this. It is so easy to get upset with people for targeting me. Yet to them, I represent opportunity, and herein lies the heart of the problem. I don't want to represent anything. I want to meet them as equals, and yet we are not equals. Simply by virtue of where we were born. I am a visitor in their country, officially welcomed with a U.S. passport that allows me to travel almost anywhere in the world. Most Malawians will never have passports nor the funds to travel abroad and if they do, a lengthy visa application process awaits them to possibly be permitted to come to the U.S.

The greener pastures of material life in the U.S. appeals to so many of them. But it no longer appeals to me. I see the strong family bonds and the connections to home villages that are lacking in so much of the U.S., where the question "where are you from?" has almost become meaningless in many places. Here people really are from somewhere, referring to "my place." I see their love for each other and their love for their land, and I see what we are missing. They are not poorer than we are because they live in mud houses, though they think they are. Stuff—and big houses—doesn't make people truly happy. A basic level of food and shelter is important, and some here are lacking even this, but beyond that, things are not a true source of happiness.

In Lesotho, I lived in my own one-room house on a family compound. I watched the family plow their fields and plant corn and raise chickens, pigs, and sheep. They hauled all their water for bathing, cooking, and doing dishes from a village pump. They cooked by fire. No machines helped them with any of these tasks. Yet I never heard them complain. Instead I heard their laughter and saw them sit with each other and talk. I saw that they always had time for anyone who stopped by.

Occasionally, we see a local cyclist or a motor vehicle, but most people are walking. Several children have distended stomachs, the first I've seen in more than two years in Africa. Many Americans join the Peace Corps thinking they'll live in the developing world and learn what it's like to be poor. But in reality, we find out what it's like to be rich. We receive a monthly living allowance that is roughly equivalent to a local teacher's salary, a hundred or so dollars a month in Lesotho. Yet most teachers support their families on their salaries, not just themselves. And as volunteers we always have the option of quitting. Tell the Peace Corps you want to leave and within 72 hours they'll have you on a plane back to the States. This isn't learning what it's like to be poor. It's learning what it's like to be a privileged American.

Most of us will never have to take in and raise eight nieces and nephews because all our brothers and sisters have died of AIDS. Most of us will never watch our kids' hair turn orange because they're so malnourished. As volunteers, we are exposed to poverty, but we don't learn what it's like to be truly poor ourselves; we learn what it's like to be rich.

Lots of aggressive "give me money" children run toward and sometimes after us as we ride by. It is harder to turn down their requests when they're so visibly malnourished, but I don't want to help turn them into beggars, and so I ride on. I remember asking a couple of the local teachers with whom I worked in Lesotho what they thought about my always saying no to people asking for handouts.

"That's what you need to do," they said, "We've gotten so much aid, it makes some people lazy. They need to learn to work, not to beg."

We pass sunflower fields, then tall brown grasses as we finally near Jali, my legs more than ready to stop for the day after eighty-one kilometers. As it's getting dark, we stop at the Jali police station to ask about a place to stay. A policeman outside is just getting off duty.

"There is a resthouse. I will escort you," he says as he hops on his bike.

"Great, thanks," I reply. Otherwise, we would have had to ask for permission to camp somewhere.

"It is not up to tourist standards, but it is the best around," he says.

The resthouse is on the main road but completely unmarked and hidden from view by a cement wall around the property. It is a basic place, but what I expect from the short bike tours I've done in Zimbabwe, Uganda, and Tanzania. The rooms consist of a twin bed and just enough floor space for a bicycle against the wall. A bare bulb hangs from the ceiling. Shared restrooms are squat toilets and bucket baths. They let us choose our rooms amongst the vacant ones, and I pick the ones with the least-worn sheets and mattresses and make sure the keys they give us really work.

Paul and I are both very hungry, so hungry I'd say starving if we hadn't just cycled by those kids with distended stomachs, and too hungry to wait for water to be heated to bathe before going to dinner.

"Do we have to change out of our shorts for dinner?" he asks me.

"Yes." Outside of white South Africa, adults don't generally wear shorts in southern Africa. They're acceptable for sports but definitely not for going to a restaurant or walking around a village. Even cycling, we don't wear Lycra because only prostitutes wear Lycra here. Paul wears regular shorts over his Lycra cycling shorts, and I wear loose-fitting mountain bike shorts with a padded liner. As white people here, we'll never entirely blend in, but this doesn't give us license to be culturally offensive, and I believe cultural sensitivity is an important part of staying safe.

After he changes into pants and I put on a sarong, we ask about a place to eat dinner. A teenage boy is told to escort us to a nearby restaurant, about the equivalent of two blocks away. When we arrive, they tell us all they have is *nsima* with chicken. When I first moved to Africa, remaining vegetarian was one of my biggest concerns, and I wasn't sure that I'd be able to do it, but now that I've lived here for two years, I'm not ready to give it up. Generally,

I've found it easy to get *nsima* or rice with beans or cabbage. But I'm feeling pessimistic now. The food stores are probably closed. Someone else comes out to talk with us and asks if I eat eggs. I do, and she offers to make me an omelet with cabbage.

As we wait, the owner, a stocky man, sits down with us, and we chat. He wants to know about our trip. Jali is one of those villages not mentioned in guidebooks, where not many foreigners stop, so meeting us is a special treat for him.

When our dinner is served, Paul looks at the chicken with *nsima* on his plate then at the huge omelet filling my plate and immediately says, "I want one of those, too."

Everyone laughs, but he says, "I'm serious," and they agree to make him one.

The restaurant owner is also a teacher and teaches standard three, or second grade, at the primary school down the road from 7:30 a.m. until noon. He has 65 students in his class, not an unusually large class.

"Are the students fed at school?" I ask, thinking about the failure of the school feeding programs I worked with in Lesotho.

"No," he says, "but some bring food for their break."

While he teaches, his wife runs the restaurant. His younger brother also works there. He tells us that there are four universities in the country, for a population of ten million.

"Does Jali have a chief or a council?" I ask.

"Both," he replies.

"Are there any women chiefs in Malawi?" I ask, thinking about the lack of women chiefs in Lesotho.

"Yes, there are many."

Perhaps sensing my interest in his country, he sings us a song about one *tambala* coins—Malawi's smallest coins, and to the *kwacha* what pennies are to the U.S. dollar—then asks if we have seen any. He shows us a couple, saying they are not really worth anything anymore and are no longer in circulation. As we're leaving, he tells us to keep them.

"Are you sure?" I ask.

"Yes," he responds, nodding.

"Thank you." It feels weird to be given money, but the coins are a great lightweight souvenir, and I don't want to insult him by turning down a gift.

I have always remembered my high school history teacher, Mr. Drake, talking about his Peace Corps experiences. I no longer remember what those experiences were or where he served as a volunteer, but even now, more than fifteen years later, I remember the enthusiasm with which he spoke, although it had been years since his volunteer service.

I remembered him when I considered applying to the Peace Corps right out of college, and I remembered him again almost four years ago now when I was sitting at lunch with a friend at a sidewalk cafe in Washington, D.C. I was thinking about leaving what had turned into an unhealthy work environment.

"What will you do if you quit?" asked my friend.

"Maybe join the Peace Corps," I replied. This thought came to my mind only as I said it, but once articulated, I knew it was right.

"Why?" asked my friend.

"I've always wanted to, ever since listening to a high school teacher talk about it. I looked into it after college, but at that time, I think they would have wanted me to teach English in Eastern Europe and that wasn't what I wanted to do." In addition to studying in Germany, I also studied in Poland during college, and I majored in Central and Eastern European Studies, but I had zero desire to teach English.

"What would you do with them now?"

"I don't know. I'll have to look into it."

"Where would you want to go?"

"Probably Africa. I'd love to see more of it." I'd been on a two-week bicycle tour in Zimbabwe that summer.

I looked into it and found out that my non-profit background was a perfect match for the Peace Corps' Non-Governmental Organizational Development Volunteer profile, and a year and a half later I was on a plane to Lesotho.

While there, I was assigned to the Ministry of Education's School Self-Reliance Feeding Unit. My job was to help schools manage income-generating projects that were supposed to raise enough money for them to feed the students lunch. But with parents, and to some extent teachers, unable to prioritize these projects, the program failed on a national level. The Peace Corps pulled out of it less than six months after I arrived but told us, "We're still supporting you as volunteers, not sending you home. Do whatever projects you want for the rest of your two years here." So I found things to do with my schools, and now I wonder what long-term impact they will have.

I wonder if any of the students at my schools will remember me, or more importantly my projects, with such enthusiasm fifteen years later. Will any of them became bankers because the banker from Hlotse took the time to come to their village from the district capital and speak with them on Career Day? Will any of them take better care of the environment because Sesotho Media came and showed them educational videos? And will any of the newly trained AIDS Peer Educators save lives with their newfound courage to distribute accurate information about HIV and AIDS?

When Paul and I return to the resthouse there are buckets of hot water for bathing waiting for us. The smell of smoke from cook fires lingers in the air. Restaurants and others who can afford them generally cook with propane stoves, but most villagers cook over open fires. After bathing I relax in my room and think about how nice it is to have my own private space, even though it's only a small space, after a day in view on the road.

After some overnight and early morning rain, leaving Jali is slow going on the now wet, sandy road. We ride in the tracks of other cyclists, occasionally stopping to walk our bikes into a better track when one gets too muddy and our bikes sink too deep to pedal. I can't look around at the scenery while riding because I have to focus on the tracks in the road to stay upright. Paul gets ahead of me, as has become his habit. This doesn't bother me. I included riding at our own paces in my tour proposal. It's too hard for people who've never met to commit to riding at someone else's pace for a months-long tour. And even though Paul rides ahead, I still feel safer than I think I would if I were alone. People who see me riding alone have likely seen him go by earlier, and thus know, on at least some level, that he could be just around the next corner waiting for me or on his way back looking for me.

When I catch him waiting by the side of the road, he says, "The touring bike is faster than the mountain bike in mountain bike terrain."

"I think the mountain bike rider is more tired than the touring bike rider."

The ride to Zomba is almost twice as long as we expect, twenty-seven kilometers rather than the fifteen kilometers the policeman we met yesterday said. It's still a very short riding day, but twice as far as expected always seems far, even when it's not a long distance.

Zomba, a large town with a population of about 75,000, is Malawi's former capital. Like many African towns, it's a mix of modern Western establishments, including banks and what we Americans would consider small grocery stores, and traditional African businesses, including healers and a large outdoor market. When we arrive, we stop at a telephone bureau along the main tar highway, and I call Elias, whom I met on the plane. A friend of his, whom I also met on the plane, answers and tells us to go to the Gymkhana Club, just off the main road, to meet Elias "now." As we wait, we regret not getting something to eat before calling.

"Now" frequently means "soon" in Africa, and sometimes it just means "today." We could have a long wait, but after half an hour Elias pulls up in an old, dusty, blue pickup truck. He's wearing military fatigues and introduces us to his wife, Chimwemwe. He's on his way to drop her off at her job and suggests that Paul and I eat at Caboodles while we wait for him to return.

Caboodles is a cafe geared towards travelers, with Western food and an English book exchange. It serves coffee and pastries and has a stay-and-browse feel. We're happy to see pizza on the menu but disappointed by the wimpy size of our personal pizzas. Food is fuel for cyclists, and this looks more like a snack than a lunch, but at least it takes the edge off our hunger. Paul browses through the book exchange while we wait for Elias.

When Elias arrives, he offers to take us to look at places to stay. My hope that he might offer us a place is quashed when he tells us he lives on the army base and they aren't allowed to have overnight guests, or at least not foreigners. We put the bikes in the back of his pickup, since he says it's hard to give us directions through the twisty streets. As we drive off the main highway, we pass the large market.

African markets are a hodgepodge of wooden homemade stalls with people selling all sorts of goods that together defy categorization: fruits and vegetables, perhaps fresh bread, roots used as traditional medicine, kitchen wares, household goods (some new, some used), mechanical parts that I'd have no idea what to do with—really anything that can be sold. Women selling produce may not have stands and simply sell it out of circular plastic basins. Busy markets can have a hectic feel, as competing sellers all urge, "Buy my bananas. Buy from me."

Elias turns down a side street and stops at the Ndindeya Motel. A clean room with two beds and a private bathroom meets our budget goal of five dollars or less per night each. We're still near the center of town, so we can easily explore on foot without our bikes, and we decide to stay here rather than spend more time looking around.

Elias gives us time to settle in and shower, then returns to show us around. I'm expecting a tour of Zomba, but apparently he meant to show us where he hangs out rather than show us the sights. He drives us to Annie's Lodge, which is outside of the center of town, to see the expansive view of the forested hillsides rising above Zomba. The sparkling clean bar, lounge, and restaurant are in a central airy building, and thatched-roof cottages are scattered about the landscaped grounds. Over drinks, Elias introduces us to Annie, a plump, robust light-skinned woman wearing a light sweater over a patterned dress. While Elias talks with Paul, I have a long conversation with Annie about women in Malawi. I wonder if this separation of the sexes is intentional or just natural, but I enjoy getting to know Annie, who is a member of parliament.

"How many women are in parliament here?" I ask.

"16 of 193," she replies.

"Do you work on women's issues?"

"We try, but when we come back to our home districts, the men don't always listen."

She bought this place a couple years ago and designed and built a lot of it herself. She tells me about her personal life. She's forty-four and was married to a man from the UK for twenty years. She was happy with him until he got restless and played around.

"I told him not to come back," she says with confidence.

I'm heartened to hear about her strength. So many African women stay in marriages no matter how badly their husbands treat them. She tells me she now has a "very nice boyfriend" who keeps her from getting lonely.

When he's ready to move on, Elias takes us to the officers' mess at the army barracks. He shows us a bit of one building then takes us to the bar that he repeatedly tells us "used to be a morgue," and introduces us to the few other officers there. They buy us each a drink. Paul has a beer, and I have juice. Elias' friend from the plane is there, as is the colonel in charge of the base. I'm a strong proponent of non-violence and am somewhat uncomfortable in this military setting. I make the best of it and talk with the colonel about the Malawi army and learn that Malawi is part of the UN peacekeeping forces currently in Congo and Kosovo.

After drinks, Elias takes us back to Annie's for dinner. As we're walking inside, Elias strides ahead. Paul whispers to me that Elias and Annie made some sort of deal that he'd bring us back, she'd overcharge us for dinner, and we'd pay for him to eat with us. This reminds me of his suspicions of James trying to overcharge us. Is he suspicious by nature? Or is Africa or Malawi bringing out this distrust?

Elias says he is not hungry and waits in the bar while we eat. I'm disappointed that Annie isn't around. I would've liked to talk more with her. I have no trouble getting a vegetarian dinner—a big plate of veggies—here. We are not overcharged. Paul must've misunderstood whatever he overheard.

I've sensed some tension from Paul, and I wonder if this trip isn't what he was expecting. Looking back years later, I'll wonder why I didn't directly ask him. But now I simply don't think to. Perhaps I am too tired from a draining end to my Peace Corps service to clearly analyze my current situation. Perhaps I am afraid of the answer. What would I do if he says, "No, it's not?" So instead I think back to my proposed tour description I emailed to him and other interested cyclists:

"Cycling 30-60 miles/day—tending towards 30-40 earlier in the trip and on rough roads and 40-60 later in the trip and on well-paved roads. A combination of dirt and paved roads...Taking time to really see and get to know the areas we'll bike through. This is not a race...Taking some time to meet the locals but also frequently choosing less populated routes for their serenity...A combination of camping and basic but hopefully clean and quiet backpacker lodges or hotels. Biking 5-6 days a week. Taking one day/week to really rest our muscles and possibly another day for another sport, such as hiking, kayaking, or snorkeling..." Sounds like this trip so far. What could possibly be wrong?

I tell myself that things are fine. They have to be.

Eleven years ago, I biked across the U.S., thinking it would be the big bike trip of my life. I thought that it would satisfy my craving to do a long tour, and that afterwards, I'd settle down with a job, only two weeks of vacation per year, and some semblance of a normal life. But I was wrong. It didn't satisfy my craving. Instead it created a desire to do an even longer trip, a desire that stayed with me. I worked two part-time jobs with flexible schedules for awhile and was able to take extra unpaid leave, which I always spent bicycle touring. These trips were never more than a month long, though—and usually only two weeks. So when I joined the Peace Corps, I still had this desire to one day do another months-long bike trip in the back of my mind. Sometime in Lesotho, I realized that after the Peace Corps would be the perfect opportunity. I didn't have a job to go back to or any other commitments, and I wanted to see more of Africa. It all came together.

This is a trip I've been dreaming about for years, and we've got another three plus months to go. Things have to be fine. I disregard the tension I've felt.

chapter three

AFRAID OF THE DARK?

As I reach into one of my front panniers the next morning, I discover that my front rack is broken near where it attaches to the dropout of my bike's front fork. My bike fell over yesterday while we were waiting for Elias, and this is probably when it broke, though it must have already been weak. Paul suggests staying in Zomba another day to both fix my rack and explore, and I agree.

During breakfast at the hotel, we decide to look for hose clamps in town to repair my rack then hike the potato path—so named because it's used by locals to bring produce to the Zomba market—up to the plateau outside of town. Things frequently seem to take longer than planned in Africa, though, and by the time we buy water, find hose clamps, and check our email, it's almost noon. Standing on a street corner, we talk about whether it's too late to start the hike. Taxi drivers approach us as we talk.

"You want to go to Ku Chawe?" Ku Chawe is the hotel on the top of the plateau.

"Maybe, but we might walk."

"Potato path is dangerous," they say. "There are bad men there."

There was a time in my life when I would have shrugged off this warning as a case of people thinking things they don't do are dangerous. Africans walk a lot but only because it's either their sole transportation option or their sole affordable one. They don't generally hike for fun.

But now I've spent the past two years with the Peace Corps and the Basotho people telling me things aren't safe, and we've read about potential robbers in our guidebook, which recommends hiking with a group or a local. One taxi driver explains that early in the morning there are a lot of locals using the path—villagers who commute into Zomba—so it's safe then.

"But in midday," he says, "only a few people use the path, and the bad men hang around waiting to attack people for their money."

Knowing this, I don't think I'd enjoy the hike because I'd be wondering about our safety and on alert rather than relaxed and enjoying the scenery.

"1300 *kwacha*," they tell us. For 1300 *kwacha*, they will drive us eight kilometers up the road to Ku Chawe.

I'm not sure what it should cost, but I'm sure it's not this much. I tell them, "No, too much."

While Paul and I talk about what to do, the price gradually comes down to 900 *kwacha*. This sounds more reasonable.

I'm tempted but have another idea, "Why don't we call Elias, ask him and Chimwemwe to drive us up and offer to buy them dinner as a thank you?"

"That's a great idea," says Paul.

Late in the afternoon, Elias, Chimwemwe, and their seven-year-old daughter Arevo pick us up. Elias tells us we need to buy him gas. Paul silently looks at me but complies. We ride in back of their pickup. Along the way, we pass several men transporting firewood on their bikes. As the road steepens, the men get off their bikes and push them. The firewood is stacked as tall as the men. We stop at the Mulunguzi Dam.

"It opened less than two years ago. It's great," says Elias.

It looks like a regular dam to me, but I nod in agreement. Africans tend to be proud of their countries' engineering projects, and there's no reason to dampen his pride.

"How about if I take a picture of all of you here?" I ask.

Back in the pickup, the air cools as we ascend through pine forest on the aptly named one-way Up Road. The Ku Chawe Inn is on the edge of the 1800-meter plateau, 1200 meters above the valley floor below. We walk around the upscale hotel and its grounds. Arevo wants to see what's down every path and through every door. Marred by thick gray clouds, the views of evergreen hillsides are not spectacular, so it's good to have the enthusiasm of a child along.

Elias is too tired from staying out drinking until 3 a.m. after he dropped us off last night, so only Chimwemwe comes to dinner with us. We return to Annie's. African names frequently have meanings, and I ask Chimwemwe about hers. She tells me it means happiness.

Paul listens attentively. I sense that he's letting me take the lead in these conversations with locals out of respect for my knowledge of their culture.

I ask Chimwemwe about their lives.

She's thirty-seven and Elias is forty.

"How'd you meet?" I ask.

"I mistakenly called him. It was a wrong number, but we got to talking. That was in 1995," she continues, "Arevo isn't really our daughter. She's one of my five sisters' daughters. I had an operation two years ago and can't have children, so my sister gave her to us to raise."

How beautiful, I think. How many Americans would do that for their sister?

"We used to have some white friends, but they moved away," she says out of the context of the conversation.

"What does Elias think about you working and going back to school?" She is getting her university degree.

"He supports me," she says.

"Is that common here?"

"No, a lot of men want their women to stay home."

She talks about her country. She liked Banda, Malawi's former military ruler, because the economy was better then, and the *kwacha* was much stronger. Malawi has recovered from last year's drought, and there is plenty of maize meal now. She thinks lots of things are dangerous, including Zambia, boats in Malawi, and leaving cars parked in Blantyre and Lilongwe—where there's lots of car theft.

Back at our hotel after dinner, I finish hose clamping my front rack to the fork of my bicycle. The repair is stable enough to carry my gear for now but isn't permanent.

"We've both had bike problems so early in the trip," says Paul.

"What would Steffi think if she were here?" I joke. Steffi is our third person, the one who disappeared from contact after committing to the trip.

"Maybe she'd be having problems, too," he replies with a smile.

Then he asks, "What was that comment about having white friends that Chimwemwe made about? Is having white friends cool or something?"

"It doesn't entirely make sense to me, considering our history as oppressor, but black Africans do sometimes find it cool to have white friends or even just to hang out with white people. It seems to be a status symbol of sorts." I tell him about an experience I had in Lesotho:

I was walking down the main dirt road to my village when a woman walking towards me on the other side of the road suddenly crossed the road, veered toward me, and stopped directly in front of me. Usually people would just yell a greeting across the road. I greeted her, and she asked me a couple questions about what I was doing then went on her way. I imagined her going home and bragging to her family that she'd met the white woman living there.

Paul and I stop at a bank to exchange money before leaving town. We're carrying travelers' checks and some dollars to exchange as we go. Credit cards are generally accepted only in some tourist-oriented places in larger towns and cities, and, thus, are of no use for our day-to-day expenses. ATMs, where they do exist outside of capital cities, are only for that bank's customers and are not on any international systems, so are also not of use to us. Thinking that I need to get a new rack before mine breaks any further, I call Peace Corps/Malawi and ask where they get spare parts for their mountain bikes. Nowhere in Malawi, they say, and they give me the name of their South African supplier who ships them parts from Johannesburg. Our last task before leaving town is buying bottled water. Though we're carrying water filters, we've gotten into the habit of buying bottled water rather than taking the time to filter tap water.

From Zomba, it's an easy ride with lots of downhill to Liwonde. As we cycle north through grassy hillsides, my rack starts rubbing and I nervously pull over. A hose clamp has come loose and only needs to be tightened.

After a late lunch at the Liwonde Park Motel, we ask where the Mvuu Camp office in town is. We're on our way to Liwonde National Park. Bicycling isn't allowed in the park, but one of the camps in the park—Mvuu— is accessible by boat from outside the park, and we hope to be able to stay there. Liwonde is known as Malawi's best wildlife park, although Malawi is not known for its wildlife. An escort from the motel takes us to a hut, which we never would've recognized as an office, on the Shire River. An older man, with touches of gray in his slightly frizzy hair, tells us about the camp and its boats. One boat leaves from this hut every morning and travels along the river to the camp. The other one leaves from outside of Ulongwe, about thirty kilometers north, and only crosses the river to the camp on demand. He assures us that we will be able to take our bikes on either one.

It's generally much easier to take bikes on transit in Africa than in the U.S. There are rarely rules about whether bikes are permitted and at what times. Sure, you can take your bike—or your chickens, or your goats, or your new mattress, whatever you need to bring with you. Nothing is prohibited. People here are accommodating and want to make things work. Limited means does not mean limited ways of doing things.

"Let's go to Ulongwe today," says Paul.

"I think it's too late," I reply.

"We haven't ridden very far today." 52 kilometers.

This doesn't sound like the self-described flexible guy who volunteered in an email that he'd biked anywhere from 20 to 125 kilometers a day in New Zealand and whom I was expecting.

"We got a late start. It's already 3:30 and we still need to get groceries here to bring into the park with us." It gets dark between 5:30 and 6:00, and not having planned to bike at night, we don't have bike lights with us. In the U.S., I would've been more likely to push and more comfortable getting in at dusk. But not here. Not after two years living in a southern African country where it generally wasn't safe to be out in the villages after dark. And not now, when we've both been having bike problems. I can't think of a single reason to go on to Ulongwe today.

"Are you afraid of riding in the dark?" asks Paul with more than a hint of condescension in his voice.

"I don't think it's a very good idea."

This is our first stark disagreement. It, along with the tension I've been feeling, makes me wonder how things would be different if I'd gotten a group together for this trip, if it weren't the dynamic of just the two of us disagreeing.

I corresponded with a few others who were very interested in the trip, but when it came time to commit, to buy the plane ticket and schedule the time, none did. For some, it was money or time. For others, it was the talk of imminent war in Iraq and an apparent corresponding fear of traveling outside the friendly confines of the U.S. while at war.

This is a notion I have trouble relating to. The war in Iraq, which started three months ago now, has not affected day-to-day life here in southern Africa at all. And I am probably safer from terrorism here in Africa than I'd be in the States. When I heard from friends while in Lesotho that they were worried about me post-9/11, I told them that I didn't think Osama bin Laden was going to pick a country most Americans have never heard of for his next terrorist attack. Unfortunately, the Peace Corps didn't share my confidence and banned us volunteers from going to Lesotho's capital, Maseru, making both doing our jobs and communicating with friends and family back in the States more difficult.

We stay at the Liwonde Holiday Resort, which is a resort in name only. Our room with two beds and no other furniture costs us 150 *kwacha* each. The worn plastered walls are bare.

After we pay and wheel our bikes in, the manager says, "You want a bath? Hot water costs 50 *kwacha*."

"Isn't it included with the room?" I ask.

"No, cold is included. Hot costs extra."

I hesitate, thinking that he should've told us when we asked about the price, not now that we've already taken the room. But I don't need to be this cheap. My monetary philosophy on this long trip is that it's a budget trip but not a pinch-every-penny trip. It's okay to occasionally spend more on things like game drives in national parks. We bypassed the motel up the road that charges the equivalent of twenty U.S. dollars for a room, but it's worth an extra sixty cents to have a hot bucket bath. Paul chooses not to pay for hot water and takes a cold bucket bath.

We have dinner at the resthouse's restaurant. It is a fairly typical Malawi restaurant. Old posters decorate walls with fading paint, and worn tablecloths cover plastic tables. It's family-run, with the waitress related to the cook. Chicken with *nsima* seems to be the most commonly served dish. Rice or French fries can sometimes be substituted for *nsima*. Here they are still French fries (or more commonly, chips), not freedom fries. Beef is sometimes available.

I've gotten into the habit of ordering either an omelet or rice with vegetables (usually cabbage). Neither of these is normally on the chalkboard menu but suddenly becomes available if I ask for them. Southern Africans don't generally understand vegetarianism. Many rarely eat meat, but because they can't afford it, not because they don't want it. If they have the money to eat out, they want meat.

"Can we talk about our route from here?" asks Paul after dinner.

"Sure." I get out my map. "I'm still thinking about continuing north to Monkey Bay, taking the Ilala north for a day or two on Lake Malawi to Nkhata Bay, then heading inland then south to Lilongwe, then over to Zambia." The Ilala is a large passenger boat that goes up and down Lake Malawi once a week in each direction.

"That sounds good except I don't want to wait around at Monkey Bay for a few days." It looks like we'll arrive in Monkey Bay a few days before the Ilala.

"What if we ride to Chipoka and get on there instead, if that works better for our schedule?" I say, though I'm thinking that I wouldn't mind just hanging out somewhere for a few days.

I started this trip mentally tired, more so than I'd expected. In addition to moving out of my mud-dung home of two years and saying all my good-byes, my last weekend in Lesotho, I attended the funeral of one of the head teachers with whom I worked. He died of AIDS, though no one would openly admit it. At the funeral, people spoke of his sickness as if it was a mystery illness. Their denial depressed me. Although I spent a few days in Pretoria on my way to Malawi to meet Paul, I didn't have any real rest after the end of my Peace Corps service. A few days resting appeals to me, but I know it's not what Paul came to Malawi for, and I did suggest our start date.

Paul looks puzzled.

I explain, "Then we'd be biking for a couple more days instead of waiting around. We'd just need to make sure we can bring our bikes on in Chipoka."

"That could work," he agrees

Maybe this trip will work out, I think, not realizing that our differences will be not so much about the route itself but about where and when we stop for the day, our daily pace and mileage, and days off the bike.

SLOWED TO AFRICA'S PACE

"Hello. Hello. Hello," kids lining the sandy dirt road to the park are yelling. Their voices ring out in unison. "Give me money."

"Hello," I say as we ride by.

"Hello. Hello. Hello." They run alongside our bikes.

I am silent.

"Hello. Hello. Hello."

"Hello," says Paul.

"Hello. Hello. Hello. Give me money." They stick their hands out, palms up.

I look away from them and wish I could be alone outside, at least occasionally. And I look forward to feeling like less of a spectacle as we ride into less densely populated areas as the trip progresses.

We leave the hello chorus behind at the park entrance, then ride another kilometer to the river. At the river, we load our bikes onto the green boat with yellow trim and three bench seats across. We are the only passengers and take over the boat with our bikes and gear. Paul lays his bike in the middle of the boat. I put mine in the front. The front wheel nestles in one corner and the rear wheel perches on the top of the other side of the boat. The boat takes us across the river to Mvuu Camp.

"You are welcome here." Porters greet us as the boat docks and help unload our bikes and gear. They walk us along the short path to the reception, restaurant, and bar area—a rectangular open-air structure with low cobblestone walls and a thatched roof.

"Welcome to Mvuu Camp." The man at the check-in desk greets us.

All this welcoming reminds me of the Kenyan safari my parents took me on when they came to visit. There's an understanding of customer service here that's lacking in a lot of rural Africa. Here we are treated as we as Americans expect to be as guests. No one stares at us or asks us for anything.

We camp for the first time since Blantyre. As I set up my tent, it feels like home. There's something soothing about setting up one's own home for the night. We have a mellow afternoon at camp—eating a picnic lunch, doing laundry in a sink, cleaning and lubing our bikes, taking hot showers, and resting. While Paul goes on a game drive, I go over to the bar overlooking the river to watch for hippos. I feel enveloped in serenity. I'm relaxed, clean, and feeling good after an easy forty-three kilometer ride, a hot shower, and some time alone. It can be hard to spend so much time with someone I've just met.

Later we're cooking dinner with our camping stove when Paul looks up and says, "There's a hippo."

I turn following his gaze and see it, only fifteen meters away. Standing next to a white thatched-roof rondavel—a round, one-room building—the hippo is munching on grass, its pink chin moving as it chews. It looks so peaceful, I almost forget hippos are one of the most dangerous African animals. We watch it without approaching any closer. It plods along out of sight and we go back to cooking.

Paul asks me if I'll be ready to go on from here tomorrow after the morning boat safari that we've booked. I say I will, and he asks how far I want to go.

"Maybe Mangochi." 59 kilometers.

"Or maybe stay here awhile, then only go back to Ulongwe." 17 kilometers.

"That'd be fine." I am amazed that he suggests a shorter ride than I do.

In the morning, we go on the motorboat safari. The river is central to the park, and animals congregate near it. The boat glides along, and I peer into the brush lining the riverbanks and look for animals. There's a sense of peace, of nature's balance, here. We pass a nude palm tree, dead and palm-less but still standing. Hippos surface to breathe, only their eyes, ears, and noses sticking out of the water. I take a deep breath with them and exhale as they sink back under the surface. Birds gather to fish. We spot fish eagles, pied and malachite kingfishers, and white-breasted cormorants. I feel a peace among these birds and animals that I rarely feel among groups of people. Although elephants live in the park, we do not see any.

Over hot chocolate at the bar after the boat ride, Paul and I agree to hang out at Mvuu for awhile rather than leaving right away. I sit at the bar writing a card, watching birds in the birdbath, and reading. This is exactly the kind of experience I imagined having time for on a no-firm-schedule bike tour. I'm thinking about how nice it would be to spend the rest of the day sitting here when Paul comes over.

"I'm all packed up and ready to leave," he says.

"I thought we agreed to stay here awhile," I respond with a note of surprise in my voice.

"It has been long enough. I'm hungry and need to get to Ulongwe to buy food." His tone of voice hardens.

"But you told me to bring enough food in case we wanted to stay here tonight." A bit of confusion creeps into my voice—and mind.

"Well, I have food but it needs to be cooked and I'm already packed up. So where do you want to go today?"

"I think just Ulongwe," I say evenly, though I'm astonished that he got all ready to leave without talking with me about it first.

"Last night you said Mangochi. I want to go to Mangochi." His body tenses.

"After I said that, you said maybe just Ulongwe. When we agreed to hang out here awhile, I figured we weren't going to Mangochi today," I say.

"I want to go there." He crosses his arms over his chest.

"I don't think we have time." I'm not persuaded by his hardness.

"I think we need to talk about this trip later."

"Good idea."

I grudgingly agree to get packed up. My peace here has already been disturbed anyway.

Why does Paul feel such a need to move on? For me, part of what a no-firm-schedule trip is about is being able to stay places we like longer, making those spur-of-the-moment decisions not to go on, not worrying about how many—or few—kilometers we've come, being able to simply say this is a nice/good/fun/interesting/whatever place: let's stay a little while. I think I feel more of a need to absorb places than Paul. I like to absorb energies, and there's a positive feeling here. He seems to have a we've-seen-it/it's-time-to-move-on attitude, whereas really getting to know a place can be about lingering to me. Hanging around/watching people/exploring. I don't have the same need to be always "doing something," "getting somewhere," or "making kilometers" that he does.

After taking the boat back across the river and cycling to Ulongwe, we arrive at 3:30 in the afternoon. Paul still wants to go on to Mangochi, but I refuse. We should have time to make it to Mangochi, but what if either of us has a bike problem and we need to stop and fix it? Paul also seems to have a need to push things, to get as far as possible in a day, ride until late afternoon.

I don't share this desire. I like some time to relax during daylight hours after finishing a day's ride.

I think back to having to be home by dark in Lesotho. In a way, I hated it. I felt restricted, especially when I was away from my village and had to catch an early enough mini-bus taxi to be home by dark. At times, I wondered if it was really necessary or just the Peace Corps being overly careful in this lawsuit-happy era. But some of the schoolgirls who liked to come by and play with my almost shoulder-length light brown hair told me only "boys with knives" are out after dark. The teachers I worked with confirmed that they didn't go out after dark. One day, I went on a field trip with one of my schools to a track meet. The bus got back just after dark. No problem, I figured, everyone else on the bus is walking home now, too. But a neighbor who chaperoned the trip insisted that she walk me home.

In another way, I embraced having to be home by dark. Evenings became my time alone. Without a phone, I could read or write uninterrupted. I developed an almost daily yoga practice, knowing no one would come knock on my door, as could happen at any time during daylight hours.

We stay in a resthouse in Ulongwe. As usual when we ask for a restaurant recommendation, a boy is told to escort us. He takes us to a small, darkish restaurant with only a couple tables.

"Is there anywhere else?" asks Paul.

Looking surprised, our escort says there is.

"Let's check it out. Just for kicks," says Paul, looking at me.

I'm hungry and would rather just stay here, but I humor him. Our escort takes us to another restaurant, but it's lifeless, so we return to the first one. I'm expecting to have "the talk," but our escort hangs around to translate for us and Paul buys him a soda.

I'm not sure why we don't have the talk when we get back to the resthouse, but we don't. Neither of us brings it up, and we go to our separate rooms.

Checkout time is an early seven a.m. and we're out by seven-thirty. I think we're finally going to get an early start, but Paul realizes that he has lost his bike lock and wants to look for it, so we retrace yesterday's wheel tracks through town.

"Let's check with the police," he says.

"Why?" I ask.

"Just in case someone turned it in."

"No one will have. If someone found it, they'll find a use for it." I sigh, thinking that people don't generally turn lost locks into the police, not just here in Malawi but around the world.

"Well, let's check. Just for kicks."

The policeman listens politely while Paul explains that he's looking for a lost lock.

"No one has turned it in," he says.

"That's what I thought," I say.

He smiles at me.

We find a telephone bureau—a wooden shack with a phone that a woman charges people to use—for Paul to call Mvuu Camp. He leaves them a message asking if they've found it.

Once we're on the road, it's an easy, essentially flat ride on a tar road. Early in the ride, my rear rack comes loose. I pull over, glad we weren't riding this stretch late yesterday. A small crowd gathers to see why I've stopped. A man offers to help, but I decline. As I try to tighten the allen bolt, it spins. The dropout threads must be partially stripped. I take out my spare bolts and find one with a nut that fits. It seems to hold. My audience watches raptly, as if they've never seen a woman fix a bike before. They probably haven't.

As we ride north, gently sloping, rounded mountains are to the west, on our left, and Lake Malombe is to the east, on our right. I ride by a baobab tree and wonder how far ahead of me Paul has gotten. Baobab trees are sometimes known as upside-down trees. Their scraggly branches that stretch towards the sky look like roots reaching down into the earth. As I ride on, I'm surprised to see a billboard polluting the landscape here. Advertising a place called Sun and Sand, it must be geared towards tourists heading to Lake Malawi.

Baobab Tree

We stop in Mangochi for lunch. While looking around, we cross a bridge over the Shire River. Suddenly we're surrounded by blue water and green marshes—a stark contrast to the dry landscapes we've been cycling through. Over lunch, Paul and I talk about how far to ride this afternoon.

"Did you see that sign for Sun and Sand?" asks Paul.

"Yes."

"It looked cool. Let's stay there."

I'd never give this as a reason to stay somewhere, and I realize that appearances and the need to be cool are much more important to him than to me. I'd prefer to stay here and explore Mangochi. But I can imagine his response of "You want to stay here? We haven't gone anywhere yet today," and I agree to go on.

Back on our bikes after lunch in the shady restaurant, the midday sun feels burning hot. I'm taking dioxycycline as an anti-malarial, and one of its side effects is increased sun sensitivity, definitely less than ideal for a bike trip. But I prefer it to lariam's potential psychological side effects. Stopping to put on more sunscreen, I'm surprised to see two hand-cycles—bicycles driven with hand cranks rather than pedals—go by and wonder where they came from. Handicapped accommodations are generally nonexistent here.

Sun and Sand is a real resort. It's set on the beach on Lake Malawi and has chalets, a camping area, and an open-air restaurant with sharply dressed waiters wearing dark dress pants and white button-down shirts. As we set up camp, a few other backpackers arrive, and we all hang out together. Later we meet two South African families camping. Meeting other travelers takes some of the pressure off of Paul and me traveling together.

Camped on the beach, I fall asleep to the sound of waves constantly crashing on shore. Early the next morning, I sit outside my tent watching the sunrise through the clouds over Mozambique across the lake, and I daydream about doing this trip with a friend, someone more agreeable and with a friendlier way of expressing differences. I accept that compromise is part of having a travel partner, but I wonder if Paul does.

While riding to Monkey Bay I see, appropriately enough, vervet monkeys scampering across the road and then later some in a tree. They are the first wildlife we've seen along the road. After lunch at the New London Cafe, which is not at all European, we're surprised to find out that there's no internet access in Cape Maclear, where we're headed. The only web access in Monkey Bay is at the Venice Beach Backpackers, a hostel about two kilometers down a sandy road. Hostels are called backpackers here in southern Africa. Both needing to communicate with friends in the U.S. about potentially having bicycle parts shipped ahead to us, Paul and I feel compelled towards the sandy road.

The sand gets deeper as we cycle away from the tar road. Our tires sink in and slow us down. As we get close to the backpackers, the sand gets so deep and loose that we have to walk our bikes. We arrive at the seemingly deserted backpackers and find it still under construction. There is no signage. Is there an office here? We yell hello, and a tall European man with long, brown hair pokes his head out of a door. Surprised to have guests at this time of day, he greets us and confirms that we can use his laptop for internet access. The sluggish laptop has a few broken keys, an awkward mouse in the middle of the keypad, and some strange screen configurations. It's a slow connection and keeps disconnecting. It takes Paul over an hour to send his messages. Getting into my account, writing and sending messages about my broken rack to my best friend and dad takes forty-five minutes more. Just before I log off, I see that my best friend has already replied, telling me that he'll work on it right away. Suddenly I don't feel so far away.

Our quick four-kilometer detour to send a few emails has turned into an all-afternoon event, and it's 4:30 when I finish.

"I guess it's too late to go to Cape Maclear today now, and we need to stay here tonight," says Paul.

"Yep," I readily agree, relieved that he realizes that going on today is no longer a good option.

Africa has slowed us to her pace. The sandy road has told us "Don't plan too much," and today we have listened. We chose to check our email, and it's as if Africa has chosen that we will not go any farther today. I remember one of my Peace Corps trainers saying not to be frustrated on days when we only get one thing done but rather to look at it as good that we got that thing done. So now email is done, and the day is a success. I unfurl my yoga mat that I brought along to double as a sleeping pad and do yoga in my room. As I stretch and loosen my body, my mind also loosens—and lets go of the tension of traveling with Paul. I wish I could find the time and space for yoga every day on this trip, but it is only when I have the privacy of my own room that I even consider it an option.

Several backpackers arrive after we decide to stay, and a partyish atmosphere develops. With music blasting from the bar and the scent of marijuana hovering in the air, I quietly eat an omelet and think that this is not the Malawi I've come to see. Paul also eats an omelet. Though he hasn't become a vegetarian, liking omelets for dinner is one thing we have in common.

"Where do you want to stay in Cape Maclear tomorrow night?" Paul breaks our silence.

"I think Chembe Lodge," I reply, straining to speak over the music.

"I want to stay at Fat Monkeys," he says resolutely.

"The camping at Chembe sounds much more scenic."

"I've heard it's less secure," he counters.

"I haven't heard that," I say. Fellow travelers have recommended both Chembe and Fat Monkeys. The consensus I heard from them is that Chembe, at the end of the road, is more scenic but Fat Monkeys is more social and, thus, cooler.

Paul doesn't respond.

"Why don't we check them both out before we decide?" I'm hopeful that it'll be easier to agree after we see both than it is now.

"I want to stay at Fat Monkeys," he repeats.

A hilly road leads us to Cape Maclear. A couple of the hills are steep enough that I think about walking, but I keep riding even when it's no faster than walking. I prefer to be on my bike. This is the quietest road we've been on in Malawi. There are almost no "give me money" kids or villages. There is lots of local bike traffic.

Paul is waiting for me with his bike leaning against a wooden fence outside Fat Monkeys when I catch up to him.

"I want to stay here," he says.

"I'd still like to check out Chembe," I say. "Don't you want to see it 'just for kicks?'" I grin. "We can come back here if we want."

"I'm not going there." He grabs his bike and wheels it into the Fat Monkeys compound and straight to the registration area.

I don't want to argue and risk making a scene in front of all the people staying here, so after a moment's hesitation, I follow Paul to the registration area. I wonder, though, about his decision-making process and where I fit in.

From Fat Monkeys' backpacker camping area, we have views of the bar area and mostly South African 4x4s parked by their motor vehicle campsites.

After I set up my tent, Paul returns from the office and says, "I got us a double kayak for the afternoon."

"I'd prefer two single kayaks," I say. We talked about kayaking on Lake Malawi while here but not a double kayak.

"Well, they didn't have many kayaks left, and I wanted to be sure we got one, so I reserved a double," he says definitely.

It's nice to know that my opinion means so much.

After settling in, we walk over to get our kayak and he asks, "Have you ever done this before?"

"Yes."

"Then how about if you steer?"

I get it now. Easier to ask me to steer than to teach him to steer his own kayak.

Lake Malawi is Africa's third-largest lake and covers almost a fifth of Malawi's total area. It contains more than 600 species of fish, attracting snorkelers and scuba divers. Cape Maclear is a top backpacker destination along the lake for its long sandy beaches and scattered nearby islands.

We row to an island that Fat Monkeys recommends as a good place for snorkeling. I snorkel from the beach but don't see any fish. Paul doesn't snorkel because he doesn't want to risk getting bilharzia, a disease caused by parasitic worms that use snails as intermediate hosts. Bilharzia is known to exist in Lake Malawi and can cause serious organ damage over several years if untreated but is easily cured with medication.

We kayak to a rocky area, where we see other snorkelers. They are feeding the fish, lots of brown ones with some fluorescent blue. The fish are so close that we watch them from the rocks without snorkeling. It feels fake to me. I want to snorkel in a more natural environment, not where fish are being fed. We row around the island a bit more. An otter pokes its head out of water.

That evening, we wait over an hour and a half for our pizza for dinner at Fat Monkeys. I've gotten much more patient since living in Africa, but I start to lose my patience. It shouldn't take this long to get pizza, even here. I'm too hungry and it's not even particularly crowded. While we're waiting, we meet some white South Africans, also waiting for pizza.

After hearing about our trip, one man says, "You two are either going to love each other or hate each other at the end of three months."

I laugh, thinking there's some middle ground. Paul glares, perhaps knowing there's not.

chapter five

A Different View
of Life

In the morning, as I wait more than half an hour for Paul to get ready for what turns out to be an eight-thirty departure from camp, the notion of love certainly never crosses my mind. He sure likes to push to get farther in the afternoon but generally not to get going in the morning. We retrace our tracks on the only road in and out of the cape, then turn onto a dirt road reportedly in bad condition and head west to Mua. Some sections of this fairly flat road are rough washboard, but we can usually ride around them, much easier to do on a bike than in a car. There are lots of bike tracks to follow. It's not so much the dirt road but the distance that challenges me. It's too early in the trip for an eighty-eight kilometer ride, and I'm dragging. My legs want to

The Road to Mua

stop going round and round, stop pushing the pedals, long before we get to Mua. They don't tend to get sore, just tired.

In Mua we camp at a mission that was founded in 1902. We join the older, white priests and a couple fellow travelers for a dinner of potato soup, green beans, chips, pasta with a carrot-tomato sauce, cole slaw, and a banana. Almost two weeks into the trip, my appetite is insatiable. I consume a large plate of food and am not even stuffed. I sit next to David, one of the priests who's probably in his fifties or sixties, and we talk about AIDS in Malawi. He tells me he has recently been to a meeting with a bunch of different groups and was heartened by the concern he saw from them all.

"What's the government doing about AIDS here?" I ask.

"Nothing. All the government does is line their own pockets."

Malawi gained its independence from Britain in 1964, and the leader of the independence movement, Hastings Banda, became prime minister. Banda consolidated his power and in 1971 declared himself "President for Life." His oppressive regime jailed political dissidents and essentially ignored basic human rights. Government ministers who questioned Banda were fired for "disciplinary offences." People who openly disagreed with Banda disappeared. Legislation made discussing politics or family planning illegal. A dress code, which applied to both locals and tourists, forbade women to wear pants and men to have long hair.

Demonstrations in the early 1990s, along with donor countries cutting off all non-humanitarian aid, led to Banda's agreeing to relinquish total control. Over eighty percent of eligible voters took part in a referendum in 1993, and a strong majority voted for multi-party rule over Banda's autocratic rule. Banda accepted the vote, constitutional changes were made, and a general election was held the following year.

The new president, Badkili Muluzi, freed political prisoners, permitted free speech and a free press, and instituted economic reforms. Food prices soared as subsidies were reduced. Unemployment rose as companies closed. Crime, especially robbery, increased in urban areas. The three political parties bickered with each other. The press reported massive corruption and mismanagement. Some said little had changed from Banda's rule.

Although David is not a native, he's a long-term resident, and his comment is indicative of the lack of faith many here have in their government. He tells me he's doing some research on AIDS and that I'll see it in the museum. He says Islam is a problem in the struggle against AIDS, but before I have a chance to ask him what he means, someone interrupts us and changes the subject.

In the morning, Paul and I walk over to the Chamare Museum at the Kungoni Art Craft Centre. The museum consists of three rondavels adorned with exterior murals inset in brick frames. Inside, our guide, Francis, explains that the exhibits detail the three different cultures in Malawi—Chewa, Yao, Ngoni. The exhibits include statues in traditional dress, paintings, and animal effigies. Placards explain their rituals of birth, initiation, marriage, death, anointing a new chief, traditional healing, and rain dancing. For example, the Chewa are matriarchal and the husband joins his new wife's family. If tribes intermarry, the traditions of the woman's family are followed.

I don't see anything about AIDS at all. When I ask Francis, he says that he doesn't know of anything except that some of the masks that have traditionally been used to ward off promiscuity are now being used to ward against AIDS since promiscuity spreads it.

The Centre teaches woodcarving to the locals, and the showroom is full of intricate wood carvings—statues, animal figures, and masks. I buy a mask that is small enough to easily both rest in one hand and carry with me on my bike.

Exhibits in the Chamare Museum

We get groceries at the market for lunch. I buy tomatoes and buns to make sandwiches, and fatcakes, which are fried dough. Even after last night's large dinner, I feel a need to eat some grease to get more calories.

After lunch, we cycle to Chipoka and confirm the Ilala schedule. The Ilala is named after a boat used by the Scottish missionaries who founded a mission at Cape Maclear in the late nineteenth century. That first boat was named after the place where the explorer David Livingstone died in 1873. The current Ilala consists of cabins, a first class deck that includes seats and some shade, and the economy lower deck. It arrives here at one tomorrow afternoon and departs at four.

At the Chipoka Beach View Lodge, we get our own rooms with a shower, toilet, and toilet paper, which is a rare commodity at resthouses, though easy to find in shops. The rooms are basic, but it's a treat to have our own bathrooms rather than shared ones down the hall. I'm surprised to see pasta on the dinner menu at the restaurant. Perhaps the lodge is a little more used to European tourists than the local village restaurants we've been eating in.

After a lazy morning at the lodge, we buy first-class deck tickets for the Ilala, pay a small surcharge for our bikes, and wait at the port. It's over an hour late. I watch the red, white, and blue boat approach and remember that today is the Fourth of July, my Mom's birthday. As we board, the crew directs us to store our bikes in the crew area. We lock them to a railing, ensuring that they'll be secure even in rough weather, and climb the ladder to the deck. While looking for a spot for my panniers, I notice how easily it looks like stuff could fall through the metal railings and off the boat. I keep them away from the edge. We spend the rest of the afternoon chatting with other passengers and relaxing. Until we depart from Chipoka, a Malawian named Goodwin hangs out on the deck but then goes downstairs because he only paid for economy class. I talk a lot with Jonathan, a U.S. college student who just spent a semester in Cape Town—another American who understands Africa.

The classes on the boat have different food options. We're presented with a short menu for first-class food, which will be served to us if we order it. But it's expensive (650 *kwacha*), so five of us venture down to economy class instead. Going down the stairs, we leave the fresh sea air and bright sunshine. Descending into the engine fumes, I have my first view of life in economy class. It's dark and crowded. People sit against their sacks of cassava and luggage crowds the aisles. Stepping over the sacks and past people sitting in the walkway, we make our way to the cafeteria. Separate giant metal cauldrons contain beef, beans, *nsima*, and rice. For 100 *kwacha,* I get a plate of rice and beans. We bring our food back up to the deck. I'd hesitated about buying a first-class ticket, not liking the segregation that the price structure creates and thinking that maybe I wanted to experience the Ilala like the locals do, but now I'm glad I didn't. Fifteen minutes of crowds and fumes was enough.

The Ilala makes four stops between Chipoka and Nkhata Bay—Metangula and Cobu, Mozambique; Likoma Island; and Chimzimulu Island. Traveling on the lake gives a different view of life than what we get from the road. The Ilala is the primary commercial link for some of the villages—the main way in and out for both people and goods. As we approach Metangula, under a light pink early morning sky, waiting crowds line the shores. The lake here is too shallow for the Ilala to dock, so smaller boats ferry people and goods to and from it. Some people wade from the small boats to shore. As I watch, the sun rises enough to light up the scene.

I have a restful morning napping, reading, and watching the scenery. As we head north, closer to the equator, the hills of the Mozambique shoreline get greener. Small fishing boats, usually with only two people in them, bob on the lake.

Although the Ilala sways a lot at times, it's good to not have anywhere to go and have a restful day and a half, no decisions to have to make with Paul.

Ten of us white people get off on Likoma Island for a couple hours while the Ilala is stopped there. The Ilala doesn't dock at Likoma, so we take a small boat to the island. Getting on the small boat is chaotic, as people push and some throw heavy sacks that land with a thud onto the boat. As our boat brings us to the shore, stacks of crates with empty glass Coke bottles wait to be ferried to the Ilala.

Likoma Island became a Christian missionary base in the 1880s when the missionaries took refuge from attacks by local tribesmen. In 1903, they started building a cathedral the size of one in Winchester, England. They used bricks made on the island and mud from anthills as mortar. Without knowing this, we go to the almost 100-year-old church and find it huge for an island. There is a mellow, comfortable feel to the island, and the kids don't ask us for money. I think I'd be happy relaxing here for a few days. I seem to be thinking this a lot.

To get back to the Ilala, we ride a barge that also carries a car. After we board the Ilala, the car is winched up onto it. And we asked if we could bring our bikes.

In the evening, while we are waiting for more beans to be cooked, the boat hits a rough section. Thinking I was about to eat, I've just taken a dioxycycline and feel nauseated. A Canadian couple gives me a Dramamine and the Ilala enters a bay of calmer water. I slowly recover. Leaving the bay, we re-enter rough water. As the boat sways, a large red backpack slides towards the edge of the boat. It's heading for the gap under the railing and is about to go overboard when someone grabs it.

We dock at Nkhata Bay at 2:30 a.m.. The captain makes an announcement confirming what we were told the previous evening: everyone should stay on the boat until five. A collective restlessness seems to invade the group of us sleeping on the deck. It's as if some don't trust him. If they allow themselves to fall back asleep, the boat will leave early and with them still on it. Though I don't think it would it be so awful if we did go on to the next stop, this restlessness keeps me awake.

I overhear Paul telling one of the other backpackers that we're going to Njaya—a popular backpackers' hostel—only for breakfast then riding to Mzuzu.

"What was that about going to Mzuzu today?" I later ask.

"We've got all day. What else would we do?" he says with that trademark exasperation creeping into his voice.

"We haven't talked about anything other than staying at Njaya when we arrived," I say, tiredly.

"That was when we thought the boat got in late at night."

"We never talked about another plan when we found out it didn't. I don't want to ride fifty hilly kilometers after being awake since 2:30 a.m.."

His disapproving silence fills the air between us.

"I thought you wanted to take the time to see places along the way, too," I add, thinking back to our pre-trip email correspondence.

Paul had mentioned that he started his recent New Zealand bike trip with a group but had split up with them because his riding style was different than theirs, that he wanted to see more sights. He said they never wanted to sightsee anywhere that wasn't directly on their route. Maybe what he really meant was that he had trouble traveling with a group whose interests were sometimes different than his, and maybe I should've asked him if he was sure he wanted to bicycle in Africa with other people.

"I'd rather be spending the time someplace I like better," he says.

Is this the underlying problem? He doesn't like Malawi much, so we're spending too much time here. I'm happier and more comfortable here than he is. In all fairness, I did suggest three weeks per country, and we are on a pace to spend more than this in Malawi, but it was only a loose suggestion with a caveat to spend longer at places we like. I had planned to make these decisions by group consensus. In a group of two, however, there's no consensus when we disagree. He may still be adjusting to Africa, whereas I'm used to it. I wonder what can I do about this other than try to be patient and try not to take his comments too personally.

In a few years, I will write down this story. I will re-read Paul's emails, and I will understand that he was so agreeable by email because he was so unfamiliar with the conditions here. He asked me what was possible here and accepted my recommended distances. But once here, he found the distances were easier than he expected, and without even realizing what he was doing, started trying to make the trip into a higher mileage trip than I'd suggested, and he'd readily agreed to. If he had asked me nicely if we could do some longer days, we probably could have worked out a compromise. But instead he ridiculed me, and my defenses sprang up: the classic fight-or-flight response. I felt attacked, and I could either fight back or run away, which in this case meant withdrawing more into myself, and thus protecting myself from more barbs rather than chumming around and facing ridicule.

chapter six

THUNK THUNK THUNK

At Njaya, five fellow travelers from the Ilala invite me to explore Nkhata Bay with them, but I decline. I just want to rest. I'm so tired, even after a mellow day on the Ilala. I think it's mental strain.

"It must be tough traveling with someone only for safety reasons," says Jonathan.

What? I wonder if this is what Paul is telling people and if he has felt this way all along or if it has evolved over the course of the trip.

I sit on the deck at Njaya relaxing, looking at the lake, writing, and thinking about ordering lunch. I watch a woman at a nearby house use a large piece of wood to grind something, but I can't see what. I think about how there's no place like Njaya, with a deck overlooking a lake to relax undisturbed on and to eat veggie food at backpacker prices, in Lesotho. The portions aren't bicyclist-sized here, but there are a lot of veggie options on the menu—and it's a good break from rice with cabbage or beans.

From here, we're headed to Lilongwe, Malawi's capital. We can either go south along the coast of Lake Malawi then turn west to go inland, or go inland from here then head south. We choose the latter for a variety of scenery through a less touristy area. Leaving the coast for the mountains is our most difficult day of cycling so far. It's fifty kilometers to Mzuzu with almost 1200 meters of cumulative elevation gain, including several steep hills. It becomes our first day riding in some rain, but at least we are on a tar road so it cannot turn to mud. My legs feel drained for the last ten kilometers. In the evening, I'm exhausted.

The next morning the waiter at the Chinwanja Resthouse restaurant asks me what I want for breakfast.

"I'd like an omelet," I say.

"No omelet."

"But it's on the menu." Could they possibly be out of eggs? This doesn't seem likely.

"The cook doesn't know how to make omelets."

I pause, never having heard this before in Africa. "I'll have fried eggs then."

Ten minutes later, he brings me an omelet. I don't ask how the cook learned so quickly.

Leaving Mzuzu is another difficult ride, with more climbing and steep hills than I expected. The road meanders through a pine forest. We pass only a few small villages but many men carrying large stacks of wood on their bicycles. The people are either friendly or quiet and no one requests anything.

As usual, Paul gets ahead of me and I ride along alone. I think about how pressured I feel—pressured to keep a schedule that he's happy with and pressured to catch up to him after he rides ahead. I take a break at the top of a climb, and it hits me that something is really wrong. Here I am on my dream trip—exploring southern Africa by bicycle with no real schedule and no plane ticket back to the States or anywhere else—yet I'm unhappy. This isn't how it was in my dreams. I've been trying not to admit this to myself, but maybe Paul and I just aren't compatible travel partners. We thought we were, or at least I thought we were.

Now what? I tried to put together a group because I didn't think I'd feel safe doing this trip alone and wanted company. But with the only company I've got so negative, should I suggest we split up? He told me in Blantyre that he wouldn't have come to Africa alone, so now I feel responsible for his being here. Maybe I just need to focus more on my own enjoyment on the trip and not let myself feel pressure. So what if I'm slower? I'm riding a slower bike and not in a rush. Why shouldn't I take my time? I suggested mountain bikes for this trip, and he chose to bring his touring bike. Why should this be my problem?

I haven't seen him for hours, longer than usual. I'm both enjoying the solitude and wondering where he is when I see him stopped up ahead.

"I was about to turn around and ride back to look for you. I've been waiting here a long time. Is something wrong?" Paul looks slightly concerned as he leans on his bike by the side of the road.

"No. I'm just taking my time enjoying the scenery, taking breaks and photos." Figuring this will just be a quick stop, I straddle my bicycle.

"Well, it's four o'clock and we've only come forty kilometers." An annoyed look crosses his face.

"Really? Is that it? It feels much farther with all the hills and getting such a late start."

"Your computer still isn't working?" He furrows his eyebrows. My bike computer stopped working in yesterday's rain.

"No, it must need to dry out more. And I guess I'm still tired from yesterday's ride."

"I didn't think that was a hard ride. We've still got more than twenty kilometers to go. At this rate, we're never going to make it."

"Maybe we'll have more downhill soon." I try to smile optimistically.

"I don't like camping out by the side of the road." His negative vibes fill the air.

"We might not have a choice."

"I'm almost out of water."

"Maybe there's a village up ahead where we can get some if we aren't going to make it to the lodge tonight." I scan the hills ahead.

"What do you want to do?" he asks.

"Let's keep riding for now. There's no reason to stop and camp here. We've still got almost two hours of daylight left," I say.

"I want to get to the lodge, and I don't mind riding after dark."

"In the U.S., I might keep riding after dark. But not here. We'd be too vulnerable."

"So you're afraid of the dark?"

"No, but we don't even have good bike lights with us and it's going to be pitch dark out here. It'd be too easy to ride off the road and get hurt." This is my reality, but it is clearly not his. When two people's realities don't mesh, it is probably best for both that they not travel together. Yet here we are together, neither of us understanding the other's perspective.

He silently stares at me.

I continue, "Plus we don't know this area well enough to know if there are bandits roaming around after dark. Let's keep going for now. Maybe we'll get to the lodge or find a village with a resthouse."

We get back on our bikes and ride on. The road starts going downhill more than it goes uphill, but the uphill sections have steep climbs that slow me down a lot. We've gone sixty-one kilometers by about 5:40. Just after watching a brilliant sunset as we ride, we reach a small village. Two men are standing around outside, and we approach them.

I greet them in Chewa, and they return my greeting in another language, which I guess is Nyanja. They speak a bit of English, so we are able to communicate with short sentences and sign language.

I ask, "Lodge how far?"

They talk amongst themselves and the one wearing an orange vest says, "Nine kilometers."

I look at the darkening sky and say, "Dark. Far. Village with resthouse near?"

The same one answers, "Six kilometers."

Paul and I look at each other. I know he wants go on, but we've learned from experience that Malawians don't really seem to know distances. I tell him we can't be sure of these distances. We can see the road rising away from the village, so we know it's a climb out of here. Even if it is only six kilometers, it's not an easy six k and it's rapidly getting darker.

"If you want to stay here, you ask," he says.

I look back to the men. "Place here camp? Have tents," I ask and make a triangle with my hands to indicate a tent symbol.

Yes, they nod, okay. Where? They show us an area where a few wide paths converge amidst some brush.

Noticing the lack of trees, I ask, "Bikes—place to keep tonight?"

"Bikes. House," the same one answers. At some point, he identifies himself as the community police officer.

Paul's annoyance is again emanating from him. The trip doesn't seem to be going the way he wants or thinks it should. Yet it doesn't really surprise me that we didn't get to the lodge. One thing I came to accept over the course of my Peace Corps service was that sometimes in rural Africa, you can only get one thing done per day.

This might sound crazy, especially to a high-powered American, but things just take longer here. People don't have the same sense of urgency, and time doesn't have the same importance. We took the morning to check our email, do a bit of shopping, and exchange travelers' checks. When I had to wait more than an hour at the bank because they didn't yet have today's exchange rate and couldn't use Friday's rate because it might have changed a lot over the three-day weekend, as they said, I realized that we had too much planned for today for Africa's pace. Errands plus what we expected to be a hilly sixty-five kilometer ride. Before I lived in Africa, I also would have thought no problem, but here it felt like too much, too out of tune with the natural rhythms of the place. I remembered one of our Peace Corps' cultural trainers explaining people's thinking, "If I don't do it today, I'll get to it tomorrow, or the next day, or next week, or whenever." At times this had been infuriating, especially when I had to wait days for things to happen that allowed my projects to go forward. But traveling with another American, one who has never before been to Africa, I am realizing how much I have changed, how much more patient and accepting of things being the way they are here I've become. This morning I thought about suggesting to Paul that we spend another night in Mzuzu and have the afternoon free to explore or relax rather than still try to do our planned day's ride in only the afternoon. But I didn't. I knew I was thinking more like an African than an American and that he wouldn't be able to relate. I didn't want to hear his complaints about the pace of the trip or see his look of exasperation, so I didn't even suggest it.

I'm surprised that they're offering our bikes a house but not us, so I clarify, "House?"

"Yes, house. Bikes in house." They nod.

Paul still looks resentful.

"Is it okay to stay here?" I ask, looking at him.

He shrugs, looks away, and utters a sigh of resignation.

I know he's unhappy, but I'm relieved to be off the road before it's completely dark. I'd also prefer a lodge or resthouse over village camping for the privacy of a room and the opportunity to bathe, but I accept this as part of the experience of cycling long distances in Africa. There aren't always accommodations available at bike distances. Part of the adventure of this kind of trip is not always knowing where we'll spend the night, even when we think we do.

A small audience of seven or eight gathers to watch us put up our tents and store our panniers inside them. The kids crouch, peering in our tent doors, and giggle. I ask for water. One girl runs off and returns with a bucketful.

The community police officer seems to have put himself in charge of the situation. He takes me and the bikes to a nearby house and introduces me to its occupant, Chief Ngozi, who tells me our bikes will be safe in his house tonight. Outside I encounter the village drunk, who keeps trying to take my arm as I walk back to the tents. Someone yells at him, and he wanders away.

When I return to the tents, Paul asks, "You're more comfortable with our bikes in a house we can't see from here than right outside our tents overnight?"

"Yes, I am. I locked them together."

"Well, I'm not," he counters.

"There aren't any trees here to lock them to. If we just left them outside our tents, anyone could come along and wander off with them," I say.

"No, they couldn't. I'd hear them if they tried." He stares at the ground.

"I'm a sound sleeper, and I'm more comfortable with the bikes inside. Besides, it's too late now anyway. We can't ask for them back to leave them outside. That would be too insulting to the chief."

Years later the realization that traveling by bicycle is an opening, enlivening experience whereas traveling with someone who ridicules you is a deadening one will come to me as I listen to my body and prana—life force—guiding me into surrendering into the pigeon pose on my yoga mat. But for now all I know is that I am simply uncomfortable traveling with Paul. My body knows and is telling me, but as ironic as it might be on such a physical undertaking as a bike trip, I am not listening to my body. I am listening to my brain, to logic reminding me that I tried to put together a group for safety reasons and that Paul wouldn't be here, traveling in Africa now, if I hadn't placed that ad. And so, I listen to logic, taking responsibility for the consequences of my actions and not realizing that logic doesn't know what is truly best for me, what is healthiest for my soul.

Paul and I cook our emergency pasta for dinner by moonlight. The police officer returns and asks us what time we will leave in the morning. We're not sure. He says four o'clock is a good time. I can't figure out what he's talking about. He can't be asking us to leave that early because it's still dark then. He tells us to pick up our bikes at six. I don't understand why, but say okay. After he leaves, Paul asks me if we have to leave at six. I tell him I don't think so, the chief probably just wants the space in his house back or maybe he's going somewhere.

It's winter in the mountains and has been rapidly cooling off since the sun set. As soon as we finish eating and washing dishes, we crawl into our tents to get warm. I'm glad my sleeping bag is rated for freezing temperatures. It's not that cold, but I get cold at night easily and like to be cozy.

I drag myself out of my tent at six in the morning to pick up the bikes. It feels way too early to knock on someone's door, but the chief isn't surprised to see me, so I guess we got the right message.

Before we leave, I turn to the girl who brought us water yesterday, hand her a pen, and say "Thanks. Water." I want her and the others to understand why she is getting a gift. It's not a handout. It's a thank you for work. She bows to thank me.

It takes us forty-five minutes to ride nine kilometers to the village with a resthouse, and it's another five kilometers to the turnoff for the lodge from there. I'm glad we didn't go on yesterday.

It's another hilly ride with some steep climbs, but the tar road gradually flattens out after about forty kilometers. It doesn't get flat, just less hilly. We descend into a drier zone. The grass is browner and scrubbier shrubs replace the pine trees.

There are some villages along the way but still not many people. People continue to be friendly without asking for things, a welcome change from all the repetitive "hellos" and "give me moneys." Here people simply greet us or wave, maybe because we are off the tourist route, or maybe because of the different culture in this region.

Arriving in Jenda after a longer-than-expected ninety-two-kilometer ride, we stop and ask a policeman where the best resthouse in town is. It's fun to be able to ride into a town, ask for the best resthouse, and know that it's easily affordable. In Jenda, the best is clean and well-kept but has no running water or electricity. Later, I find the owner in her house with the door open and ask for a restaurant recommendation.

"I will cook you dinner," she says, "I have some meat to cook for you." She holds up a chunk of raw meat.

I flinch inside but hide my repulsion. "I do not eat meat. My friend might want some, but would you cook me eggs?"

"I do not have any but will cook them if you buy them."

She wants to make some extra money but doesn't seem to be willing to work very hard for it.

"I will let you know if we find some eggs."

Paul and I walk across the dusty dirt road to a nearby store. It doesn't have any eggs, so we wander around town. Street vendors are selling fresh chips (French fries) and salads. The chips sizzle in oil and their greasy smell penetrates the air and tempts our bellies, but they wouldn't be filling enough for a post-ride dinner—and I wouldn't trust a salad here.

We walk down the main tar road and go into a restaurant.

"Do you have omelets?" we ask.

"We can make you some if you want."

"Do you have eggs?"

"No, but we will get some."

Pleased that they are not asking us to find them eggs, we agree. We're both still thinking about the chips, though, and I go to buy some for an appetizer while Paul waits in the restaurant and journals in his Palm Pilot.

As I walk toward the chip stands, a few young men yell to me in Chewa. I don't understand their words, but I do understand the sexual overtones. They aren't threatening, just harassing. I ignore them, not even glancing their way and keep walking. This is my first time out alone after dark in Malawi, and the change in the atmosphere surrounding me is palpable. Now I'm a woman alone—an available woman—whereas when I'm with Paul, men assume I'm really with him and leave me alone. Uninterested in brief flings or one-night stands, I consider this a fringe benefit of having a male traveling partner.

Ignoring the catcalls, I keep walking. I realize how different this trip would be if I were traveling alone. Paul's presence protects me from sexual comments. In a way, this isn't much different than in the States, where a solo woman at a bar will be approached by all sorts of men, whereas one with a man will be left alone. Except here, it's as if the whole country is a bar after dark: a solo woman out alone is subject to harassment.

If I were traveling alone, I probably wouldn't always be comfortable walking back to a resthouse alone after dark. Even if I were safe, this evening is evidence that I most likely would be hassled or harassed as a woman out alone. Is trading these hassles for the hassles of Paul worth it? I don't know, but I'm not thinking this way at this time.

The following day is a Thursday, Jenda's market day. By six in the morning, thousands of tomatoes, lots of potatoes, some onions, and cabbage are already displayed on makeshift wooden tables that sprang up in a dusty lot. As the early morning hours unfold, more sellers arrive with textiles, pots, and bike parts.

I feel good riding, like my legs are finally getting into touring mode. Although there are still some hills, it's an easier ride than the past two days. I get in a good cycling groove and cover fifty kilometers by noon, but I occasionally hear a rubbing noise coming from my rear wheel. It gets worse, so I stop to check it out. I can't find anything wrong. The wheel spins freely and doesn't rub on the brake pads. I go on. The noise gets worse.

Thunk. Thunk. Thunk.

I stop again and standing on the other side of my bike this time, I discover

Jenda Market

that my rim has cracked and buckled. I stare at the crack. This is bad, not something that can be repaired by the side of the road, or anywhere else. I'm going to need a new wheel, or at least a new rim. The question is when. And whether I'll be able to find one that's compatible with my bike anywhere in Malawi. How far can I ride with the rim like this? How long until it cracks through, into the tire and tube? What now? I may as well ride some more and at least try to catch Paul whenever he next stops, then try to get a ride into Lilongwe, more than 160 kilometers away. I get back on my bike but don't make it much farther.

Pop. Hissssss. My tire goes flat as the rim bends into it.

Just as I start trying to flag down a ride, Paul comes back looking for me. He'd stopped up ahead and gotten concerned when I hadn't caught up. He decides to go ahead to the next town to try to arrange a ride for me and send someone back. I tell him I'll keep trying here. I hope to be able to find someone going all the way to Lilongwe. We arrange a fallback meeting point—Kiboko Camp—in Lilongwe for tomorrow in case we don't see each other tonight. He rides ahead.

I try to flag down every private vehicle that goes by, but not one stops. Don't I look stranded? Whatever happened to wanting to help a damsel in distress? What is probably only fifteen minutes feels like an hour in the midday sun. Cycling provides a natural breeze but stopped off the bike, it's downright hot. And I'm miserable. How could my bike break now when I was finally feeling so good riding? I don't really want a ride. I want my bike to magically fix itself. A local comes by and tells me he'll get me a ride. He flags down a mini-bus taxi. I don't tell him that I was trying to find a more direct ride than a taxi, which will make many stops. The driver and conductor put my bike behind the backseat and tie the door as shut as it can get. I ask the driver to stop when we pass Paul, so I can tell him I've gotten a ride. He doesn't seem to understand, and speeds by. I yell out the window and wave.

The taxi only goes to Kasungu, still 130 kilometers from Lilongwe. It's mid-afternoon. I could get a mini-bus taxi to Lilongwe, but by the time it fills up and possibly stops at many places on the way, I might not get in until after dark. Not an appealing option for arriving in an African city taxi rank, especially an unfamiliar one, where thieves may be lurking.

I walk through town and consider walking out of town and trying to hitch a ride. But it's a big town and off the highway.

"I fix bike," boys and men say as I walk by.

"No, you cannot," I say, knowing that they think I only have a puncture and am a helpless woman who can't possibly know how to fix it.

Some follow me. I stop and ask a man wearing a suit if he speaks English. He tells me the boys can fix my bike. I show him that the wheel is broken and can't be fixed. Even in a land where everything can be fixed, where things are jerryrigged in all sorts of innovative ways, this can't be fixed. He translates for the crowd that my wheel is broken. No one offers to fix it. Then he recommends the Dumadasi Motel and tells a boy to escort me. Two other escorts appoint themselves and they all walk me to the motel.

As I'm checking in, the man at the hotel reception says, "You shouldn't let men escort you."

"Another man asked them to. He gave them directions."

"They are thieves."

What a contrast to the "you are very welcome here" of Mvuu Camp. The possible thieves didn't steal anything from me. I think they thought it was cool to escort the white woman with the broken bicycle. I suppose the receptionist is trying to be helpful, but his negativity is the final trigger on an upsetting day. I shut the door to my room, lean my bike against a wall, and sit on the bed in tears. What if I can't find a new wheel in Lilongwe? I'll have to get one shipped from South Africa. This could take awhile—or be very expensive. Why did my wheel have to break here? Why couldn't it have broken in Pretoria three weeks ago? In more than 60,000 lifetime miles, this is the first time

I've ever had to get a ride because my bike is too broken for me to fix. I really don't need to be told that I was just escorted by thieves. Things are already bad enough.

chapter seven

DON'T YOU HAVE A
HUSBAND?

While I'm waiting for the six a.m. bus to Lilongwe, a man wearing a light blue jumpsuit walks over to me.

"That's the bus," he says pointing, "The driver is not ready, but come with me and I'll load your bike before everyone rushes to get on."

He takes me to the bus before it's officially loading and has me put all my gear inside, then he ties my bike onto the roof rack. When the bus drives over to where people are waiting to board, I'm all set up—sitting with my gear in the front two-seater.

"I work for the bus company in Blantyre," he explains.

Many people board in Kasungu, but everyone gets a seat. The bus departs at 6:30. As we go along, more and more people get on, and it gets crowded. The conductor tells a small girl to sit next to me. People crowd against my legs. At one stop, not everyone who wants to get on is allowed to push in.

When we arrive at the old town bus stop in Lilongwe, boys climb up to the roof of the bus and hand my bike down to me.

"Two hundred *kwacha*," says one. This is more than my ticket cost.

"No, you didn't do any work," I say, shaking my head, "I'm not paying you for handing me my bike."

An onlooker nods in agreement. I consider taking a private taxi with my bike but don't see any and want to get away from the bus stop. I consulted my guidebook map on the bus and know the way to Kiboko, where Paul and I agreed to meet. As I walk, I notice a boy following me. I turn around and stare at him a few times and he goes away. Some bicycles with multi-speed hubs are displayed outside small shops. I stop to look at them, but none are eight-speeds, like my bike. My arms get tired of pushing my bike, but I keep walking until I get all the way to Kiboko.

After setting up my tent and locking my bike to a tree, I walk into the center of old town. I go to the Peace Corps office, introduce myself, and tell them about my trip. I ask if their bikes have eight-speed hubs and if so, could I buy a rear wheel from them? They tell me their bikes do have eight-speed hubs but whether they can sell me a wheel is up to their Administrative Officer (AO)—and he's out to lunch. I ask to use the internet while I wait, but the IT guy says it's only for current volunteers. Welcome back to the land of U.S. government bureaucracy. While I wait, I go to an internet cafe then have a veggie burger for lunch at Nando's, a South African chain. When I return to the office, the AO says he can't sell me a wheel but I can have one from one of their old bikes. They have just gotten new ones. Wow, I think, this was too easy.

And it was. They show me one of the bikes—and it has a seven-speed hub. Eight-speeds aren't seven-speeds with one more gear added to the end but rather they are eight closer-together gears in a similar amount of space as a seven-speed. My eight-speed shifters will not properly align my chain with the cogs of a seven-speed. I may be able to combine the two wheels into one that will work with my bike, but not quickly. I get permission for Paul and me to stay at the house Peace Corps has for volunteers when they're in Lilongwe, starting tomorrow. There we'll have access to the extra Peace Corps bikes and tools.

I bring a wheel from one of the bikes back to Kiboko with me. It will at least be a lot easier to push my bike around with a tire that holds air. When I return to Kiboko, Paul is there—and impressed that I have a wheel and access to bikes and parts and permission for us to stay at the Peace Corps house.

In the morning Paul is feverish, achy, and queasy, but he still wants to move to the Peace Corps house. I put my "new" wheel on my bike. Just as I expected, it fits but the gears don't work.

Over the course of the next few days, we hang out at the house to fix my bike, get Paul some rest, and relax, and we wander into town for meals out, groceries, and internet cafes.

Paul and I try to move my gears to a Peace Corps wheel, but the gears don't fit on the freewheel. Our only other option is to rebuild my wheel so that we can use a Peace Corps rim with my hub, gears, and spokes. Fortunately, Paul has some experience rebuilding wheels and Peace Corps has a truing stand. He loosens all the spokes on my wheel while I remove all the spokes from a Peace Corps wheel. He then replaces my broken rim with the Peace

Corps rim, tightens the spokes, and trues the wheel so that it spins without a wobble. I adjust my brakes to accommodate the wider rim. The front rack my best friend arranged to have sent from South Africa arrives, and I replace my broken rack, too.

While spending time at the house, we meet several Malawi volunteers, including Maryann, who was a volunteer in Lesotho from 1998 to 2000, and Justine, whose dream is to bike around Namibia. I feel more connection and camaraderie with them in a few days than I've felt with Paul this entire trip. Justine is a third-year health volunteer, and she talks about loving and hating Malawi, loving the friendliness but hating the lack of motivation. She shares an article that she wrote about her experience in Malawi. She lives near Monkey Bay, where the men leave their families for extended periods to fish. While away, they earn lots of money but squander most of it on alcohol and other women instead of bringing it home to their families. So their wives prostitute themselves to support their families. Nonetheless, the article is largely positive and about hope—the hope she sees in the eyes of a baby AIDS orphan and the hope she gains from a man with whom she works. This man sets a positive example by taking care of his family and spending his money on them. She also writes about how she lives close to nature by cooking and washing dishes outdoors and frequently uses her bicycle for transportation and loves it. She tells me that she didn't bicycle at all in the U.S. and now would rather bike sixty-five kilometers than take a minibus.

After spending five days in Lilongwe, Paul and my bike are both healthy enough to get back on the road, and we depart the Peace Corps house late one morning. Once we weave our way out of the city center, we're on a smooth flattish tar road. I cruise along, with both my new wheel and rack working perfectly. It feels good to be back on the road. Surprisingly, I arrive in Namitete, forty-nine kilometers from Lilongwe, ahead of Paul.

I notice a police station on the left and pull over. The police in Malawi have been good sources of information about accommodation. There's a tall, thin officer hanging around outside the station. Our conversation starts fairly typically.

"Good afternoon, Sir."

"Good afternoon. Where are you coming from on that bicycle?"

"Today, Lilongwe, but I've taken the long route from Blantyre over the last four weeks." I lean my bike against a low cement wall and settle in for a chat.

"All on bicycle? How many kilometers a day?" Surprise fills his voice.

"Usually fifty to eighty but sometimes more or less."

"Do you like our country?" he asks with pride.

"Yes, the people are very friendly."

"Yes, we are the warm heart of Africa. Are you alone? Don't you have a husband?"

"My friend is coming. He's back there. He'll probably be here soon." I look down the road, scanning for Paul.

"You mean he is slower than you?" he asks, and I hear his question as how is it possible that a man is slower than a woman.

"Not usually but today he is. He has been sick." I continue, "Is there a resthouse here?"

"Yes, there are two. They are near. The first one is better." He smiles.

"And what about in the next village or anywhere else before Mchinji?"

"Not in the next village but in Kamwemba. It's not so good. Mchinji is better," he says.

"But Mchinji is too far for today by bicycle. How far is Kamwemba? It's not on my map."

"Maybe thirty or forty kilometers. Is that too far?"

The police have not been known for giving us accurate distances. Thinking that thirty or forty means it could easily be fifty, I reply, "It's farther than I'd like but possible. Maybe we'll stay here. My friend should be here soon, and we'll decide."

While I'm discussing our plans to cycle in Zambia with the policeman, Paul rides up. He looks surprised to see me here, and one of his annoyed looks crosses his face. Why are you stopped here, it seems to ask. Yet last night's plan for today had been to ride to Namitete, find out whether there were any other resthouses before Mchinji, and decide here whether we were going to go on today.

"Is everything okay?" he asks.

"Yes, I was just asking about resthouses." I share the information I've just gotten from the police with him.

"I already know that. I talked to someone who knew last night and decided we should go to Kamwemba today."

"Thanks for letting me know."

"Do you want to stay here?" His voice is laced with frustration.

I wonder if he thought I'd just keep riding without stopping in Namitete because he had a secret plan. "I'm not sure. Ideally I'd like to go a little farther but given the options, maybe."

"If we stop here, then we'll have to do 115 kilometers with a border crossing tomorrow. Is that what you want to do?"

"I'm not sure." I'm not thrilled with any of the options.

"Well, we'd have to. Our visas are expiring and we have to get to Zambia tomorrow. We can't stop in Mchinji tomorrow."

"I can extend them for you," interjects the policeman.

I give him a huge smile. He can't know that Paul has been talking about our thirty-day visas expiring for days and that I've told him we could easily get them extended.

Paul ignores him. "I want to go to Kamwemba today. I'm the one who has been sick, and I'm not tired, so you can do it."

"It's not about being tired. It's about sometimes wanting to do shorter and easier days, especially when we get late starts."

Paul continues to look peeved.

"I'll go on today, but I'd appreciate it if you don't ridicule me when I suggest riding distances that were included in my tour description."

"Ridicule you?" He looks genuinely surprised. "I don't know what you're talking about, but we can talk about it later if you want." He rides away.

The policeman also looks surprised by my assertive comment.

I thank him for his help and go on. I ride along, thinking maybe this is what Paul and I need—to talk things out. I also think about cycling through Zambia alone. Should I suggest we just split up, acknowledge that it isn't working, that maybe we're not compatible? But I know he's hesitant about Zambia and concerned about safety there even with two of us, and he did just rebuild my wheel.

I realize I expected we'd become friends, and we just haven't. Although we got along well enough initially and can still be friendly towards one another, we've never clicked as friends. And at this point, the only possible desire I have to be friends with him is one of proximity and convenience, certainly not of personality or admiration. This trip is probably too long and too difficult to do with someone who isn't a friend, or who doesn't become one along the way.

Forty-five kilometers from Namitete, we reach Kamwemba. It's late afternoon and Paul confesses to being worn out. The owner of the resthouse doesn't speak much English, but he understands that we want two rooms. He seems confused, though, because he keeps telling me that their rooms have 3/4 beds. We've heard of these beds in other resthouses. They're the size of 1½ twin beds. It must be routine for couples here to share them. The possibility of our not being a couple doesn't cross his mind, but he gives us keys to two rooms. Now that we've got rooms, bathing would be great.

"Is there hot water?" I ask.

"Cold?"

"No, hot?" I repeat.

"Cold?" Perhaps he thinks I am asking for drinking water.

"No. Hot. For a bath." He looks confused, so I get my towel out of my room and ask again, "Hot water? Not cold."

"Is coming."

He knocks on my door when it's ready and shows me the bucket in the bathroom.

After bathing, I ask him where a restaurant is and as usual when the restaurant is not within sight, he appoints someone to escort us. At the restaurant, we again have some communication trouble. But as usual when we are having trouble, someone appears who can help. This time a woman who speaks decent English comes out of the back of the restaurant. I order rice, cabbage, and an omelet. Paul orders rice and chicken.

Just after we order, a man and two women who recognize us from the resthouse arrive. They join us at our table. It's common to share tables with strangers here. Sedgwick introduces himself and asks about our trip. He's Zambian and happy we're on our way to his country. He tells us they live in Chipata, where we're headed tomorrow. Our food arrives while we're talking and my plate includes an unordered chicken leg. I guess they didn't understand vegetarian after all, but eggs again save me. It'd be hard to be a vegan here.

Both women are quiet until I draw them into the conversation. I turn to Sedgwick's wife and ask her what her name is. It's Ann. She tells us about her two children and that she's retired from the Ministry of Education. She talks about her kids as if they aren't there. This confuses Paul and me because we've been thinking the much quieter, younger woman traveling with Sedgwick and Ann is their daughter.

I turn to her, and she must sense my question because she says, "I'm the second wife."

Even after more than two years in Africa, this surprises me. Traditionally, it was very common in many African cultures for men to have multiple wives, but it has become much less common.

It's still very common and much more acceptable than in the U.S., though, for men to have affairs, especially men whose jobs take them away from their homes for long periods, such as truckers and miners. This is a huge factor in the spread of HIV/AIDS throughout the region. Men get infected when they are away, then bring the disease home to their wives, who culturally cannot say no to their husbands' sexual advances even if they suspect that sex is a death sentence.

AIDS is usually still a death sentence in rural Africa since treatment is frequently unavailable or too expensive. Death by stigma is also a reality, as infected people are shunned. All this is changing somewhat as governments are coming to accept the need to deal with AIDS, with twenty to thirty percent of most southern African countries' adult populations HIV-positive. The sheer number of deaths are bringing them out of their years of denial.

This woman is the first African woman to tell me that she's a second wife. I'd love to ask her and Ann how they like this arrangement, but it seems inappropriate with their husband here. Instead I ask her about herself. She also has two children. Before getting married, she was a police officer in Malawi. Now she's a teacher in Chipata and is on strike for higher wages, along with all other government employees in Zambia except the police, she tells us. I ask them more about Zambia. They are all dissatisfied with their current president but won't give specifics.

After dinner, they give us a ride back to the resthouse. Along the way, Sedgwick says to me, "You could be my third wife."

"I'm not really into husband sharing," I reply, and everyone laughs.

Zambia

chapter eight
INTO ZAMBIA

The Malawi immigration officials quickly stamp our passports and send us on our way. We ride the twelve kilometers through no-man's land to the Zambian border post, where there's a short line to get visas. Zambia is a landlocked country shaped roughly like a tipped-over hourglass. We're entering at its southeast corner and planning to head southwest. When I get to the front of line, I hand the official my passport and a $20 bill for the visa.

"We only take the new twenties. Don't you have any?" He frowns.

Knowing that he means the newly designed twenties, I look at the few other $20s in my wallet. All old bills.

"Not right here," I say. "I have never had a problem using these. They are still accepted everywhere in the U.S.A.."

"Our bank does not take them. I can only accept new bills."

I think about the cash in my money belt and look around at all the people seemingly watching me. African women frequently keep extra money in their bras for safekeeping, but I never got into this habit, and it's probably just as well that I don't pull sweaty cash out of my bra while biking anyway.

"I might have one tucked away. Is there a restroom around here?" I ask, as Paul listens in.

"It's inside, down the hall and to the right," he says.

I find a new $20 bill in my money belt and return with it. He smiles and stamps my passport with a visa.

Sometimes border changes are geographic, such as at rivers. Frequently they are arbitrary lines in the sand, especially in areas such as southern Africa that were once divided amongst colonizers. But sometimes they are distinctly marked by cultural changes, such as is the case cycling from Malawi into

Zambia. Soon after we leave the border, a local, male cyclist rides up next to me. I expect another harmless but silent tagalong cyclist, as was always the case when this happened in Malawi. Instead this cyclist starts a conversation.

"Where are you going?"

"Namibia."

"You must be very strong."

Wow, I think. What a refreshing change from the expressions of disbelief my destination usually elicits. My new companion tells me he is a twenty-four-year-old orphan. He's going to Chipata to sell groundnuts (peanuts) and strikes me as motivated and articulate.

Suddenly he asks, "Are you interested in buying stones or a leopard skin?"

I smile at his opportunism. "No, thanks. But I would like to learn about your country. What is the main language you speak in this area?"

"Nyanja."

"Would you teach me a few words?" I glance over at him.

"*Bwanji* means hello. *Muli bwanji* is how are you. *Ndili bwino* is I'm fine."

"What about thank you?"

"*Zikomo.*"

We ride up and down small rolling hills together as I practice speaking Nyanja.

A few days later after a side trip by truck into South Luangwa National Park, I sit at a wooden picnic table in Chipata finishing my dinner. Paul comes out of the club, which is more like a rotary club than a nightclub, and joins me.

"I just found out that a Swiss cyclist was killed on the road to Lusaka last year," he says, sounding ruffled. We're headed to Lusaka, Zambia's capital, 605 kilometers from here. "What do you think we should do? Is it safe?"

"Where was he killed?" I ask with a bit of a frown. A dead cyclist is never good news.

"I don't know." Paul looks away, perhaps realizing that he doesn't have much information.

"Was he traveling alone?" I ask.

"Yes."

"What happened?"

"I don't know."

"Without even knowing where or what happened, I don't think there's anything we can do. He might have been riding at night, or done something culturally offensive," I say.

"Do you really think we're safe here? Some South Africans I met in England also warned me about Zambia."

Zambia, formerly Northern Rhodesia, gained its independence from Britain in 1964 but inherited a multi-million dollar national debt, underdeveloped public health services, a poor communication infrastructure, and a minimally educated population. The new republic's first president, Kenneth Kuanda, attempted to decolonize through nationalization. This resulted in inefficiency, corruption, and decline, but police-state measures protected his autocratic rule. Foreign exchange reserves were largely exhausted, inflation became rampant, and serious shortages of food and fuel became the norm. White travelers were frequently hassled at roadblocks.

The collapsing economy, political frustrations that included violent street protests, a coup attempt and food riots in 1990 led Kuanda to legalize opposition parties and set an election for 1991. He was defeated by Frederick Chiluba and stepped down. Foreign aid returned to Zambia but with conditions of austerity measures. For many Zambians, life did not improve and government corruption remained a fact of life. Gradually, though, Chiluba's government encouraged economic diversification and sold the formerly state-owned copper mines. The police stopped questioning backpackers based on their looks. A more relaxed, and welcoming, atmosphere developed in the country. In 2001, Chiluba was term-limited, and Levy Mwanawasa was elected the new president.

"I don't have any reason to believe Zambia is any less safe than the rest of the region. When I talked with the Zambian Peace Corps office before we started our trip, they didn't have any particular concerns about cyclists, and the Peace Corps tends to magnify dangers, not downplay them," I reply.

"Well, I just want to get through this country as quickly as possible." His voice reflects his hurry.

"If it turns out that we don't feel safe, we can take a bus. But I felt very safe on our ride into town after crossing the border." I sigh, thinking that bike touring is not supposed to be about getting through places as quickly as possible.

Paul's fears keep us on the main tar road to Lusaka for the next week or so. I'd like to explore the backroads and get deeper into the country to more dramatic landscapes and off the well-traveled road, but he has no interest, so we stay on the main road. It's still the dry season, and the road winds its way through landscapes various shades of brown and muted green. Fading green leaves cling to many trees, and hillsides with enough trees appear greener than those covered in long, light brown grasses. An occasional tree with red leaves catches my attention for its rarity. As we traverse the hillier areas, I'm frequently amazed at the road's ability to find a flatter path through the hills than looks possible.

It's the Zambians, though, rather than the landscapes that make a lasting impression on me. Although English is one of the official languages in almost every southern African country and is taught in schools, it's frequently not spoken fluently and not nearly everyone goes to school. But in Zambia, with seventy-three ethnic groups and twenty languages, eight of these official languages, English is widely spoken and viewed by many as necessary to interact with one's fellow countrymen. I find it much easier to have lengthy, nuanced conversations with locals here. Whereas in Malawi, we could always find someone to translate for us if necessary, here we are always meeting people who want to sit down and talk with us, really talk about things, not just practice their English.

One afternoon when we stop to ask for directions to Zulu's Kraal, a nearby campground, we meet Moses. Like most Zambian men, he's dressed in a western fashion, wearing long pants and a button-down shirt. Even in the hottest weather, men wear pants, not shorts—only boys wear shorts. Moses tells us he's coming to the campground later and will visit us. The campground caters to foreigners on overland trips, but the restaurant also attracts a few locals. He joins us while we're waiting for our dinner at the open-air restaurant.

Moses tells us he works for the Ministry of Agriculture in this district and is in the area doing field training for farmers. He's planning to go on strike, along with many other government employees, at the end of this month over a housing allowance that they aren't receiving. He tells us that the last government sold a lot of housing to get votes. Some houses were sold for as little as 15,000 Zambian *kwacha*—about three U.S. dollars.

He and his wife have three children of their own and are raising eleven orphans—all children of his three dead sisters. He doesn't mention AIDS. He doesn't have to. At least one of the sister's husbands is still alive but has disappeared. One of the orphans is now pregnant, and the father of her child is refusing to marry her.

Moses talks about wife-beating and child-beating being common. He says most rapes aren't reported, but the police pursue those that are. Child abuse is illegal, but this isn't widely known.

Moses asks us about our trip.

Paul starts to answer, then turns to me and asks, "Are you writing a book about our trip?"

"No," I answer, thinking that I'm not. If I were planning to, I'd be taking a lot more photos and writing many more details in my journal. Some days, I write only that it's a scenic ride, not realizing I won't know what this really means when I read it years later.

After Moses leaves, we meet Joe, an accountant who works for a USAID (U.S. Agency for International Development) organization in Chipata. He's trying to get a scholarship to study further in Canada, or maybe the U.S. He likes the Zambian president for taking a tough stand on corruption, and he likes all American presidents because they give good speeches.

A couple days later, eighty-five kilometers into what Paul insisted would only be a seventy-kilometer ride to Bridge Camp, he's standing by the roadside waiting for me.

"My stupid map was wrong," he insists.

Nothing is ever his fault, and I know I'll never hear him say, "You were right."

Arriving in a tiny town whose center consists of only two worn cement buildings, I find Paul waiting for me along the side of the road. This is our agreed upon decision point for the day. As usual, he wants to go on, and I'm not so sure. I'm concerned about running out of daylight if we go on and anything goes wrong. On a trip where we've both had so much bike trouble already, it's hard not to think about the possibility. Since Paul likes to check out alternatives, it's easy to agree to look at the resthouse here. As we walk our bikes over, I notice there isn't any glass in the windows, only burglar bars. A woman comes over from the restaurant next door and shows us a room. The bed is a wooden plank with only a flimsy piece of foam for a mattress, and the room is covered with dust. I'd be more comfortable sleeping in my tent on the floor.

"May I see the key?" I ask the woman.

She gives me a key. I try to put it in the lock and it doesn't fit. I wiggle it around, but it's not even close. I think about the leering looks on the local men's faces as they'd watched me walk over with Paul.

Brothel comes to mind, and I turn to Paul and say, "Let's go on to Chongwe." This'll make today a 125-kilometer day, our longest of the trip and farther than I'd like, but I'd rather be on my bike for the next few hours than here.

He smiles.

Five kilometers down the road, my rear tire goes flat. Almost as soon as I pull off the road, a local cyclist wearing spandex and Lycra and riding a shiny racing bike comes along and stops to see if I need help.

"No, thanks. It's just a flat tire. I can fix it," apparently doesn't convince him and he hangs around.

"I haven't seen any other Zambians wearing cycling clothing," I say, as I take my wheel off my bike. "Are you going far?"

"Lusaka."

"When will you arrive?"

"Late tonight. I am training." It's eighty kilometers. Paul and I plan to get there tomorrow.

"Where did you start?"

He names a village about fifty kilometers back then asks about my trip. He seems unfazed when I tell him we've come from Malawi and are going to Namibia. As we talk, I replace my punctured tube with a new one, preferring to patch the puncture later in a resthouse rather than by the side of the road. I check the tire to make sure nothing's stuck in it that will cause another flat. He holds my bike as I put the wheel then my panniers back on. We ride together for a bit. Soon Paul appears, riding back down the road.

He stops and looks at me quizzically.

"I had a flat. It's fixed now," I reply as the cyclist and I stop.

"I was waiting up ahead. When you didn't come, I got worried something bad had happened. I thought those drunks along the roadside back there might've gotten you."

"I didn't see any drunks. They must've moved on, but thanks for checking." It's nice to know he still cares about my safety.

The three of us ride together briefly until the local cyclist goes ahead. Paul and I ride into Chongwe in the dusk, racing the setting sun, and find a clean resthouse with real beds and a door that locks.

Downtown Lusaka

Riding through the outskirts of Lusaka, Zambia's capital, I'm struck by how modern it looks. There's a distinct lack of visible poverty. Sometimes it's the outskirts of African cities where poverty is most visible, in the shantytowns where tin sheds are crowded homes for many. But we pass well-kept gated compounds and strip malls lining the four-lane road.

In town, we stay at the Chachacha Backpackers' hostel and meet Rob, a towering, broad-shouldered Canadian cyclist with a belly, who is two years into a solo around-the-world bicycle trip. He regales us with stories from his adventure. One day in Colombia, he was thrilled to find M&M's and had just started munching on some when he turned around and met a man from the Canadian version of the FBI, who said,

"You can't be here."

"But I am."

"You can't be."

"I am."

"You can't be. It's too dangerous. You need to get out of here immediately."

"I'm biking around the world."

"You need to get on a plane out of here. The situation is deteriorating. The Canadian government is now recommending against all travel to Colombia."

"I've biked here from Canada."

"Well, if I can't persuade you, take my card. Have your kidnappers call me when you get kidnapped." *When* you get kidnapped, not *if*.

Rob took the card but never needed it. I ask him if he felt safe in Colombia.

"Yes, but I know my presence made many people uncomfortable. It's the only place farmers ever refused me permission to camp on their land."

Now Rob is considering cycling through a 100-kilometer stretch of the Congo. He asks if I think it's safe. When I say no, he jokes, "Well, I still have that guy's card with me. Maybe I can call him from Congo."

I note the admiration in Paul's eyes as he listens to Rob talk about solo travel.

chapter nine

WHERE IS HE?

The morning we leave Lusaka, Paul decides to get his hair cut and tells me to go ahead without him; he'll catch up or meet me in Kafue—the day's destination. The tar road going south out of Lusaka goes through an industrial area and a poorer section of town. Though I briefly wonder if this is the best area for me to be cycling alone, no one pays much attention to me and riding alone is refreshing, knowing that Paul isn't up ahead waiting for me.

As I near Kafue, woodcarving stands dominated by giraffes line the road. Arriving in town, I stop and ask a policeman about places to stay. He tells me there are two. This will make it easy for Paul to find me—only two places to look. The first resthouse has neither electricity nor hot running water, so I go on and find the Rima River Motel, an expansive hotel complex that allows camping.

That night at dinner in the hotel restaurant, Paul and I are joined by two men from the Ministry of Education who are here for a four-day food and nutrition seminar. Their role is to bring information back to schools in their areas and help them implement school feeding programs by having the students grow their own food at school. The schools are given money by the Ministry of Education to use for buying seeds.

"What is the biggest health threat to students here?" I ask them.

"Malaria," one says, "Bilharzia is also a big threat, but the Ministry of Education is able to provide bilharzia medication through the Ministry of Health."

"Are students taught about AIDS?"

"Yes."

"Are teachers resistant to teaching about it?" I ask, thinking about the teachers I worked with in Lesotho, who weren't comfortable talking about sex with their students.

"No, they're not, because AIDS is out in the open now."

"We've heard teachers are on strike. What's happening?"

"Some teachers are on strike over a housing allowance, while others, who have government housing, are still teaching. The government has started to disburse the housing allowance funds, but money might run out."

Planning to find a resthouse in Mazabuka, we see a sign on our way into town for Cane Break, a place with camping ten kilometers farther along. We haven't heard about it, so we stop at a police station to inquire. They recommend it over the local resthouses.

The place seems like a good choice when we arrive. We have the grassy camping area with a picnic table to ourselves, and access to a refrigerator and bathroom in the guesthouse. Plus, there's a restaurant where we can have dinner. We set up camp and take turns going inside to shower. As we sit outside writing in our journals, I don't think anything of it when I see our hosts drive away after receiving a visitor.

"I'm ready for dinner, but I don't think they've come back," says Paul awhile later.

I look over at the guesthouse. "I guess you're right. Their car isn't back."

Paul frowns. "Let's see if anyone's inside."

We walk over to the house. Paul tries to turn the doorknob. "It's locked."

"Are you sure?" I ask in surprise.

He wiggles the doorknob again. Definitely locked.

"That's weird," I say. "I wonder if there's another door."

We walk around the house, but there's no other door. Not only isn't there anyone here to cook us dinner at the restaurant, we can't even get in to use the restroom.

"Maybe they'll be back soon," I say, perturbed but optimistic. "Why would they tell us we'd have bathroom access and dinner if we wouldn't?" It feels more like something is wrong than a trick, especially since the police recommended this place.

Paul stomps back over to our camp.

They don't come back. Eventually, we give up on the possibility of dinner in the restaurant and cook our pasta for dinner. We're alone out here. Tonight I'm glad to have the security of Paul's presence. I think I'd be spooked alone.

The proprietors return when we're just about ready to leave the next morning. They apologize, saying something came up and they hadn't expected to be kept away.

As we cycle to Chisekesi, I keep hearing locals say a word that sounds like *lehooa*, which means white person in Sesotho, the language I learned as a Peace Corps volunteer in Lesotho. We're now in an area where people are speaking Tonga, and I wonder if it has similarities to Sesotho.

At a restaurant in Chisekesi, I think back to Blantyre, Malawi and the first night of our trip. Paul and I discussed the route I'd proposed. Tracing it with a finger on my map, I said, "From near Livingstone—southern Zambia, we'll ride into Botswana. Bicyclists aren't allowed in Chobe National Park, so we'll have to go south to Nata then west to Maun, the gateway to the Okavango Delta. Then we'll have a choice of going north and stopping at the Tsodilo Hills, reputedly southern Africa's best rock art site, on our way to northern Namibia. Or we could continue traveling west and go through the Kalahari into central Namibia. Or we could potentially skip Botswana, stay in Zambia a bit longer and ride into Namibia through the Caprivi Strip. It sounds like it's safe enough now." The Caprivi Strip is part of Namibia that until recently received spillover violence from the civil war in Angola. Travelers were required to join vehicle convoys to travel through part of the strip. These convoys have now been disbanded, and independent travel is once again allowed.

"I don't want to ride through the Caprivi. And Botswana is one of the countries I came to see," Paul said.

Also wanting to see Botswana, I readily agreed. And it was settled. Or so I thought. Until now.

"We need to talk about our route," he says. "I want to go through the Caprivi Strip."

"What?"

"Botswana sounds too boring. I've been talking to people. I don't want to go there," he says in a tone that implies finality, as if the decision has already been made.

"There'll be some long dry stretches, but we can take side trips off the bikes into Chobe and the Okavango Delta, two places I'd really like to see, then also go to the Tsodilo Hills if we choose that route," I reply, while remembering that Rob the Canadian rode through both Botswana and the Caprivi and recommended Caprivi.

Unconvinced, Paul stares at me.

I continue, "I don't want to skip a country just because some people think it's boring. I've also heard a lot of good things about it, and part of traveling is seeing for yourself what a place is like."

"I just want to go through the Caprivi and get to the rest of Namibia."

"I thought we'd already agreed on our route."

The conversation fades away as we fail to convince each other and both focus on the omelets in front of us.

Entering Choma, I pass pottery stands lining the road and slow down as I ride by the museum. It's set back from the road, and I peer into the grounds, looking for Paul. We'd talked about possibly stopping here, but I don't see him. I remember him just yesterday saying that he wouldn't go into a place without making sure I knew he was stopping. So I ride on, thinking he might've wanted to find a resthouse first and then return. I pass turns for a couple resthouses but don't see him anywhere. People excitedly wave to me, and I feel their genuine surprise at seeing a white cyclist. It doesn't feel like he has been here. After a couple kilometers, I come to the outskirts of town. I ask a couple pedestrians if they have seen him, and they say no. I return to the gas station I noticed a few long blocks back and approach a woman working outside.

"Have you seen another white cyclist with lots of stuff on his bike ride by recently?"

"No, I haven't seen him, but I just got here, so I'll ask the others." She goes into the mini-mart, then returns, "No, they haven't seen him. And they would've noticed. He hasn't been by here."

"Thanks." Such a definite answer is what I was counting on. Sometimes there is a benefit to being so conspicuous as the only white people around— and on bicycles. "He must've stopped somewhere."

I ride slowly back through town, scouring the streets, sidewalks, and storefronts, looking for him. I can't help wondering whether he's having a cold drink in the shade somewhere while I'm riding back and forth looking for him. He has come back to look for me a couple times when he was concerned that I hadn't caught up to him riding ahead. But this is different. I didn't ride ahead and wait; I somehow passed him without seeing him. Where is he hiding? I get all the way back to the museum without seeing him and stop outside, unsure what to do next.

A uniformed security guard whom I hadn't noticed walks over and says, "Your friend is inside. I told him I saw you ride by."

"I've been looking for him. Why didn't he wait? Would you punch him for me?"

His face betrays his surprise. Perhaps unsure if I'm serious, he replies, "I can't punch him. He is a guest in our country."

"Oh, I know," I mutter, "I just feel like he deserves it. But thank you for telling me he is here, Sir. Where's his bike?"

"Over there—around the corner." He nods his head towards the entrance to the building.

I park and lock my bike near Paul's, then buy a ticket and go into the museum. I start to look at the exhibits on Zambian history and Tonga culture instead of looking for Paul, but I have trouble focusing on them.

Paul comes along and says, "Here you are."

"And how was I supposed to know you were here?"

"I thought you saw me turn into the store, then when you didn't come, I thought, well, I don't know where she is, but I want to see the museum. I figured you'd find me."

It hits me that our differences are irreconcilable if this is his attitude. How can two people travel together if to one the trip is all about his wants and needs? Perhaps I shouldn't have come back looking for him. Perhaps I should've just kept riding right out of town, never looking back.

But I did come back, so now I'm stuck with him. We stop at a small store on our way to a resthouse. After leaving the store, Paul gets ahead of me. I watch as the bag of buns bungeed to the back of his bike slips free and lands on the dusty dirt road. I yell out to him, but he doesn't hear me. I stop to pick them up and bungee them to my bike. I arrive at the Choma Resthouse to one of his what-took-you-so-long looks.

I silently get off my bike, unbungee his buns, and ask, "Are you missing something?"

Shock flickers across his face. "How'd you get those?"

I tell him.

"Well, I don't know how they fell off" is all that he says.

Have I ever heard him say thank you? I can no longer remember. I used to feel that he respected at least some of my opinions and valued my knowledge of Africa, but I'd have to say that gratitude was never a dominant character trait.

The next day I ride along, realizing I've been so focused on my frustration with Paul that I haven't noticed the scenery at all. My most vivid memories of Zambia, where we've been for two-and-half weeks now, are of my disagreements with him. That night, I write in my journal, "I wish I were brave enough to suggest we split up."

chapter ten

A GOOD OMEN

At Fawlty Towers Backpackers in Livingstone the next day, we can't agree on whether to stay here or at another backpackers, which Paul went ahead to check out on his way into town. I want to stay here—it's clean, welcoming, and has a big, green lawn for camping. Paul wants to go back to the other one. Although the camping area isn't nearly as nice, they run shuttles to Victoria Falls.

"We haven't decided on our route from here anyway. We could just split up. I feel comfortable on my own now," he says.

"That would be fine with me," I immediately reply.

There it is. Suddenly, after weeks of wondering if this is going to work out, if I should suggest splitting up, it is done.

"I'll stop by later to talk," he says and rides away.

I set up my tent wondering what I've done. Relief is mixed with apprehension, but I can no longer deny that I'm feeling awful physically. I threw up this morning just before we left, then felt weak and queasy while riding. Now I'm feverish too. Pushing myself to keep going, I was in denial. But now with no one to have to catch or coordinate with, I collapse in my tent, concerned that I might have caught bilharzia snorkeling in Lake Malawi a month ago. I have the right medication for it and decide to take the pills tonight rather than risk getting sicker while traveling alone. But they need to be taken with food. After a rest, I force myself to get up and walk a couple blocks to a pizza place.

Livingstone is Zambia's gateway to Victoria Falls. While tourism to neighboring Zimbabwe, across the Zambezi River, has plummeted during the past few years as President Mugabe's campaign to drive the white farmers out of the country has created instability and food shortages, Zambia has been successfully promoting itself as the alternative access point to the falls.

With increasing tourism comes increased numbers of western hotels and restaurants, and so here I am at a pizza place. It sometimes strikes me as odd that people travel thousands of miles away from their homes to eat at restaurants that remind them of home. But today I'm just happy to see a pizza place. It's a welcome break from the routine of omelets or rice and cabbage at local restaurants and pasta on a camp stove.

Returning from the pizza place, I walk into the lobby of the backpackers and hear a familiar voice say, "Heather." Not knowing anyone here, I wonder if I'm mistaken or maybe there's another Heather staying here. Then I see Katie, one of my Peace Corps friends from Lesotho, and her boyfriend, Will. They just flew up from Johannesburg this afternoon to spend a few days here and see the falls. She tells me she saw two other Lesotho volunteers' names on the reservation list for tomorrow. What a great time to run into friends. After talking with Katie, I take my medication then sleep for twelve hours.

Four other touring cyclists are also staying here, three more than Paul and I met the entire seven weeks that we traveled together. If I believed in omens, I'd have to say this seems like a good one.

In the morning, I feel much better, no longer feverish, though my stomach still hurts off and on. I join the other cyclists sitting on the grass and we compare notes. Stefan and Adan are Swiss; they started their journey in Bulawayo, Zimbabwe and are planning to ride all the way back to Switzerland. British James started a ten-year walking trip in Cape Town, South Africa. He's following the footsteps of early man, going north through Africa, then south through South America. He's cycling because he hurt his foot but will resume walking when he can. Norwegian Marian has been cycling alone through southern Africa for the last five months. If she can do it, so can I, I think, though I also suspect her flat chest has gotten her mistaken for a man many times—and kept her safer for it.

I think back to my Peace Corps training in Lesotho, when my bike became a huge issue. There was a lot of concern amongst the trainers that I'd get attacked for it.

"If men here see a woman with something they want, they'll go after her for it. But if they see another man with it, they might not, because they'll be afraid of looking foolish if the other man is stronger. They never think that a woman might be stronger than them," explained Ntate Bernard, the lead cultural trainer.

I had almost left Lesotho early, but I stayed, worked with the Peace Corps, limited my riding, and was safe.

In the evening I go out to an Indian restaurant with my Peace Corps friends. With doubts lingering in the back of my mind, I tell them more about Paul and our split.

"What a jerk," says Nancy, "it must be such a relief."

It is a relief, I realize, as tension oozes out of my body and soul.

With a new feeling of lightness, I know I am going on.

INTERLUDE

chapter eleven
An Island Respite

Feeling a bit nervous but free, I leave Fawlty Towers after saying good-bye to Katie and Will. I'm really on my own now. No one will know if I disappear but no one will know if I ride slowly and take lots of breaks either.

I'm headed to a camp on Bovu Island on the Zambezi River. The only access to the camp is by boat, and I got directions to the boat launch from the camp office in Livingstone yesterday: go fifty kilometers on the tar road towards Botswana and Namibia, turn left at the microwave tower, follow the only track for five kilometers, and they'll meet me at the power lines. I'm cruising along paying more attention to my thoughts of freedom than to the landscape when I suddenly look up and see the microwave tower looming above me. This doesn't feel like fifty kilometers. I check my odometer: 40 km. Hmmm. There can't be another tower in ten kilometers, can there? I haven't seen any others along here at all, and there is a dirt track off to my left. This must be it. I turn in and see a man walking along.

"Bovu Island?" I ask.

He nods yes.

The track soon gets sandy. I determinedly try to keep cycling, but after only a couple wheel revolutions, my bicycle stops despite the pressure my feet are applying to the pedals. I get off and walk a few steps then try again. Same thing. Pedal. Pedal. Stop. Once more. As my bike stops, I almost fall over. This convinces me that trying to bike is futile. Hoping that the track will get less sandy up ahead, I walk. Even if I do have to walk the whole five kilometers, I've got plenty of time. I can hear Paul's complaints. He'd be ready to bail, if he ever even would've agreed to go to a camp down a track. But I think of my groceries that I left with the camp office to bring out in their truck later today. And more importantly, I think about how much I want to spend tomorrow resting on an island. I go on.

After half-an-hour and two kilometers, a Land Rover-type of vehicle approaches from the other direction. I move off the track. It stops.

"Are you going to Bovu Island?" asks the white man driving alone.

"Yes. This is the way, isn't it?"

"Yes. I just looked across the river at it, but I don't have time to stay tonight. I'm on my way to Botswana. Their directions are awful, though. I'll draw you a map."

He draws a map that shows the track splitting then going off to the left then reaching a T.

"It's about thirteen kilometers total from the tar road," he says.

"Thirteen kilometers? They said it was five. I don't know if that's worth it. Maybe I'll just turn around."

"The road gets less sandy up ahead. You can probably bike after another three kilometers."

"Thanks. Maybe I'll try it."

"Do you have enough food and water?"

"Yes, I'm okay."

"Are you sure?" he says sipping an Energade, which is like Gatorade. "It's hot out here."

"Yes, I've got plenty of water."

"Well, why don't you take a couple of these anyway? They're cold," he says as he reaches into a cooler and hands me two Energades.

"Okay, thanks. Cold sounds great."

I go on, pushing my bike in the carwheel tracks, which are just firm enough that my bike rolls slowly along as my feet sink into the looser sand next to them. Scattered trees emerge from the sandy soil. Their yellow and rust leaves indicate a lingering touch of fall. Somehow getting off the tar road, the colors have come alive. There's a brightness and clarity in the autumnal rusts of the leaves and tall grasses that was missing along the tar roads of Zambia. Is the air really different here or am I just seeing more clearly without Paul fogging my vision?

After about five kilometers, the road does get less sandy, and I can bike most of it. I walk a few steps through several short sandier stretches. In another couple kilometers, the track veers to the left but the most recent car tracks go straight—and I haven't seen any other cars than the one coming from Bovu Island. I haven't seen anyone at all since then. What a contrast from southern Malawi, where there were people everywhere. Now there's no one to ask. Maybe this isn't where I'm supposed to veer left? I follow the car track for about half a kilometer until it suddenly turns sharply right. I go back and take the left fork. As I follow it, the track becomes less clear. I wonder if I'm going the right way even as it also becomes less sandy and more bikable.

I keep following the track as it winds through a more desert-like landscape of whitish sand sprinkled with small sparse trees. From the man's directions, I expect to get to the T intersection about ten kilometers from the tar road, but I get to it sooner. A couple people are walking off to the right. Although I think I'm supposed to go left, I follow them to ask.

"Hello," I say as I get close.

"Ehhh!" yells the woman as she turns toward me and jumps back. "Oh, you scared me. We didn't hear you coming."

"Sorry," I say, "I'm looking for Bovu Island. Is it that way?" I point back the way I've come.

"We'll show you," says the man.

They start walking back the way I've come, and I follow. In only a few minutes, we get back to the T.

"Keep going straight. You'll get to a village. Bovu Island is across from the village."

"Thank you."

Their directions are perfect. I reach a small village, ride through it, and the track takes me to a clearing on the riverbank. Across the river on an island stands a man with a dugout canoe. He waves, then paddles across. I take the gear off the back of my bike. We load the bike with the front panniers still attached into the center of the canoe, and I hold it upright as he packs the rest of my gear around it, then paddles us back across to the island.

As I put my gear back on my bike, a white man with crew cut dark hair and a smile approaches on a path.

"Hello. I'm Gabriel. Did you find us okay?"

"Well, it was more of an adventure than I expected. I wouldn't call this five kilometers down a track. But it all worked out okay."

"Is that what they told you? Come on, I'll show you around. Where are you from?" His accent is so familiar yet also so unexpected that it takes me a minute to realize that he's American and is asking me where in the U.S. I'm from, not what country.

"I grew up in New Jersey but lived in Washington, D.C. before joining the

Vervet Monkey on Bovu Island

Peace Corps more than two years ago. I haven't been back to the States at all, and Africa feels more like home to me now than the U.S.," I say.

"I know what you mean. I'd been traveling around for more than six months before I landed here. I loved this island so much I got a job here. My visa is about to expire, though, so I'll have to leave soon."

We walk through riverine evergreen forest populated with gnarled waterberry and fig trees. In a clearing stand the main bathrooms with walls made of reeds. A rope hangs next to each doorway, and Gabriel shows me their system of pulling the rope across to a hook on the other side of the doorway to indicate occupied. Once inside and around a corner, they look like modern bathrooms: flush toilets and hot showers. Reed huts for some guests are down one path. The camping area is down another. We pass the kitchen and bar where meals are served, then walk through the lounge to the larger bar area for drinks. All the buildings are open-air structures.

After getting set up and showered, I cook an early dinner with a charcoal stove. Harriet, the cook, fills the stove with hot charred wood-charcoal and gives me some free popcorn for an appetizer. The stove Paul and I had been using was really his stove, so now that we've split up, I'm without one of my own.

I wander over to the bar after dinner and meet Gremlin and Brett, the long-haired hippie owners of the camp. When he hears that I'm cycling, Brett also asks if I found them okay. When I tell him about the directions I was given by the office, he is livid.

"They told you what?" he almost screams. "I'm going to talk to them."

He tells me they get a lot of Zambian Peace Corps volunteers and about some who came for New Year's without getting permission to take leave and were then kicked out of the Peace Corps.

"Sounds like the Peace Corps. They can be pretty strict in Lesotho, too," I say.

"They were all doing good work here. It's a shame."

I both agree and disagree. It is too bad when volunteers doing good work and enjoying the country they are serving in are kicked out.

"It is a job though. What other job can you just go on vacation from without telling your boss?" asks Gabriel, echoing the rest of my thoughts.

As we talk, gunshots ring out. I look around.

"Poachers in Zimbabwe," says Brett.

I tell them of my plans to go on into Botswana, then Namibia, alone.

"I hope you aren't afraid of lions?" says Gremlin.

"No, not really. I know not to get out of my tent at night in lion country. I'm more concerned about two-legged animals and finding places to camp."

"You'll be able to find places, and Botswana's very safe. I spent a lot of time there before deciding to open this camp here," he says.

In the morning, I wander into the lounge with my journal.

Gabriel walks in and says, "If you're looking for a good book, I can recommend this one." He picks up *Don't Let's Go to the Dogs Tonight* by Alexandra Fuller.

"I've never heard of her." And what kind of grammar is that, I think. Don't let's?

"It's new. A few other people have read it recently and all liked it. It's about growing up in Zimbabwe."

That piques my interest. As I look around, none of the other books grab my attention, so I pick it up and am sucked in by the opening as Fuller describes her parents telling her not to wake them up suddenly during the night—because they might shoot her by mistake. What a different life. My reading on this trip so far has been focused on guidebooks and the occasional story in a collection, but I didn't realize how much I needed to immerse myself in someone else's story as an escape until now. And so I sit on a comfy sofa with pillows and read. It's good not to have anywhere to go, or even much of anywhere that I can go. The island is only about one kilometer long. Sedentary is a good choice for now.

I intend to stay only two nights, but the rhythm of a relaxing day spent reading, wandering, and taking a sunset dugout canoe trip with a few other guests convinces me I want more of this. This is the type of rest and relaxation that I craved after I finished my Peace Corps service but never found. Now, after traveling with Paul, I need it even more. Why rush on to Botswana? It's not going anywhere, and I'll enjoy it much more if I wait until I'm ready to travel onward. I wonder if fear is creeping into my decision to stay here longer. Am I just putting off traveling alone because I'm unsure whether I really want to go on? I don't think so. I think I'm recognizing a deep need to rest—and to take care of myself. I've been focused on the mental strain of traveling with Paul recently, but the physical strain of biking more than 2100 kilometers over the past almost seven weeks has also taken a toll. I'm in so much better shape now than I was starting out that the biking feels much easier, but my body feels worn down from whatever illness I had arriving in Livingstone and my leg muscles could also use a few days to rejuvenate.

So here I stay. I want to be fresh to tackle the rigors of solo travel, such as needing to find safe places to camp every night in a country where distances between campgrounds or lodging are frequently more than a one-day bike ride apart. Despite all of Paul's annoying habits, I believe he would have been there for me if I ever got into a bad situation and really needed help. Now I'll have only myself to rely on, and I want to be fresh for the challenge.

I choose not to return to the mainland for a village tour with a couple other guests. I don't want to leave the respite of the island. It is a decision a part of me will later regret: an opportunity to compare and contrast this village to the one I lived in in Lesotho. But right now, I need a break from everything more than I need to tour what feels like "another" village.

I spend the next couple days doing yoga, reading, eating, journaling, and occasionally wandering around the island. Inspired by the confluence of cyclists at Fawlty Towers, I start to think about continuing this trip into South Africa. I never had an exact endpoint in Namibia in mind and now that I'm on my own with no schedule, why not continue to Cape Town?

One night over a Mexican dinner of tortillas with a bean, okra, and potato mix, salad, and a custard dessert at the restaurant bar, I meet an older Dutch couple. They've been traveling around Malawi and Zambia by public transport, and I ask them their impressions of the two countries.

"We are impressed with Zambia. The transport is better and less crowded with people who don't smell."

"Less crowded? You must not have taken a truck to South Luangwa?" I smile.

"No, we didn't. People here in Zambia also seem to have a lot more pride in whatever they are doing. Maybe because they've never been as repressed as Malawians were under Banda," they continue.

"I'm not sure why, but I've also noticed a higher level of motivation here," I say. "Maybe they don't have as much of a donor mentality here."

After three lazy days, my legs start to get restless. On my fourth morning, feeling that staying any longer would be dawdling rather than resting and rejuvenating, I take the camp shuttle out to the tar road. It turns to go back to Livingstone, and I get off and point my bike in the other direction, to the border, ready to ride into Botswana alone.

Part Two

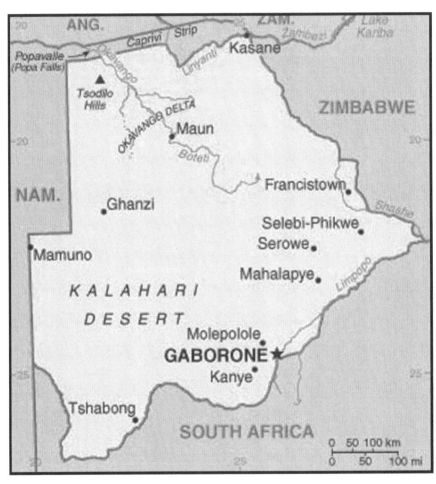

Botswana

chapter twelve

On My Own

"...**a** bandon any ideas you may have about a Botswana bicycle adventure. Distances are great...the climate and landscapes are hot and dry; and even along major routes, water is scarce and villages are widely spaced...the sun is intense...cyclists may literally be blown off the road...and cyclists may encounter potentially dangerous wildlife while traveling along any highway or road." –Lonely Planet's *Botswana*

In a way, it would be easy to follow this advice. Easy to just go home, back to the U.S., rather than going on alone. Easy to say, "well, I tried and it didn't work out." Easy to blame Paul for misrepresenting the kind of trip he wanted to do. Easy to choose the illusion of safety in quitting rather than the uncertainties of solo travel.

Yet neither this trip nor my life has ever been about taking the easy route, making the easy choice. If I make that choice here, I will always wonder, "What if?" I refuse to be one of those people who turns old with a litany of regrets and a list of trips never taken. Trips put off until there was more time, more money, a safer world, retirement, whatever. Trips put off until the time was right—and then it never was. Anything could happen at any time, making postponed trips no longer possible. This single factor is a driving force behind my decision to go on. If it isn't fun or doesn't feel safe, I can end the trip later without regrets. But now I can't end it without any.

There's a subset of travelers for whom Lonely Planet is their bible. I am not among them. I believe in the usefulness of guidebooks for ascertaining some basic info about places, but I also believe in forging my own path and figuring out what's right for me. Taking some advice but leaving other advice.

Botswana's reputation as exceedingly safe, even for women traveling alone, and my interest in its wildlife and rock art make it the right choice for me, the right place for me to truly start the solo portion of my journey, the portion that I never intended to take place. These factors far outweigh Lonely Planet's pessimism and a few warnings about boring roads I received from other travelers. Warnings about boring roads don't concern me too much. Warnings about bandits might, but boring roads and needing to carry lots of water, I can handle. And so I board the ferry at Kazangula, Zambia and cross the Zambezi River into northeastern Botswana, alone.

I am truly alone, so alone that not a single person I know is aware what country I am in at this moment. My parents and best friend received emails about my plans to split with Paul and go on alone, but at this exact moment that I am crossing the border, they wouldn't be able to say whether I am in Zambia or Botswana.

There is something inherently freeing about this type of solo travel. No commitments. No restraints based on anyone else's wants or needs. No more "you don't want to do that, do you?," "it's okay if we do this, isn't it?" or "why would you want to go there?" Suddenly, I am free, free to do the trip as I designed it and free from criticisms. Free to ride slowly when I want to without being asked if something is wrong. Free to take a day off the bike simply because I am ready for a rest. Over the next few months, I will meet many travelers who will tell me that I am brave. Yet I never intended to be brave. I intended only to continue leading the life I want to live, living my dream trip rather than abandoning it. I am doing exactly what I want to be doing with my life. How can I give this up to any hesitation about going on alone?

After getting off the ferry and having my passport stamped in Botswana, I am stopped at the veterinary checkpoint. Now that I've cleaned my mind, I need to clean my bike tires. An officer instructs me to wheel my bicycle along the side of what looks like a large puddle in a concrete ditch, and to make sure my wheels stay in the puddle. The puddle is a cleaning fluid to keep animal diseases, such as foot-and-mouth, from spreading to Botswana's wildlife. This theoretically could happen, but has not been proven. Still, every vehicle entering Botswana has to have its tires cleaned. If only the officials wanted to wash the frame of my bike for me, too, I wouldn't mind. But it's only tires and shoes they are concerned about. After walking my bike through the vehicle puddle, I stand in the shoe puddle and wipe my soles on a mat in it. Why I couldn't just walk through the vehicle puddle with my bike, I don't know. This is the way it's done here, though, and I'm reminded that Africa isn't always logical.

I remember a story Rob, the Canadian cyclist, told me in Lusaka about his arrival in Botswana. He put his passport on the immigration counter. The official picked it up, saw its Canadian cover, threw it and her hands up into the air, and screamed, "SARS! You have SARS! SARS! You have SARS! Go away! Ehhhh! Go away!" As she tossed away the passport as if it might contaminate her, she jumped up but was so overweight that her chair stuck to her butt. In her effort to escape SARS, she moved faster than she probably ever had in her life, according to Rob, and backpedaled across the office with the chair sticking out behind her. Rob explained to her that he hadn't even been in Canada since the SARS outbreak and she could look at all the visa stamps in his passport to confirm this, but she just keep screaming, "Go away! You have SARS!" Eventually, someone else stamped Rob's passport and he was allowed into Botswana. With clean tires on my bike and a smile on my face, I ride into Botswana.

Landlocked Botswana, bordered by Zambia, Zimbabwe, Namibia, and South Africa, is about the size of France and has a population of 1.6 million. Seventy-five percent of the country is the semi-arid Kalahari region. Botswana is known among Africa aficionados for its wildlife, national parks and the Okavango Delta.

I spend my first two nights in Botswana camped at a lodge in the town of Kasane, just outside of Chobe National Park. Chobe is renowned as one of southern Africa's best parks for seeing wildlife. Bicycles are not allowed in Botswana's wildlife-oriented national parks, but it is possible to camp at lodges outside the parks and join game drives into the parks from the lodges, and this is what I do here.

In Kasane, I stop in at the Botswana Information Office and tell the man there about my plans to bicycle through northern Botswana. My projected route will take me south to Nata, then west to Maun—from where I want to take a dugout canoe trip into the Okavango Delta—then north to the Tsodilo Hills and finally across the Namibian border.

Looking resigned, he responds, "We don't recommend cycling on the road to Nata because there are sometimes animals, especially buffalo, very close to the road. They can be dangerous."

I look at him, and he seems to sense my question.

"There have never been any incidents with cyclists, but we still don't recommend it. How far can you ride in a day?"

I shrug. "More than 100 kilometers if I need to, but I prefer less."

"We recommend you do three 100-kilometer days from here to get to Nata. There are a couple lodges with camping in Pandamatenga, then there's a forestry camp 100 kilometers from Panda. They let cyclists stay there, and they have water. Don't camp in the bush. There are too many lions around."

I thank him for the advice, which is surprisingly detailed for something he's recommending not doing. I wonder if the recommendation is only a formality because of liability concerns.

I walk back to the lodge thinking that I need to reassure my parents about my safety traveling alone. I know the email I sent them from Livingstone telling them I was splitting up with Paul has them concerned. My mom is a natural worrywart. She worries about airplane crashes so much that until recently, she'd never fly anywhere with my dad and either my sister or I but not both of us because she didn't want the other one of us to be an adult orphan if the plane crashed and everyone on board died. The logic that three of us were much more likely to die in a motor vehicle crash together and are actually safer in a plane than a car couldn't persuade her. And so I know that if she's going to worry about my traveling alone, it's beyond my control and simply who she is. But still, it would mean a lot to her to hear my voice telling her that my ride into Botswana alone went well and about Botswana's reputation as safe. The sign on the pay phone outside the bar at the lodge says phone cards are available inside. I go inside and ask for one.

The bartender tells me, "The phone cards are finished, but you can get one at the front desk."

I walk to the front desk, which is about fifteen minutes away through the sprawling complex.

The man there says, "The phone cards are finished but you can get one at the bar."

Generally this lack of coordination and preparation wouldn't surprise me in Africa. But Botswana has a reputation for being more developed than other southern African countries outside of South Africa, so my expectations were higher. Pay phones with international capability, even pay phones at all, at lodges are a step up the development ladder from Malawi and Zambia. Too bad there's no way to use them.

The next day, I leave Kasane and turn onto the road to Nata. It takes me through a dry landscape of tall brown grasses and some small trees, not much taller than elephants' raised trunks. Cycling, I can feel the road gradually climbing then gradually descending, but in a car, it might seem flat. Physically, it's easy riding, except for the headwind that's trying to push me back to Kasane. The challenge is to keep going, 100 kilometers a day for three days. It is farther than I prefer to ride every day, and this is the road I've been warned is the most boring. But, the possibility of seeing wild animals doesn't seem boring to me. And the lack of people along the road is a refreshing change after the constant attention in Malawi and much of Zambia. Still, I can understand why people think it's boring. The scenery doesn't vary much and could be considered drab, since it's mostly shades of dusty brown. There are only a few villages and no attractions to stop at.

As I cycle along, I relax. There's always a bit of trepidation mixed with the curiosity of experiencing a new country. But as I ride along, adjusting to the rhythm of a different country, I begin to feel calm and confident.

I'm happy to be on my own, doing my own thing at my own pace. I think about Paul and how ironic it is that we split up now. One of the sources of tension was his desire to do more longer days, and now I'm doing longer days alone. I'm not too concerned about the dangers of wild animals because I've cycled through their territories briefly on an earlier trip to Uganda. I'd been much more concerned about problem people. For the past few days, when I told people I was headed for Botswana and planned to spend about three weeks cycling here, they usually responded with the questions, "Aren't you afraid of animals? What about lions?" I was more relieved that no one thought that anyone might harass a solo woman cyclist than concerned about wild animals.

Botswana has a much lower crime rate than the rest of southern Africa. Perhaps this is because of its peaceful history. Many of its neighbors fought bloody wars to gain their independence, but Botswana's transition to independence was peaceful. Violence just isn't much of a part of the society here.

I constantly scan the landscape for animals. I don't want to ride too close to any and startle them. James, the walker I met in Livingstone, told me that when he walked along this road, there was a lion lying on it. Knowing that he should not approach the lion, he waited until it moved away, then he continued on. I pass a couple of baboons, off to one side of the road. Unlike the Jungle Habitat baboons of my youth that rushed towards cars in an aggressive blur, searching for food, these baboons seem to simply notice me passing by and go on with their lives, unconcerned, uninterested, and unconditioned to being fed by humans.

A slight movement in the brush catches my eye. There's a large elephant in there, only about fifteen meters from the side of the road. It screeches at me, rears up, and raises its trunk. With an adrenalin rush, I wonder if cycling on this road was the right decision. After a momentary pause, the elephant crashes off through the brush to its right—in the same direction that I am going. Is it going to chase me? I remember Rob saying something about being chased by an elephant in the Caprivi Strip, but I'm sure he never finished that story. I suddenly wish I knew how he got away, but I somehow suspect the elephant just wanted him out of its territory and stopped the chase when it was satisfied. This elephant crashes away and I exhale.

I come upon a large group of another twenty or so elephants. I'm humbled by the presence of these huge beasts who could easily squash me if they chose to. They seem so gentle now. Yet I know this could change in an instant if they feel threatened. I cautiously ride by, staying to the far left of the road, away from them, and trying to project a sense of calm that I don't entirely feel. Some turn away, but none screech, and I am reassured by our friendly coexistence.

My thoughts turn to lions. I feel a special almost kinship with lions. Before I left for Africa, my best friend gave me a lion necklace as a going-away present, wishing me "strength in Africa." He would later compare me to a lion, habits-wise but thankfully not eating-style wise: someone who has a lot of energy and expends it in spurts, vigorously pursuing activities, but who also takes periods of rest. Then when I arrived in my village in Lesotho, the teachers with whom I would work for the next two years had to, according to their culture, give me a name in their language. Without knowing about the necklace, they chose the last name of Tau, which means lion in Sesotho. I have since seen lions from a motor vehicle on safari in Kenya. This convergence of lions in my life has made me wonder whether I'm destined to see one on my bike.

The elephant shrieking at me earlier today, though, has rattled my nerves. I'm not exactly relaxed as I cycle along and suddenly see a shape moving slowly along a ways up the road. Definitely an animal but too far away to determine what kind. "Lion" comes to mind. Not wanting to approach a lion, I pull over and stop. I peer through my camera's telephoto lens but still can't really make it out. It does have a general lion shape, but they aren't usually wandering around at midday. It's the wrong shape to be an elephant, buffalo, baboon, or antelope, the most likely suspects, so my mind keeps returning to the lion thought.

While I stand by the side of the road, snacking and thinking about what to do, I see a police car approaching and then slowing. It stops next to me, and the policeman rolls down his window.

I expect him to ask me what I'm doing out here with the lions, but instead he says, "Are you tired?"

I shrug and say I'm just taking a break. He asks where I'm going today, and my response of Pandamatenga brings relief to his face. Relief that I'm not planning to camp in the bush in lion country, I think.

Then he asks it, the question: "Are you afraid of lions?"

No longer as confident as I'd felt earlier, I reply, "Not exactly, but is that one up the road?"

"No, it's a cow. It's too hot for lions at this time of day. They're sleeping in the bush now." He tells me to stop in at the police station in Pandamatenga if I need anything, wishes me well, and drives away.

A cow? Now I feel silly. But what on earth is a cow doing in lion country, I wonder. Not even the cows are logical here in Africa.

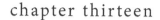

chapter thirteen

MIRAGES IN THE DESERT

A s I near the entrance to a lodge in Pandamatenga, a tall white man with long blond hair gets out of a parked car and motions to me to stop.

"Are you looking for a place to camp? We have camping here," he says.

"That's what I heard. I was planning to stop."

"Great. I'm going to pick up a couple things. I'll talk to you later."

This lodge, like most of Botswana's tourism infrastructure, caters primarily to South African and European tourists. Botswana's government has chosen to focus on promoting upscale tourism rather than mass lower-budget tourism geared towards backpackers. Where there are lodges, they generally have Western standards and frequently Western prices for rooms. My plan for Botswana is to camp at lodges where they are available and to free camp with permission where they are more than a day's bike ride apart. Another irony of Paul and me splitting up when we did is that one of the reasons I wanted a riding partner or group for this trip was to be safer free camping, and now that I've gotten to the part of the trip that involves free camping, I'm alone.

In the evening I order a vegetarian meal at the lodge's restaurant and am served a plate of seasoned carrots, zucchini, mushrooms, tomato, cauliflower with cheese, rice and salad. This is probably the most variety of vegetables I've seen on one plate in Africa—and a stark reminder that I'm not in rural Zambia anymore. Here I trust the salad and eat heartily. The blond-haired man, who turns out to be from New Zealand, introduces himself. He's currently working at the lodge, has traveled a lot, and likes to talk with other travelers. Traveling solo, it's nice to have a bit of company while I finish my dinner.

The only wildlife I see the next day is an impala and several birds, including two malachite kingfishers. That evening I stay at the forestry camp recommended by the tourist officer. It's not a campground, but they let cyclists camp here. It's enclosed by a fence, which is important in lion country, and there's water available from a rain catchement tank. Three men live in block housing reminiscent of a small resthouse. They greet me when I arrive, then keep to themselves. I set up my tent on the other side of the camp. When I walk over to get some water from the tank, I ask one of them what their jobs are.

"To protect the trees," he replies.

This makes sense for a forestry camp, but there aren't many trees and nothing I'd call a forest here. I'm tempted to ask what trees but don't. They've been respectfully leaving me alone, and I'd like to keep it this way. Here I am in exactly the kind of situation that I wanted a riding partner for: informally camping in a very rural area with only a few local men and no women around. In Lesotho, I wouldn't have felt safe in this type of situation. Yet here I do. There's a different sort of feeling in the air, one of respect rather than opportunism. The lack of attention, lack of even looks, is reassuring. My choice to cycle into Botswana alone feels like the right one.

The following day is my happiest day of cycling on this trip—and I make up a song about people saying there's nothing here, but I'm seeing nature and animals and that's not nothing at all to me. I see a puku—a type of small antelope—and six ostriches. One of the ostriches is trapped between a fence along the side of the road and me. It runs in the same direction as I'm cycling and keeps looking back at me. I slow down to try to let it get ahead, but it seems to slow too. So I stop. It keeps going and finds a bush to hide in while I pass. I wonder if it really thinks I don't know it's there. What do ostriches think?

Four people in cars stop to talk with me. They're mostly white South Africans who are surprised to see a cyclist along this road and want to know about my trip. One man stops and tells me there is a "lion, elephant" along the road up ahead. I soon see a large elephant. It ignores me as I ride by. There is another veterinary shoe and tire washing stop. More people want to know about my trip. Now that I'm alone, my trip seems to be more interesting to people than it was when I was with Paul. Women traveling alone are a rarity in Africa, especially off-the-beaten-track. A woman who works at the stop tells me there was a leopard in the road yesterday, but they haven't seen it today.

I cycle an extra ten kilometers through Nata to camp at a lodge that has been recommended by fellow travelers. As I round a bend, the road to the lodge gets sandier. Did the sign really point me in this direction, I wonder.

I shift into my lowest gear and keep pedaling. This doesn't make sense. I don't think two-wheel drive cars could get through here, and the lodge isn't supposed to be four-wheel drive only access. But stubbornly, I ride on—for a few minutes, until the sand gets so deep it stops me. The road has practically withered to a track.

Like a mirage, a horseman appears up ahead, riding towards me. He's an older man with a weather-beaten face who probably lives in a nearby village and may have never left this area of his native Botswana. I'm thousands of miles away from the country others insist is my home, although it no longer feels like it to me. I wave, and he stops.

"Hello," I say.

He looks at me blankly. Perhaps shocked to see a lone white woman on a bicycle.

"*Lumela, ntate,*" I say, remembering where I am. Hello, Sir. When I first arrived in Africa calling all adult men "sir" felt funny to me, but now it comes naturally.

His Setswana response sounds enough like the Sesotho "*Lumela, 'me*" that I know he has understood me. Setswana is the most commonly spoken language in Botswana and is similar to the Sesotho I learned.

"*Tsela lodge?*" Is this the road to the lodge?

He shakes his head no.

"*Lodge o kai?*" Where is the lodge?

He looks at a fence to my left, and I understand the lodge is in the compound, though I cannot see any buildings.

"*Kea leboha, ntate.*" Thank you, sir.

"*Kea leboha, 'me.*" Thank you, ma'am.

He rides away on his horse. I pick up my bike, turn it around, and ride back to find the entrance to the lodge that I must've missed.

I arrive at the lodge to find out the water is out. So much for a hot shower to clean off the dust of the past few days. My stomach suddenly feels unsettled, and all I eat for dinner is apple juice, bread, and crackers. I feel better later in the evening, and the water is fixed, so I get a hot shower after all.

After three consecutive 100+ kilometer days through the dry heat, I'm ready for a break and rest at the lodge the next day. I luxuriate in having the freedom to do so. Now instead of being tired of my riding partner, I'm just tired—and this is much easier to recover from. In the morning, my stomach is again queasy and I'm exhausted. But as the day goes on, I feel better. I oil my bike chain and derailleurs, do laundry in a sink, and filter water. I have an omelet for lunch at the lodge's outdoor bar then spend most of the afternoon sitting in the shade by the pool, resting, reading, and writing.

That night after dark, I hear a group of South Africans come in and set up camp near me while I'm reading in my tent. In the morning, one comes over, says she hopes they weren't too loud last night (they weren't), and asks me about my trip. She returns with a care package consisting of an energy drink, an energy bar, an apple, a brownie, a muffin, several cookies, and a couple other unidentified edibles. They're on a religious mission and she wants to bless my trip. Is this how missionaries do their work these days, by giving out food? I graciously accept the package, which comes without a sermon.

I ride the ten kilometers from the lodge back to Nata then turn west towards Maun, embarking on the second of the three legs of my Botswana adventure. It's another 300⁺ kilometer segment that I'm planning to do in three days because of lack of services along the way. Today's landscape is less colorful than the road from Kasane to Nata: the browns are grayer, less golden, and most of the trees growing from sandy soil are barren. After I bike by a stretch of tall, brown grass, an early sidewind turns into a slight headwind. Whenever I stop for a break, flies buzz around. I see cattle and occasionally people but no wildlife. There are fewer large trucks on this road, making for quieter traffic. It's a long, hot, hazy, flat, dry day of cycling. Pushing myself to go more than 100 kilometers a day isn't fun. I'm ready to stop after eighty. And knowing I've got another two of these days coming up—without any official place to camp along the way— doesn't help.

I camp at the Gweta Rest Camp. I sit at dinner thinking that Botswana's reputation as expensive isn't entirely deserved. It is more expensive than Malawi and Zambia and a lot more so if you want a bed; however, *pula* 16,50 (about $4 U.S.) for a candlelight, poolside dinner doesn't seem so expensive, even though it isn't a cyclist portion, and I eat my blessed muffin for dessert back at my tent. Rain is so valuable here that Botswana's currency, the *pula*, is named for it.

I ride out of the inhabited Gweta area to land that is fenced off on both sides of the road, although it looks deserted. As I cycle along, I enter a national park. The scenery remains so barren that it doesn't feel like a national park. The park contains saltpans, but they're down sandy tracks and not visible from the main road. I'm finding the main roads in Botswana well paved but

Heather's Bike

have noticed that all the side roads are so sandy that a bicycle would simply sink if I tried to ride on them. I struggle cycling into a headwind all day. When a man stops and offers me a lift to Maun, I'm tempted, although I immediately turn him down.

Wondering where I'll end up tonight, I find myself looking around for places to free camp hours before I plan to stop. I'm planning on riding at least 100 kilometers today but after only eighty-one, a sign with a tent symbol suddenly appears on the side of the road. I wonder if it's a mirage in the desert. Some people imagine lakes. Am I imagining a campground sign? I don't see a campground. I see a man inside a fenced-in area and ask him.

"It's right here," he tells me, "This is it."

It's a roads camp, similar to the forestry camp I stayed at my second night out of Kasane. It's fenced-in and has a water tank and latrine. This is a gift when I expected to be camping in the bush. I'm reminded to have faith that things do work out.

I think back to a couple of my first bike trips—the Maine Coast and Seattle to San Francisco—and how the leaders of those trips had, what seemed to me at the time, an incredible faith that things do work out, a faith that I not only didn't have back then but also couldn't even comprehend. Yet now this is exactly how I feel. There's something about bike touring, about how it exposes us to the world around us and leaves us vulnerable yet how we bike travelers are generally met with warmth, interest, and openness and rarely with hostility or violence, that restores my faith in humanity, in the goodness of our souls, and in the world around us. Bike touring helps me see the universe as a friendly place rather than an unfriendly one.

The local man who seems to be in charge of the camp is the friendliest Motswana (person from Botswana) I've met so far. He stands around and chats after telling me where to set up my tent. He talks about some other people who have come here—Swedes who saw lions up the road after dark, Koreans who built the camp, and Zimbabweans who come into Botswana illegally and sell things here since the *pula* is so much stronger than their currency. He also tells me that he's going to Maun tomorrow because it's payday and that the purpose of this camp is to fix potholes in the road.

He later returns to offer me his cell phone number, saying "I thought you might want to have it."

I tell him that I don't have a cell, but I give him the last of the food that the South Africans had given me. I'd discovered that it had meat in it. He looks genuinely surprised and happy. He takes a bite and thanks me.

I sit outside my tent eating a cold dinner with a huge smile on my face. It's amazing how fulfilling basic needs can lead to such happiness. I have a safe place to camp, some food, plenty of water to drink, and I'm happy. This is all it takes.

I'm finding cycling in Botswana to be very freeing. The lack of people along the roads, combined with Paul's absence, means I've really got time to think. Not going through any villages means no kids running after me, no staring adults, no tagalong cyclists. My time is really my own. Until this point, I haven't been able to get the same psychological benefits from cycling in Africa that I do in the U.S. It's hard to just ride along and think when you feel like you're constantly the center of attention. In the U.S., cycling tends to relax me and put me in a better frame of mind. In Africa to this point, it has been more for exercise (in Lesotho) and independence and a tool to get to know the landscapes and cultures. This trip starts to turn when a long day's ride starts cheering me up. The miles can be meditative.

The next day's ride is again flat, and I'm pleased to have a tailwind pushing me along. Suddenly, after seventy-two kilometers, my bike seems to slow as if the wind has turned to a headwind. I stop and discover that the rear tire is soft—a slow leak. I can't find anything in the tire or tube but put in a new tube.

Just after I re-install my wheel, a couple from Maun stops and offers me a lift. While I talk with them, I put my gear back on my bicycle. As I finish, the woman starts to wheel my bike down the road. I don't know why she does this, especially since I've turned them down, and it catches me with such surprise that I walk with her and my bike and forget to check the ground around me, as I usually do after fixing a flat. Soon after they leave and I start cycling, I realize the patch kit and tire levers I'd put in my pocket are no longer there. I go back and can't find them on the ground. The spot was non-descript, but I have an accurate idea of where it was because the man had asked how far I'd cycled today and so I'd checked my cycle odometer. I don't think they could've pickpocketed me, but I wonder if they saw them on the ground and picked them up, hoping they were something valuable. Monetarily, they're not. But I'm nervous cycling without them and dread the possibility of getting another flat. I have more spare tubes and I'm sure I could find something in my panniers to use as makeshift tire levers, but this would be time-consuming and I'm already concerned about making it to Maun by dark. I need to push myself mentally to get all the way there. One hundred and forty kilometers is a long ride on a mountain bike, even on a tar road with a tailwind for parts of the day, but I finish the ride feeling strong and fast.

I arrive at a hotel with a campground as dusk descends. Preparing to set up my tent in a secluded area away from the tour groups, I lean my bike against a fence. A man drives over and asks if I'm planning to camp here.

Yes, I say, wondering if he'd somehow already claimed this spot. Instead he tells me that there was a robbery in camp last night. At four a.m., thieves cut a hole in the fence, slashed a tent, and stole some clothes.

"Why wasn't I told this when I arrived?"

"Because if we told people, no one would stay."

"But, I'm a woman traveling alone with a bicycle, which is valuable."

"They wouldn't be after your bike, just your clothes. Besides, robbery happens at all the camps here. This is Africa. You don't know, this is just the way it is here."

It strikes me that this comment would probably not have been directed towards a black person and reminds me that no matter how much at home I feel here, I can never entirely fit in.

"Well, actually, I've been in Africa for more than two years and haven't been robbed yet." Except maybe for a patch kit and tire levers, I think.

"I'm just trying to help you out by telling you. I suggest you camp over in the more central area by the restrooms."

After he leaves, I consider asking for a refund and going elsewhere, but it's now so dusky this would mean cycling after dark. I walk over to the area he recommended and grudgingly look around. It does look safer, with lights and other campers, but I want dark and privacy. I want to be alone. But now, knowing about the robbery, staying in my original spot feels like an unnecessary risk without enough potential gain. It sure would be a drag if my tent got slashed, and I don't know if I could find a lightweight replacement here. And, so, I move, figuring that the right choice tonight is the one that protects my tent—and thus protects my trip.

chapter fourteen

LOOK LIONS IN THE EYE

I spend a couple days in Maun, a sprawling town of 35,000. It's a mix of old and new, of locals and tourism infrastructure. New shopping centers and multi-story buildings sit next to crumbling buildings and mud huts. The main road through town is tar, but most other roads are dirt. This former outpost for hunters and poachers is now the gateway for trips into the Okavango Delta. I'm able to get a new patch kit at a sporting goods store and tire levers at a hardware store. I can only find metal tire levers, though, not plastic ones, which are more rim-friendly. I duct tape the metal ones to keep them from scratching my rims. I book a tour into the Okavango Delta, a 16,000-square-kilometer area of river-fed channels and islands in northwestern Botswana. Access to the interior is by small plane and canoe only.

Flying from Maun into the Delta on a six-seat plane, I watch the landscape change from the browns and grays of a parched land to the blues and greens of an inland waterway system. It's only a twenty-minute flight, but it takes me to a different world, a world where travel is by dugout canoe and foot and where people and wild animals live peacefully with one another.

The plane lands smoothly in a clearing on Ntswi Island, where a porter from Gunn's Bush Camp meets me.

"Camp is a ten-minute walk," he tells me.

Along the way, we stop to look at an elephant track, clearly showing a very wrinkled foot, in the sand. We walk around the footprint, then he raises his hand, motioning me to stop again. The elephant is standing just off the trail up ahead, maybe fifteen meters away. We detour onto a different trail to give it its space.

"I think elephants are more dangerous than lions," says the porter.

"Why?" I ask, thinking about the elephant that screeched at me on my way to Pandamatenga.

"Because elephants are unpredictable."

Arriving at the camp, I'm greeted by a camp manager, Dion, who confirms that my reservation is for an overnight *mokoro* (dugout canoe in Setswana) trip with an additional night back at the camp before returning to Maun.

"Our guides are unarmed," explains Dion, a white South African in his thirties. "They use their knowledge of their surroundings and animals to stay safe."

The local people here have been living harmoniously with animals for at least decades and probably centuries. Giving animals their space and knowing how to deal with challenges from various species are key. Look lions in the eye, even if they're charging at you, and never run. Their prey runs from them; if you don't run, you aren't prey and they will stop their charge. On the other hand, run from charging buffalo (they never bluff charge), maybe climb a tree, or lie down and pretend to be a log if no trees are around—this will slow them down and decrease the force on impact. Get out of the water at least five meters onto land away from mad hippos. Dion's level of comfort living with wild animals is reassuring, and I wish I'd had this information when I arrived in Botswana.

I'm introduced to my guide, Luckson, who is called a poler and lives in the local village on the island. We load our camping gear, food, and water into a fiberglass *mokoro*. Traditionally, *mekoro* (plural of *mokoro*) are made of ebony, or kigeria, logs. But since these trees take more than one hundred years to grow and a *mokoro* lasts for only about five years, many *mekoro* are now being made from fiberglass. Reminiscent of a Venetian gondolier, the poler stands at back of the *mokoro*, steering and rowing using a long pole with one end flattened out like a blade. I sit in the front to balance our weight, with our gear between us. A second passenger could sit directly in front of the poler.

We glide along the channels of the delta. Green grass and lily pads with white flowers poke through the surface of the calm blue water. We pass islands of various sizes with green grasses on their shores and taller brown grasses, sometimes as tall as elephants' legs, just the slightest bit inland.

It's late August now, still the dry season. There hasn't been any rain in months. The islands are dotted with palm trees whose tops look down on shorter, scrubbier trees that take on a brownish tinge at this time of year. We pass a couple of informal camps—other visitors on overnight *mokoro* trips—

but mostly we watch the animals. Elephants wander through the water ahead of us, and we pause to let them pass. Zebras stand peacefully in the water but splash away from us as we approach, giving us plenty of room to pass. A giraffe looks on calmly from the shore. My poler identifies every bird we see, wattled cranes among them.

I enjoy the serenity, the lack of motor vehicle and other mechanical noises. This isn't my first time seeing most of the wildlife here, but the whole feeling is different than traveling in a motorized safari vehicle. This is a much more peaceful experience, immersed in the environment rather than disturbing it. I feel that the animals are my neighbors, and just like with human neighbors, if we treat each other respectfully, we can live harmoniously together.

We land on the island where we'll camp tonight. Although it's only the end of winter, midday temperatures frequently reach the low 30s °C (around 90 °F)—a good reason for a midday siesta. I set up my tent near a kigeria tree, but not under it in case any of the fruit fall. Kigeria are fruit shaped like oversize sausages that elephant eat. There's so much animal dung around that I have to clear a space big enough for my tent. Luckson sets up his tent a short distance away, within easy sight but also giving me some space. I climb a small hill in the shade of another tree and eat my lunch on the hilltop, watching wildebeests and zebras graze across the channel and baboons and red lechwe—reddish antelopes—walk by on our island. A hippo in the channel occasionally grunts. There's no need to imagine what life was like here a hundred years ago. I'm seeing it as it was then and still is today.

As the sun starts to drop from its midday high, we go for a bush walk along the sandy paths of our island, then a *mokoro* ride through more channels. Both add to the feeling of being one with nature as we watch the animals without disturbing them. An elephant shakes a palm tree with its trunk.

"Perhaps it wants to take the tree down," Luckson says, unsure.

We see giraffe, reedbuck, and kudu. Back at camp, while Luckson builds a fire to cook dinner, I watch the sunset turn the sky and the water into an orange glow. Hippos surface while my pasta cooks. They stick their heads out of the water then sink back down. Luckson cooks his dinner, and I try to talk with him about the area. His English is very good when he's telling me about the animals and I trust his knowledge to keep me safe, but he's not fluent enough to have a long, easy conversation.

"Do you have family here?" I ask.

"Yes, a wife and kids."

"Do they live in the village on Ntswi Island?"

"Yes." He stirs the fire.

"That's good, then you get to see them a lot? Between trips?" I gaze at the fire.

"Yes, I am happy. I used to guide for another camp. This is better." He smiles.

"Why did you switch?" I look around into the darkness that's enveloping us.

"I am better paid now."

Poling is a hard job and, sadly, many of the camps grossly underpay their local employees. I feel better about being here knowing that my guide is happy. I watch the stars as we talk. It's a peaceful place, this camp in the delta. I feel connected to the earth here and at one with nature.

Sometime during the night I wake up and hear roaring. It doesn't sound very close and feeling safe in my tent, I easily fall back asleep. I feel safe because I know the key to safely camping in lion country is to really stay inside your closed tent all night. Lions don't understand that tents are not solid objects, so they walk around them just like they walk around houses. But don't leave your tent door open. Then it's a hole, not a solid object, and lions will go in.

In the morning, Luckson confirms that the roars were lions far in the distance. We take a *mokoro* ride to a nearby island for a bush walk. He finds

Lion Track

lion paw prints and pauses just long enough to point them out to me before starting to track the lions. Our pace picks up, as he's on their trail. Yesterday he frequently asked me if I needed a break. Today he doesn't ask. No breaks allowed when tracking lions. Sipping from my water bottle as we walk, I wonder what our chances of finding the lions are. I see only an occasional paw print, but he moves confidently along.

After about two hours, he suddenly stops and points. There's a lioness walking quickly into the brush. She is close enough that I can clearly see her but not close enough to get a good photo, even with a 200mm lens. She continues on her way and saunters out of our sight. Then Luckson points me in another direction, where two male lions with full, flowing manes are resting in the distance. They're mostly hidden in the grass, but their heads are silhouetted above it. They are looking right at us, unfazed, just watching, not bothering to get up or move around. I look them in the eye, though they are too far away for me to really be able to see into their eyes. They accept our presence, and we accept theirs. I'm thrilled to see them but disappointed to have to turn away rather than get closer. Yet in this moment, if there is any lingering doubt in my subconscious that coming into Botswana alone was the right thing to do, it is gone. All the shades of brown scenery, all the long, hot days, all the doubts about where I'd camp, any questions about safety, are all so worth it to have stood on the African soil and looked lions in the eye, safe not because I'm enclosed in a safari vehicle but safe because I've met them on their terms and kept my distance.

As we make our way back to our *mokoro*, we get within a couple meters of a spotted hyena, much less exciting after seeing lions than it would've been before. After lunch and another midday siesta watching zebras and wildebeests at our island camp, we take one last two-hour *mokoro* ride. On our way back to Bush Camp, we see more elephants that are two-tone from walking in the water, a large sleeping crocodile, and a python.

At Bush Camp, I treat myself to dinner at the restaurant. A Spanish couple are the only other guests tonight, and we eat with the camp managers, Dion and his German partner, Anja, by paraffin lamplight outdoors. It's a wonderful meal of stuffed green peppers with a coconut cream sauce, couscous with nuts, a bit of corn on the cob, and cake with amarula sauce. This doesn't feel like the bush anymore.

"Do you all have flashlights?" Dion asks. "Leopards have been visiting the camp late at night recently." He says leopards are smarter than lions and will not attack people even at night unless by rare mistake. Shining light into leopards' eyes lets them know we are people and not prey.

We all nod yes, we have flashlights. As I walk back to my tent, I wonder where my spare batteries are.

Early in the morning, I sit on the deck enveloped in serenity. No one else is around. The sun's reflection in the water sparkles and the grass shimmers green. An antelope, maybe a red lechwe, runs in the distance. Birds, mostly black and yellow bulbets, chirp and hop about. I get word that my flight is delayed for an hour because the president of Botswana is flying. Apparently no other planes are allowed to fly when he does, but I don't mind. The feeling of oneness and harmony with nature that I have here will stay with me long after I fly back to Maun.

chapter fifteen

CAMPING WITH A DEAD OSTRICH

In Maun, I pick up my bicycle and the rest of my gear from the camp office, get groceries, check email, and then cycle out of town late in the afternoon. The twenty-one kilometers to the camp turnoff takes a bit over an hour. Expecting a quick ride to camp, I'm dismayed to find a sandy road at the sign for the camp and no other evidence of it in view. My only realistic option is to push my bike. With the sinking sun, I worry about getting to the camp by dark. I ask a local along the way how much farther the camp is.

"About a twenty-five-minute walk," he says.

This turns out to be fairly accurate, and I arrive as dusk descends. While I set up camp in a quiet spot, an overland tour group truck pulls into the adjacent sites. A tent city springs up around me and bustles with voices and clatter. It's such a contrast to the delta, and it reminds me that groups traveling together tend to become their own self-contained entities with their own social structures, moving through places together and mingling mostly among themselves. Whereas the group traveler pays the tour company to take care of logistics, even the simple—or sometimes not so simple—things like finding food and accommodation offer the solo traveler contact with the locals and a deeper sense of the area and its culture. And the solo traveler is generally seen as much more approachable by locals. So, although there are times when it would be nice to arrive in camp and have someone cook dinner for me, it wouldn't be as satisfying or as interesting. And although there are occasionally times it would be nice to be traveling with a good friend, someone much more compassionate than Paul, I'm mostly just relieved to be alone after all the tension.

I'm back in a dry landscape of barren trees and sandy soil. The sky is light blue, and the area is sparsely populated. I'm occasionally surprised to see people along the road where I can't see any houses. I feel good riding, and the road looks like it's going gradually downhill. I'm planning to camp near a lake mentioned in my guidebook, but I get to Sehitwa, which should've been after the lake, without ever seeing any water. I follow a sign for a police station and ask for permission to camp, which is readily granted. A policeman wearing a faded blue uniform directs me to a courtyard area ringed by the police station and police housing. While I set up my tent, a boy comes over and watches but leaves as soon as I finish, apparently more interested in my tent than in me. It's such a relief not to have more of an audience after Malawi, Zambia, and Lesotho. I look at my altimeter and see I gained more altitude than I lost today. I did have a slight tailwind at times, perhaps more than I realized or perhaps I had lots of energy stored up from my time off the bike.

I ask a policeman about the lake mentioned in my guidebook.

"That dried up in 1985," he says.

I later check the publication date of my guidebook. 2001.

From inside my tent, I watch two men pull a dead ostrich out of an army truck and dump it in the courtyard, probably only ten meters from my tent. It reeks of rotting flesh, and I can almost hear the burning sun baking it. The thought of camping with a dead ostrich repulses me. I'm wondering how I can possibly politely ask them to move it away from me when it's put in a wheelbarrow and wheeled away. In the evening I write in my journal, "I'm happy right now. A bit tired after ninety kilometers. But happy. Happy to be back on my bike after a good break. Happy to have had a good ride today. And happy to have found a police station to camp at." This is the most I've written about being happy on this trip so far and in stark contrast to when I was traveling with Paul. Then I always seemed to be writing about being tired or frustrated. Now I'm getting into my own rhythm traveling alone. There's so much joy in the moment when living simply on a bike tour, and traveling with Paul was never simple.

In the morning the ostrich is brought back. I ask a policeman about it.

"It was killed by a motor vehicle," he tells me.

"And why is it here? What will you do with it?"

"The meat will be sold to the public."

After I leave Sehitwa, I see an ostrich run away from the roadside and wonder if it was a companion of the dead ostrich. It's another hot dry ride, though with more green acacia trees dotting the landscape. My energy is low early on, and I stop for a sit down sandwich break in the shade. Botswana has something else I haven't seen in Africa: roadside picnic areas. They are usually tables by some scrubby trees. It's nice to be able to make use of them, though some are so trashed I keep cycling by. I feel much stronger until the afternoon heat starts to get to me. I swat at flies landing on my lips and nose.

Arriving in Nokaneng late in the afternoon, I ask about a place to camp and am directed to an unsigned police sub-station. Soon after I arrive, a mocha-colored man with short frizzy hair walks into the compound.

"I am a Bushman," he says.

Bushmen, or San, are ancient hunter-gatherers who have inhabited southern Africa for at least 30,000 years. Traditionally, they traveled in small family bands. Living a nomadic lifestyle, they followed water, wildlife, and edible plants. The early Europeans who arrived in southern Africa in the 1700s saw the San as wild animals and exterminated tens of thousands of them. Today, many San have given up their traditional lifestyle, in part due to relocation campaigns by the Botswana government. Only about 55,000 remain, about half of them in Botswana. I feel I should have thousands of questions for this man, about his lifestyle and his people, but I'm taken by such surprise that not a single one comes to mind.

"We are into hospitality," he tells me, "Do you need anything?"

I say I don't, but when I'm given warm water to bathe, I wonder if he arranged it. It's a huge surprise at a police station. Here I feel like an honored guest in the community, so different than at the campground in Maun.

Later I'm surprised to see a man wearing a suit walk over to my tent.

"I am camping here, too, tonight," he says after greeting me.

"Are you traveling?"

"Yes, I am a government employee and am handing out pensions."

I regret not having more energy to chat with him about his life, but I'm tired. People here are so much more reserved than in Malawi and Zambia. It's great when I'm riding along or walking around and get a lot less attention, but it also makes it harder to get to know people. Tonight I may be missing an opportunity.

In the morning, I have three visitors. First the Bushman comes to wish me a safe journey. Then the headman (a sub-chief) of Nokaneng introduces himself and welcomes me, explaining that he was away yesterday so couldn't come then. Finally, a policewoman stops to ask about my trip. Although I don't have long conversations with any of them, I feel so much more like I'm seeing Botswana here than I do when camping with other white travelers at the expatriate-owned lodges.

I feel the sun's warmth even early in the day now. I'm going north and it beats on my face and the fronts of my arms. I stop in Gumare at the Ngwao Boswa basket co-op, which is run by local women who make the baskets. Their wares include closed baskets with lids, which are traditionally used for storing grain and seeds; large open, bowl-shaped baskets, which are used for carrying items on their heads; and, small plate-shaped baskets, used for winnowing grain after it has been pounded. All are made from the "vegetable ivory" palm tree and are dyed shades of brown. Each basket has a tag explaining its design, with names such as palm leaf, back of the python, tears of the giraffe, running ostrich, and knees of the tortoise. Expecting to return to the States in a couple months, I buy a couple for gifts. Then I stop at a supermarket for cold juice, a treat that's hard to find. I stand in the shade of the building and savor the cold liquid coating my tongue and the insides of my cheeks before each swallow. Soon after I get back on the road, a flat tire tests my metal tire levers. They work fine, though the duct tape peels off a bit as I leverage the tire off the rim.

Heat makes me very happy to arrive in the village Etsha-6. On my way to camp, I stop at a roadside food stand and have my first meal in Botswana at a place that's geared towards locals rather than tourists: rice with beetroot and potato salad. After lunch, I follow signs to the campsite. I pull into the dirt driveway, and a slightly plump woman with her hair pulled back comes out of a cement house.

"I'd like to camp," I say.

"We don't have camping here."

"But all your signs say camping, including the one right there." I point to the sign marking the last turn.

"We planned to have camping, but when we got the tourist license, it said no camping." She sighs.

"Why is it on all the signs?"

"We'd already gotten the signs. It cost too much to get new ones."

"The tourist office in Maun told me you have camping. Can you let me camp here, just for tonight?"

"I can't allow camping." She pauses and looks towards her house. "How about if you stay in my daughter's room? She's away."

"Are you sure she wouldn't mind?" This just doesn't feel like a genuine offer of hospitality, and I'd feel awkward staying in her house. It feels like she's offering because she doesn't know what else to suggest.

"You shouldn't camp alone as a lady," she says resolutely.

"I'm really okay with camping. I like it and haven't had any problems." I smile.

"Well, you'll only stay one night, right? And what time would you leave in the morning?" She looks toward the road.

"By eight."

"Okay, go ahead and camp, but set up your tent right in front of my house. It'll be safer." She looks at her house.

There's a slight chill in the air when I leave at 7:30 the next morning, but it's gone by the time I stop in the village and buy groceries. My energy's low, and I settle in for another hot ride. I'm headed to Sepupa, where I have a decision to make for tomorrow. The Tsodilo Hills, reputed to be southern Africa's best preserved rock art site and one of my motivations for coming to Botswana, are thirty-eight kilometers down a rough road, off the main road past Sepupa. My question is just how rough is it? Is it traversable by a loaded mountain bike in a day? My guidebook describes it as a rough four-wheel drive track and lists the GPS coordinates to help locate it. I've heard from some expats I've asked that it's bad, but the long-haired man I met in Pandamatenga told me it has been improved. No one seems to have firsthand knowledge.

After getting settled in at the Sepupa Swamp Stop, I walk to the reception/ bar area to ask about the road to Tsodilo.

Renee, a pudgy white South African with short brown hair and a matching mustache, says, "I'll drive you there."

"Really, don't you have to work?" He's standing behind the bar.

"No, I can take you. I took another guest a couple weeks ago. It's easy to do as a day trip."

"I'm not sure. I'd like to bike if it's possible. But maybe. Let me think about it." In some ways, getting a ride is exactly what I want, but in other ways, it feels like quitting, or at least wimping out.

Later I sit on the banks of a stream flowing from the Okavango River. The banks are lined with papyrus-like grasses. Birds chirp, but I can't see them. Western pop music from the bar infiltrates the serenity but doesn't drown out the birds. Renee comes over and re-iterates his offer. He tells me he wants me to meet someone who is living right next to the camp.

Andries is a weather-beaten white South African who is sitting in a lawn chair outside his trailer when we approach. He has been living here with only his cat and dog for three years while waiting for some contract to come through.

"What have you been doing for all this time?" I ask. Africa has taught me patience but not this much.

"I have made three eight-day trips to Drotsky's Caverns."

I stare at him, both unfamiliar with Drotsky's Caverns and unsure how this really answers my question. What about the other 357 days a year?

"There are amazing stalactites and stalagmites there." He continues, "I needed to mark my path with string to be able to find my way back out."

As Renee and I walk back towards the bar area, he squeezes my shoulder and says, "What are you doing for dinner?"

"Making something at camp." There aren't exactly any restaurants nearby, I think, as I move away from him.

For the first time, I miss Paul's presence. Not him, just his presence effectively warding off unwanted sexual overtures from scummy men. I was a single woman while traveling with him, but men who saw us didn't know this. Now that I'm traveling solo, they assume it. It amazes me, though, that the local men here in Botswana don't seem to care and that Renee has been the first to approach me. Do the locals respect me enough as a visitor in their country not to make sexual overtures? This seems unlikely. So what is it about their culture that is different from that of their neighbors and keeps them from approaching me? I wish I knew—and could bring it to other cultures where the men aren't so hands-off, or even words-off.

"You're welcome to come to my caravan. I'll make you dinner."

"Thanks, but I think I want to be alone and rest."

I sit by my tent pondering what to do. I definitely don't want to spend a day with Renee now, but I still want to see the Tsodilo Hills. Maybe I'll just have to wait to make a decision until I get to the turnoff and see how the road looks. Maybe I can still find another ride. There are only a few other campers here but maybe someone else is going. Hoping that Renee will not be there, I return to the bar. A few men are sitting on stools and I ask if they know anyone going to Tsodilo, explaining that I'm concerned about the road.

"That road is concrete the whole way now," says one.

"Really? People keep telling me not to bike."

"Yes, it's comparable to the road in here."

"That's great. This road was fine." Sand covered a lot of the concrete, but it was cyclable. "Is the road well-marked?"

"Yes, there's a big sign for Tsodilo Hills at the turnoff. Then the road takes you all the way there. No turns."

chapter sixteen
TWO SUNRISES

I feel strong riding and cruise along to the Tsodilo turnoff, which is indeed well-marked. The road looks sandy, but I ride through the sand and keep going. I'm nervous that the road will get worse as I ride along, but it never does, and I could turn back if I really had to. Concrete tracks are generally visible where motor vehicle tires have scattered the sand. Where they aren't, the concrete underneath makes the sand bikable.

The road feels safe. This is my first venture off the main roads of Botswana, where in a sense I was protected by the watchful eyes of the passing traffic. Here I'm much more alone. If I were to run into the wrong person, I could simply disappear from the known world. But I'm confident that I won't. I know I am safe here, a knowing that isn't entirely logical, or some would say possible, but just is, like a child who hasn't yet been taught by the world to doubt her intuition.

More concrete is visible through the sand as I ride on and a tailwind helps me along. Then the concrete unexpectedly ends, and I hit red sand. Thinking that the concrete road was supposed to take me straight to the entrance to Tsodilo Hills, I'm confused by the sand road. The man at the swamp stop said no turns. So even though it doesn't feel right, I keep going and push my bike through the deep red sand. Flies buzz around and bite me. I can see the hills rising out of the plain off to my right and feel like I am going too far past them.

The Tsodilo Hills, Botswana's first World Heritage site, are four hills of quartzite schist. According to local legend, the hills were once a family. Thus, they are named Male Hill, Female Hill, Child Hill, and North Hill. North Hill, distant from the others, is said by one legend to have been an argumentative wife of Male Hill who was sent away. Male Hill, the tallest of the four, rises about 350 meters. The cliffs and walls of both Male and Female are adorned with rock paintings estimated to date from 850 AD to 1100 AD.

I stop to look at my map several times. Finally I conclude that I have most likely missed a turn. But where? Maybe in the small village I went through just before the concrete ended? I could turn around and go back, but what if I do and I haven't missed a turn? I don't want to push my bike back through the sand anyway. The ground away from the road looks harder than the sand. I lay my bike down and walk over to test it. It's hard-packed. If I walk towards the hills, I should intersect with the entrance road. I decide to go for it. I push my bike through tall grasses and around trees and bushes, whose thorns occasionally grab me, forcing me to stop and untangle my purple shirt from their grasp. Grasses scratch my legs as I walk, but this beats getting bitten by flies.

I stop and take a few conscious breaths, and my surroundings sink in: I stand alone in this dry, barren land with the Tsodilo Hills as my only landmark. I briefly wonder if I should be going off-road like this. Is this how people get lost in the wilderness, by forging ahead when they don't really know exactly where they are? Yet confident in my landmarks, I continue on, heading towards the hills at an angle at which I expect to cross the main access road. After less than an hour, I meet a rough concrete road, hop on my bike, and discover that the rear tire is flat. Not having the patience to fix it, and thinking I must be close now, I keep walking, pushing my bike along the concrete road. After another half hour, I arrive at Main Camp—and discover that my front tire is also going flat. The camp manager, a thin man probably in his twenties, walks over.

"I don't think I came the right way," I say.

He looks puzzled, and I tell him about my adventure.

"You didn't see the sign at the turn? It has a yellow triangle on it, just like the turn off the main road."

I remember riding by a yellow triangle, not knowing what it meant, and I vaguely remember the first sign. I didn't realize the significance of its yellow triangle and didn't make the connection by the time I got to the second sign.

I'm the only one camping at Main Camp and enjoy the peacefulness and eating dinner outside as the sun sets. Later I hear a "snniiiffffffffff" outside my tent. What's that? A donkey. Cows run by. All this commotion and strong winds make it hard to sleep.

In the cool morning air, I wander around, looking at the rocky hills, then go on a guided hike. I reject my first guide, telling the site manager that he

Rhino Panel

seems drunk. My new guide takes me along the rhino trail, which starts from camp and has a high concentration of rock paintings.

He points to the first painting and says, "There's the rhino."

It's so clear, with a stocky rhino body and distinctive rhino horn, that I easily could have identified it without his help. After about 1000 years, the rusty red paint still contrasts with the whitish gray rock face. I expect Tsodilo's reputation as one of the region's best rock art sites is well deserved. I've seen some rock art in Lesotho and Zimbabwe where the paintings were so faded it was hard to tell they were there. There's no ambiguity here. This was worth the ride—and the hike with my bike.

The trail climbs partway up Female Hill on the way to a water pit, where the San believe the greatest spirit knelt on the day of creation, though it's now a slimy puddle. The trail continues into a grassy valley then past several rocky outcrops before descending. Some paintings are easy to spot and identify, such as giraffes with their long necks and elands with their long double horns, but some are hidden and not as clear.

Most of the paintings are animal groupings, though there are some of humans and objects, done with a reddish pigment made of hematite and possibly mixed with animal fat, blood, marrow, egg-white, honey, sap, or urine. All were finger-painted on gray, light orangish, or white rock faces. The paintings include rhino, gemsbok, eland, giraffe, cows, lions, fish (or whales), fishnets, a tortoise, zebra, a few people, the sun, and a clock.

After the hike I sit in the shade outside the small visitor center. The site manager walks over and asks me about my hike, then when I'm leaving.

"I'm going to camp here again tonight then leave early tomorrow morning when it's much cooler." It's too hot even in the midday shade, and there won't be any shade on the road.

Staying until tomorrow, though, means that I've got to ride 120 kilometers to a camp in Namibia tomorrow. My Botswana visa is expiring. When I arrived, I answered the question on the immigration form "How long do you plan to stay?" honestly: 21 days. I'd read, though, that visitors were routinely given 30-day visas, and this is what I expected. I'd been surprised when I later looked at my visa more closely and saw that it said "21 days." Nonetheless, I didn't think this would be a problem, but now I could use an extra day. And unlike in Malawi, I cannot get it extended at any police station.

"I guess you probably don't get many cyclists here, do you?" I ask the camp manager.

"No, you are the first."

"Really?" I figured at least a hard core mountain biker or two would've been through on the unimproved road sometime.

"Yes. In the years I've been working here, you're the first. The road was just improved last December and it is very slippery in the wet season."

Wow. Now I'm impressed with myself. The first ever. Thank God Renee turned out to be a scum and I didn't take a ride in.

In the morning I depart in the early light of quarter to seven. While cycling, I watch the sun begin to rise on the left side of Male Hill. As I cycle by the hill, it blocks the sun. Once I'm past the hill, I watch the sun rise on the right side of the hill. I know this is all part of one continuous sunrise, but as I ride, it feels like watching two sunrises in one morning, and I know I am right where I am supposed to be. Alone in Africa.

Namibia

chapter seventeen

NOISES IN THE NIGHT

At the Namibian border, the tar road unexpectedly turns to sandy concrete and slows me down. With dusk descending, I think about stopping at a village and asking for a place to camp rather than continuing on to a campground only a few kilometers farther up the road. Looking around, I notice many people, including kids alone, are still out walking around. If they're not concerned about running out of daylight to get home safely, I probably don't need to be either. The thought of my first hot shower in five nights propels me to the campground.

While I eat dinner in the campground's restaurant, a woman working there tells me she walks back to the village alone every night after work and no one ever bothers her. In the morning, I talk with a man working in the office and he reassures me that this is a very safe area and that camping off the road—my only apparent option for tonight—is very safe, even for a woman alone. He tells me I'll see other people, mostly Angolan refugees, camping, and I do see some along the way. Already I like Namibia. It's such a refreshing change to be told things are safe rather than that they are not.

Namibia is shaped like a deep saucepan, with its eastern-facing handle, which reaches along northern Botswana to Zambia, known as the Caprivi Strip. I entered Namibia at the western end of the Caprivi Strip and plan to head generally southwest through this sparsely populated, largely arid land whose western edge borders the Atlantic Ocean.

Camping off the side of the road and inside my tent after dark, I hear a crunch. "What's that?" asks my mind, as I lie motionless. I strain to hear if the noise repeats itself. It sounded exactly like a footstep. Logically, I know it was just an animal, or perhaps branches settling after shifting in the breeze, like an old house settles. But I can't stop my mind from screaming, "Maybe there really is someone there. Then what are you going to do? What if someone comes after you here in the middle of the night? No one who cares about you has any idea where you are right now and it would probably be weeks before they'd get worried enough to report you missing."

I lie in my tent trying to relax. I've gotten spooked enough that I don't want to turn on my flashlight and light up my tent for anyone who happens to be around to see. I feel safer staying in the dark. My tent is set up amid barren trees far enough off the side of the road that it's out of range of any passing headlights and not near any footpaths that I saw. Tonight I'm grateful that I have a dark blue tent that blends into the dark night.

I think about how safe I felt riding after dark last night. And I think back to Lesotho, where I did not feel safe out alone after dark. I think about Patrick and Steve, fellow Peace Corps volunteers, getting attacked while camping, about the rocks that were thrown at their tent and that almost hit Patrick in the head. I realize another reason I need to keep going on this trip, going on alone, is to get over this culture of fear that the Peace Corps and the Basotho people instilled in me. For two years, I've been told that things are "not safe." I don't want to live that way or feel that way any more. But it's going to take my mind some time to adjust and accept the reality of my safety.

Eventually, I relax enough to fall asleep. In the daylight of the next morning, my fears of the night before seem silly. When I can see that I'm alone, the noises of the trees are friendly, just as the creak of an old house during the day is not at all disturbing.

From my roadside camp, I ride 120 kilometers west to the town of Rundu, where I camp at the most central lodge. From the campsite, there's a distant view across the Okavango River into Angola, Namibia's northern neighbor. I'd be tempted to cross the river and spend a day in Angola, but the nearby border post is only for locals.

The distances between services are vast now that I'm in Namibia, more consistently so and sometimes greater than in Botswana, and I need to stock up on food and water whenever I get to a town. I remember Rob the Canadian talking about how he got tired of carrying enough food for a few days and hitched a ride with a truck at one point. I'm surprised to see that the two South African chain grocery stores both sell camping stoves and replacement fuel cylinders. Their availability here in Rundu, which is not a major stop on the tourist trail, strikes me as a good sign that I'll be able to get these cylinders throughout Namibia, and I buy a stove. I'm tired of eating cold food when there's no restaurant wherever I'm camping. In the evening, I sit relaxed at a picnic table cooking spaghetti after a long bath—this is the first campground I've encountered with a bathtub. I don't think of myself as a cook, but I missed not being able to cook my own camp meals.

Leaving Rundu, I head southwest on the main tar road out of town. The blue sky is a welcome change from the gray of my ride into town. I feel cooler now that I'm going south and the sun is at my back. Namibia is so sparsely populated that I expect cycling here to be similar to Botswana in the sense of long, long stretches between towns with very few villages along the way. Instead I'm surprised to see several villages and people more constantly along the road than I have since probably Malawi. This area isn't densely populated, but there is almost always someone or a house within sight. Later I'll read that northern Namibia is the most densely populated part of country, but for now the unexpected attention is mentally draining.

I reach a construction detour. The road is being repaved. For eleven kilometers, all traffic is routed off of and just parallel to the highway. The rough concrete base I ride on is covered with sand and is very bumpy at times. Later in the ride, I pass, alternately, small villages, bush, and fenced-off farmland.

Late in the afternoon, I push my bike up a dirt trail to a tiny village—only a few mud houses—and ask for permission to camp. Camping at a village feels a lot more secure than camping alone. It's a family village. The parents and their three children and grandchildren are the only ones who live here. When I leave in the morning, the stooped grandmother with sun-baked skin says, "thank you," quickly claps her hands together a few times, and bows slightly. I do the same, and her whole face smiles.

I spend the next couple days continuing on the main tar road southwest. It takes me through a monotonous dry land of fenced-off cattle ranches and scrubby trees. The long distances in Botswana and Namibia are starting to wear me down, and my energy is low. The idea of taking a lift at some point becomes tempting. The second night I camp at a German-owned campground.

"I studied in Germany," I mention to the owners.

"*Was hast Du studiert*?" they ask. What did you study?

It feels odd to suddenly be speaking German in Africa, though German has been spoken here for more than 100 years.

Namibia became a German protectorate in the 1880s and was known as German South West Africa. In the 1890s, German farmers arrived and took over land that had been expropriated from the local people. The locals rebelled but were defeated by the German Schutztruppe early in the 20th century and fled.

The Treaty of Versailles required Germany to renounce all her colonial claims, and South Africa was subsequently given a mandate by the League of Nations to administer Namibia, which it had invaded during the war. Many of the German settlers stayed and about 20,000 of their descendants remain in Namibia.

My energy is still low the next day, and I'm struggling into a headwind when I hear the unmistakable pop of a flat tire. What a drag, I think. Unconcerned, though, and expecting to find only a thorn or shred of glass, I take my rear wheel off my bike and start to remove the tire and inner tube to look for whatever caused the flat. Instead I find that the tire has completely worn through in one spot along the bead—and looks worn out in several more. This was my spare that I've been using ever since Paul and I rebuilt my wheel in Lilongwe. I've been carrying my original that the rim tore slightly when it broke as an emergency backup. I patch the tear in that tire with a tire boot, whose package claims it's only for emergency use and not a long-term fix. I wonder if it's strong enough for the all the extra weight I have on my bike. After I pump up the patched tire, there's a bubble where the patch is. I nervously resume riding to the day's planned destination: Tsumeb, only ten kilometers away. After about a kilometer, I stop and check the tire. It looks the same; the bubble hasn't grown. A good sign, and I hope to get to Tsumeb without problems, but can't help thinking I might need to get a bus to Windhoek, Namibia's capital, to get a new tire. Even if this patch holds for now, it might not be smart to try to keep riding on it, especially in a country where getting to food and water is an issue and since I'll be getting into some more remote areas. As I get closer to Tsumeb, I gain more confidence that I'll at least make it there.

When I do, I go straight to the tourist office and find out that there is an outdoor store that sells bike stuff right here in town. Wow—what serendipity. I arrive at the store just as they're closing. They won't let me in but answer my question: they do have mountain bike tires. I return in the morning. I don't recognize the brand of tire they sell and it only costs the equivalent of seven U.S. dollars. I hope it's okay quality, but mostly I'm relieved to have a new tire.

At an internet cafe later in the day, I get an email from my dad telling me that there's a lot of tension and concern in the States about the upcoming two-year anniversary of September 11th.

I think back to September 11th two years ago, or rather it is September 12th that I think back to. Unaware that the world had changed somehow, I walked along the dirt roads and paths to one of the schools I worked with as a Peace Corps volunteer.

"What's going on in New York City?" a teacher asked me almost as soon as I arrived. "We saw planes flying around and bombs going off in tall buildings on TV."

"What? I haven't heard anything," I said, thinking about my dad, who worked in a NYC skyscraper.

They couldn't tell me anymore about what happened. I thought about going to the nearest phone, a few kilometers away, to try getting a call through to the States. But I reasoned that he saw this on TV last night and that if anything bad had happened to my dad, I would've heard; Peace Corps would have come to tell me. Envisioning something along the lines of the first World Trade Center attack, the car bomb, I went on with my work.

That afternoon there was a knock on my door. It was Susan, my nearest Peace Corps neighbor, who had walked the few kilometers from her house.

"I thought you might not have heard," she said. "The World Trade Center is no more. Terrorists crashed planes into it."

"What?"

"Ntate Seiki was watching TV last night, and he came and got me. Two planes hit the towers. They caught on fire, then collapsed. Thousands of people were killed. No planes are flying at all in the States."

I didn't know what to say. I remembered catching a glimpse of the distant towers out of the bus window on the way to JFK airport with my Peace Corps group only a few months previously. As the news sank in, I felt like I should do something. I had so many connections to the places that had been attacked. I lived in Washington, D.C. before joining the Peace Corps, and I thought of my friends there—along with my dad in NYC and my best friend in Boston.

I told my host family in a combination of Sesotho and sign language what had happened, that airplanes had crashed into very tall buildings in NYC. The looks of incomprehension on their faces were not because my Sesotho was so bad but because the concept was incomprehensible. How can you understand airplanes crashing into skyscrapers when you've never seen a skyscraper, perhaps never even seen a two-story building, and certainly never been in an airplane?

Susan and I went into the district capital, where I called my mom. All I said was, "Hi, Mom," and she broke into tears. My dad was fine. He was in Atlanta on a business trip. But my cousin had been in NYC getting her wedding dress fit, and they'd been worried about her until she was finally able to get a call out last night.

That night I sat alone in my house wondering what was going on in the States, whether there had been any more terrorist attacks as everyone seemed to fear, and realizing that I'd never felt so far away and so alone.

Now, two years later, I still haven't been back to the States. I've heard that it's changed, with an abundance of flags symbolizing a more fervent patriotism than I've probably ever seen in my lifetime, born after Vietnam War protests had become common. I worry that I won't like the country the U.S. has become, with our "You're-Either- With-Us-or-Against-Us" President. Does he have any idea how poisonous this attitude is towards world peace? Any clue how difficult it is for an Arab country to say "We're with you" if forced to choose?

I mourn the squandered opportunity of 9/11. As sad and awful as it was, it was also an opportunity to build bridges to countries that were reaching out to us in sympathy. We had the world on our side, and we had a choice to make: a foreign policy based on friendship and peace or one based on violence, and we chose violence instead of peace, or at least our President made this choice for us.

But the biggest difference I will feel when I do return is the difference in how I experienced 9/11. Friends will tell me it is unfathomable that I have never seen the video footage of the towers collapsing. Their experience of 9/11 is so wrapped up with watching it repeatedly for days on TV, impossible to avoid.

On my way out of town, I stop at the Tsumeb Cultural Museum. The inside exhibits are closed for renovation, but the manager takes me around the outdoor "cultural villages," which have houses and compounds from the different cultural groups in northern Namibia: Himba, Ovambo, Kavango, Caprivi, San, Herero, Damara, and Nama. Seeing the houses near each other, the differences are stark. The round San house is made of dried grasses, which form sloping walls that come to a point. There's no separate roof; the walls effectively become the roof. Long pieces of wood rest against the base of the walls. Large stones rest on the ground around the house. The San house is the only one with sloping walls. All the others have straight walls, some made of

Traditional San House at Tsumeb Cultural Museum

mud or clay and some of dried grasses.

The entire round Himba house, even the pointed roof, is made of clay. The Himba house is the only one with a clay roof. All the others have thatched roofs. The manager doesn't seem very familiar with all the cultures, but she does explain that the Himba are keeping their culture, not being westernized. They don't wear western clothing and don't even bathe with water. They wash with red ochre. Each wife must prepare dinner for the husband and her children every night. When she brings it to him, she must walk through the compounds of all the earlier wives, i.e. the third wife must walk through the compounds of the second wife and the first wife. The Himba live in a remote area, accessible only by 4x4 tracks, so this is as close as I'll come to them culturally.

Namibia's smoothly tarred main highways are great for long-distance traffic. But after less than a week, I've had enough of the seemingly endless kilometers of fenced-off farmland and dry, scrubby trees. I'm getting to know the country's vastness and emptiness but not its culture or the natural beauty that drew me here. Most of the sights I want to see—Etosha National Park, rock engravings, Spitzkoppe, red sand dunes—are way off the tar roads in the countryside or desert. I'm ready to get off the pavement and into the backcountry.

I don't see the turnoff for the road to Outjo where I expect it to be. I ask for directions and find what I think is the right road but still don't see any signs. I ask a slightly plump woman.

"I don't like that road. Wait a minute," she says. She goes into a nearby store and returns with a man.

"I think it's better if you take the tar road," he says, "even though it's longer."

"What do you think would be a problem," I ask, "people or the road itself?"

"People, since you're a woman traveling alone."

It can be hard to tell when something's really not safe and when people just think it's not safe because it's something that no local person in their culture ever does. I press for more information.

"Have there been any problems?"

"No," he pauses, "no one will bother you during the day, but make sure you camp on a farm at night. Then you should be fine. Don't camp by the side of the road."

His wife looks dubious but is completely silent.

I consider going around on the tar road, but this would mean a much longer ride and staying at a campground where my guidebook reports that people have been violently robbed. Here, going around on a tar road isn't a good option, and to get to some other places where only backroads lead, it won't be an option at all. I can't do Namibia if I can't do backroads, so I may as well find out now, I think. I set off down the road to Outjo feeling slightly apprehensive, no longer as relaxed and happy as I felt earlier about getting off the pavement.

About twenty kilometers along, a car of four or five men drives slowly by. Later the same car goes by me again. It spooks me. I consider returning to the tar road but realize I'm too far away: if they're going to come back after me, they'll get to me long before I get back to the tar road.

I wonder why it is that this car instills fear in me. Is it purely conditioning? From the couple's warnings? From today's society, which is always telling us that things are not safe? Or from Peace Corps/Lesotho always telling us that things are not safe? Or is there really some negative energy around these people that I'm sensing? I don't get a bad feeling about any of the other thirteen cars that drive by. My jumpiness might be the only problem. They might have slowed down simply because it is so unusual to see a white cyclist out here. I am a spectacle.

By early afternoon, I'm tired and feel like stopping for the day. But asking for permission to camp on a farm this early in the day feels too awkward, so I keep riding—and taking short roadside breaks. Roadside thorn bushes prevent me from pulling off the road and taking longer breaks. There's nowhere to stop and relax. I wonder how far along a cave campground mentioned in my guidebook is, if I might get there rather than camping on a farm.

As the sun rapidly sinks toward the horizon, and there aren't any farms in sight, I fear I've waited too long. I have visions of being stranded along the roadside without a safe place to camp as it gets dark. I kick myself for not stopping at that last farm, now that it's getting darker than I like, not knowing how far it is to the next one. It's time to acknowledge that I'm not going to get to the cave campground tonight. I fret as I cycle along, wondering if I've pushed things too far. Suddenly, a friendly-looking house appears up a hill, ahead on the left. Relieved, I gather my courage to ask for permission to camp. Though finding the farm is what I've been counting on, the moment of asking still feels awkward. A dog yaps at the gate, and I hesitate, yelling "hello." A woman motions me in but disappears before I reach the house. An older, gray-haired white woman comes to the door.

I greet her in English, but her blank look shows incomprehension. So I ask, "*Deutsch ist besser für Sie*?" Is German better for you?

She replies "*Afrikaans*" but seems to have understood me.

From its days under South African rule, many of Namibia's white citizens still speak Afrikaans as their first language. Not speaking any, I explain in a combination of German and practical sign language—making a triangle symbol with my hands for a tent and resting my head on my hands for sleeping—that I'm cycling and would like a place for my tent.

She understands and immediately says yes, telling me to set it up on the grass and showing me the toilet and water tap in a small restroom off her front porch. It's as if having a stranger knock on her door and ask for a place to camp is a normal occurrence that she's prepared for.

It amazes me how unfazed Africans—villages, police, and now a farm—seem by people unexpectedly showing up and asking to camp. They always immediately answer that there is a spot, without having to think about it. Always having a place for a traveler to stay is part of African hospitality, but I'm still impressed. I wonder how I would react if a stranger showed up at my door in the U.S. and asked to camp. Watching the sunset through palm-like trees, I set up my tent. As the stars come out, I make a pasta dinner, and I know taking this road was the right choice.

Over an hour into the next day's ride, I come across the cave and campground. I stop to see the cave, and I meet Ruth, a seventy-year-old Afrikaner. She tells me to sit on her porch, and she brings me two oranges and a pitcher of water. Her son runs the cave and he's away for the weekend, so it's not possible to see it, but she's chatty. She tells me that she and her husband moved here in 1952 and about how important their farm was during the so-called terrorist period.

Subsequent to the Versailles Treaty, South Africa wanted to annex Namibia, then still known as South West Africa, and make it a province of South Africa rather than simply administer it. In 1949, South Africa granted the white population representation in its parliament, distributed most of the viable farmland to white settlers, and relegated other ethnic groups to so-called tribal homelands. Despite pressure from the UN, South Africa refused to relent and kept its grip on South West Africa. In the late 1950s, forced laborers started to form political parties and organize strikes. The South West African People's Organization, known as Swapo, became the dominant opposition party. In 1966, Swapo initiated a guerrilla warfare campaign.

Ruth tells me she and her husband would go onto their deck from a secret inside passageway, rather than use the outdoor stairs, and map the terrorist flares by color.

"We thought the terrorists would blow up a nearby bridge—you'll come to it on your way into town—so we stockpiled extra supplies," she says.

She goes on to tell me that there are now only seven white-owned farms along this stretch of road and that they all hire four or five black families to work. All the rest of the farms are black-owned.

"They [blacks] get them very cheaply then turn them into squatter camps by inviting their families to come live on them but not working the farms," she says.

Welcome to Namibia's dark side, I think as her comment jars me. Traveling in Malawi, Zambia, and Botswana, I hadn't felt any racial tension, but I'm now reminded of South Africa and of Namibia's recent independence struggle, which formally ended only in 1990.

In 1972, the UN declared the South African occupation of South West Africa illegal and proclaimed Swapo the legitimate representative of the Namibian people. South Africa responded by firing on demonstrators and arresting thousands of activists. Eventually, the white population grew tired of the guerilla war, and the economy suffered. South Africa agreed to UN-monitored elections with universal suffrage in 1989, and Swapo won a majority of the votes. Swapo's leader, Samuel Daniel Shafiishuna Nujoma, returned from exile and became Namibia's president.

I ride north to the entrance of Etosha National Park, reputedly Namibia's best wildlife park. Unlike South Luangwa and Chobe, there aren't any lodges that allow camping near its borders. But there is a camp within the park with a waterhole just outside its boundaries where campers can watch the wildlife without leaving the camp—perfect for a bicyclist, since cycling isn't allowed in the park. Just as I arrive at the park entrance, a gray van passes me and stops.

A white man gets out and says, "I don't know if they'll let you bike into the park."

"I know," I reply. "I'm hoping to get a lift into the camp, stay there a couple nights, and watch the animals at the waterhole."

He turns to his passenger and says, "He's biking, too, but he left his bike in Outjo and is here for a day tour. We can probably drop you off at the camp."

"That'd be great."

In the van, I compare notes with the other cyclist. He's German and is in Namibia for a few weeks on a solo cycle tour. He's going on from Outjo tomorrow, headed to the coast and then south. On the way to the camp, we see giraffe, jackals, and a few kinds of antelope—kudu, impala, and gnu.

At Okaukeujo Rest Camp, the driver pays the daily entrance fee for the two of them.

"I'd like a campsite," I say.

"What's your license plate number?" asks the man at the registration desk.

"I don't have one. I'm cycling."

"Cycling's not allowed in the park. How'd you get here?" He sounds suspicious.

"I got a ride with them." I motion with my head to the German and his driver still standing nearby. "They're only staying for today, but I want to stay and camp."

"Hitching isn't allowed. You aren't supposed to do that."

"I'm cycling all around southern Africa and want to see your park. How else was I supposed to get here? There aren't any busses."

"Put my license plate on her registration," says the driver matter-of-factly. "You're really not supposed to do that," he says but does.

I thank the driver. He goes on his way with the German, and I look around the expansive camp. Outside the registration building and past the pool, it's a baked dust bowl. A tar road winds its way past a convenience store, post office, curio shop, and cottages to the campsites. The options are no shade, or a smattering of shade. I choose the smattering, provided by a short, barren tree, and set up my tent without its fly to keep it from turning into an oven.

Wondering if the park will live up to its reputation, I walk over to the waterhole. The water is an almost glacial, silty pale blue without the brightness of glacier melt. Etosha means "Great White Place of Dry Water," and the waterhole is surrounded by a white, rocky, almost otherworldly, saline desert.

Sitting in the open-air thatch-roof viewing shelter, I watch a group of ten to fifteen elephants make their way to the waterhole. They range in size from a baby small enough to stand under the others' bellies to towering matriarchs. As the herd approaches, the oryx, zebras, and impala at the waterhole move aside. The elephants walk along together, with the adults watching the youngsters, all helping to take care of the baby. When it starts to wander off, one follows it and gently nudges it back towards the herd. Healthy adult elephants don't have any natural predators, but stray babies tempt the big cats.

Using her front legs to dig and kick up lots of dust, one adult helps the baby dig a hole, like an older human sibling showing her younger sister how to build

Etosha National Park Waterhole

a sandcastle. As the baby rolls in the dust, many elephant eyes look on. As it enters the waterhole, another elephant affectionately splashes it.

I'm unsure how they decide it's time to move on. Perhaps the matriarch signals them. A few make their way to the far edge of the waterhole. Others follow. Some hang back. They've surrounded the baby, making it the center of the moving group.

As the elephants stroll away, a giraffe and some zebras approach. Above them, the setting sun is partially hidden by clouds but glows red, and beams of sunlight break through the clouds and stretch upward.

After dinner back at my site, I return to the waterhole. I've read that evening is the best time to see rhino here. I hope without really expecting to see them. But there they are: four rhino with their reflections in the waterhole. Two of them are drinking, along with three giraffe. I'd forgotten how giraffe drink: with their front legs spread apart into an upside-down V, so that they can reach down into the water with their long necks.

The camp keeps a log of visitor lion sightings. Lions are nocturnal and have recently been spotted at the waterhole between midnight and two a.m. After not seeing any the next day, I decide to set my alarm for midnight. This may be my last chance to see lions on this trip. When my alarm goes off at midnight, I promptly shut it off and fall back asleep. I wake up an hour later and force myself to get up. When I arrive at the floodlit waterhole, two giraffe are drinking and a group of shapes are silhouetted in the distance. The eyes reflect green. Are they lions? Have I come at the perfect time? No, there are too many of them. Lions don't travel in herds. As they approach the waterhole, I realize they are zebras. They drink in a jittery fashion, trading places with one another, hooves clicking as they move around. It's almost as if they are jumping, though they don't actually jump. All the zebras I've watched previously have tread more softly. Does this mean there's a lion around? Or is this normal nighttime behavior for zebras? A lone alert oryx joins them. They all—giraffe, zebras, and oryx—depart simultaneously. Two jackals run around the waterhole, and a herd of something stampedes by out of sight. A bird hops around, and others chirp loudly. Then it's still.

I get lost in my thoughts, mostly thinking about whether I want to stay here another day to give myself more of a chance to see lions. Suddenly I look up, and there's a lioness right at the waterhole. I never saw her approach. Even standing by the waterhole, she blends in with the stones. It's easier to see her reflection in the water than her. She doesn't stay long. She drinks and shifts around, then turns and walks away along a dirt path through the stones to my right, gone into the night. I linger, appreciating the moment, before heading back to my tent.

In the morning I pack up and head to the camp gate to look for a ride out of the park. My loaded bike transforms me from just another tourist amongst many here to the center of attention. Suddenly park employees and other campers want to know about my trip. The security guard, concerned that I was planning to try to bike out of the park, says he'll find me a lift. A tourist interviews me on her video camera. The park manager introduces herself and asks to take my picture with some of her employees. She says they take photos of some of their guests and she thinks it's great that I'm here. What a contrast from my welcome.

The security guard tells me he has found me a lift, and we load my bike into the back of a pickup-like truck with railings. My lift is with the white general manager of Namibia's largest security firm, who has been visiting his clients. We chat about my trip and plans. He recommends northern Namibia over the south because there are more scenic drives, less distances with "nothing," and more farms closer to the roads, making it easier to ask for permission to camp.

Back in Outjo, I stop in the tourist office. I ask the older dark-haired white woman there about the roads to the southwest, where I'm headed.

"The D roads tend to be in bad condition," she says.

Namibia's roads are all classified as B, C, or D. The B roads are the main roads, all tarred, connecting Windhoek to the larger towns and neighboring countries. The C roads are the secondary roads, mostly unpaved. The D roads are the minor roads, along which some of the attractions and natural beauty of the country lie. The backroad to Outjo was a C road, but my projected route takes me onto some D roads.

"You should find another cyclist to ride with for safety," she continues.

How unrealistic, I think, but I say only, "There aren't too many other cyclists around."

"You could find someone."

Why is she so persistent? "Do you know of any problems cyclists have had around here or anywhere in Namibia?"

"No, but you shouldn't ride alone."

Undeterred, I silently translate this comment as meaning she wouldn't feel safe riding alone.

chapter eighteen
AN AFRICAN CASTLE

I start the 130-kilometer ride west to Khorixas thinking it's too much for one day and hoping to find a farm to camp at along the way. A fast start—thirty-eight kilometers in two hours—gets me thinking about going the whole way. Riding through more fenced-off farmland, there are signs for three upscalish guest farms about halfway, but none are visible from the road, and one sign says no camping. I'm still feeling good, so I continue on. The semi-usual afternoon headwind comes along, and the ride ceases to be fun. There are occasionally run-down houses along the road but no well-kept farms, so I keep riding. Approaching Khorixas, I see signs for two places that allow camping. I briefly consider going past the lodge to the rest camp. I ask myself, "What's another four kilometers?," quickly answer "too much," and stop at the lodge.

"What's the road to Twyfelfontein like?" I ask the lodge employee who shows me to my campsite, which is surrounded by reed walls.

"That road is bad," he says. "I just took some tourists out there today. It's not in good condition, very bumpy, and it's also hilly. But you can do it."

It's nice to hear this vote of confidence, reminding me of the typical Zambian reaction to my trip of telling me that I must be strong, so unlike the disbelieving Batswana.

He recommends backtracking to Khorixas from Twyfelfontein rather than taking backroads to Uis—they'll be in worse condition. He says the backroad from Uis to Spitzkoppe is good but unused—it'll be a long time until someone comes to help if I have problems.

"Do you think I'm safe riding alone out here?"

"Yes, definitely, in Damaraland," this region of Namibia. He continues, "No one will bother you here during the day. You just need to get to a safe place to camp at night. Make sure you get to a farm when there's nothing else, then camp near the main house once there and you'll be fine."

As I use bricks to make a windbreak for my stove, I wonder why whites seem more likely to warn me while blacks seem more likely to reassure me that I'm safe.

My legs are tired when I wake up but feel strong once I start riding. The road is what is called a gravel road here, but there's not much gravel. It's a concrete base with some stones and sand scattered about by the wind. The conditions of these gravel roads depend on how much they have been used since they were last graded. The more traffic, the more washboard. This one is very bumpy at first and I briefly consider turning around, but then it improves. Some hills are steep enough that I use my granny gear—the smallest of three chainrings, which provides the group of lowest gears—for the first time since Zambia. I'm enjoying the ride but can't figure out why my front rack is shifting around. I wonder if I'm imagining it. Then the unmistakable sound of metal hitting moving rubber tells me I'm not. I stop and take a look. All the screws and bolts look like they're still tight. As I take off a pannier to check more closely, part of the rack swings out away from my bike. I discover that a screwhead has sawed off—and left the rest of the screw in my front fork. Yikes. I need to get the end of the screw out of my fork to replace it, but I can't figure out how to get enough of a grip on the protruding end to do so.

While I'm trying with an adjustable wrench, a car of Italians stops and asks if I'm okay. One of them pulls out a Swiss Army knife with ribbed scissors and offers it to me. They work well, and I'm able to get the remainder of the screw out. The screw I try to move from elsewhere on the rack proves to be too short, but a spare bolt works. I add an extra hose clamp around the fork and rack for re-enforcement. I feel good about the repair but start wondering if I shouldn't go off on less traveled roads. I think about taking this road all the way to the coast then going south along the ocean.

I stop at the Petrified Forest, which turns out to be a large petrified log and some chunks of petrified wood. It's the least shady forest I've ever seen, though this shouldn't surprise me in this arid climate. There are also two weltwitshia plants—one 400- and the other 600-years-old—with their long, fat leaves curled close to the ground.

The road deteriorates after the Petrified Forest. Though I'd been warned it was rough, I am unprepared for the constant jolting from this washboard.

Huge potholes would be preferable. They can usually be steered around and dodged on a bicycle. But these washboard ruts go all the way across the road. There is no getting around them. Every pedal stroke produces a series of bounces. How many pedal strokes per kilometer? And how many kilometers farther on this road? I forget the heat and the dryness. The washboard is my only nemesis and my only focus. It's impossible to take my mind off it. My bones feel like they're vibrating. I try to think about something else, anything else, but vibrating bones quickly bring me back to reality.

Suddenly I smile, thinking about Paul—and how he'd absolutely hate this road. I wonder if he cycled here and am glad I don't have to hear his complaints. It's a relief knowing he's not waiting up ahead to ask what took me so long.

As I go on, I realize how much I suppressed my distaste for him when we were together, at least for awhile. I was determined to make it work, so I tried to just let go of his self-centered comments. But instead of truly letting things go, I let them fester inside. They gnawed at me. Instead of making suggestions that I expected to be ridiculed, I kept things inside—and withdrew emotionally. I contracted. Now that I'm alone, I'm growing.

I realize that washboards are a small price to pay for true freedom. I love not knowing where life is leading me, other than down this road. I have a tentative route planned for Namibia and am considering continuing on into South Africa but no set itinerary, or even definite idea of when I'll return to the U.S. I originally thought November, but recently the thought of returning to the northeast just in time for winter has seemed incredibly unattractive. My plans are completely flexible, restricted only by needing to find a safe place to camp every night.

I think back to a recent email I got from a friend in Minnesota inviting me to her October wedding. This isn't the first time I'm reminded how starkly different from most my life has become. Since I've been in Africa, I've missed a cousin's wedding and have gotten baby announcements from a few close friends. I'm happy for them, but my focus in life is just different. When I was a kid and wanted a toy I claimed all my friends had, my mom used to ask me if I was going to jump off the George Washington Bridge if all my friends did. I don't think her comment was meant to lead me on a bike trip to Africa while my friends were leading more typical lives back in the States and Europe. But somehow it did, and here I am, completely unconcerned about being like my friends. Let them wonder about meeting the man of their dreams and having kids; I'm wondering just how hot it's going to get, if the wind is going to be in my face or at my back, what I'm going to eat, and where I'm going to sleep tonight.

I turn south off the washboard road and am struck by the beauty of the land: the late afternoon sun lights the gently sloping rocky mountains red and purple. I glide along on a smooth light brown dirt road, with long brown grasses fluttering in the breeze, and think that this is the Namibia I've come to see. As I near camp, cars are stopped in the road, and I slow to look around. Elephants are crossing. I stop, giving them their space, and watch as they linger by the side of the road. After they go on, I start riding again—and am surprised to go by two more whom I hadn't seen coming. They look at me. One makes a little screech. They let me pass, then keep going.

As soon as I get into Aba Huab Camp and register, I meet another touring cyclist. He's going to Spitzkoppe—along my planned route, but is leaving tomorrow, so will be a day ahead of me since I plan to camp here for two nights. He's a tour guide in Namibia and knows the roads. He says the backroads to Uis are good, like the road from the turnoff rather than the road I was on most of the day.

"There's nowhere to camp along the way, though, no camps or farms," he says, "so you really need to get all the way to Uis in one day."

This surprises me because the lodge employee in Khorixas told me there were farms, just not many. The cyclist tells me the road to Spitzkoppe from Uis is okay, although there'll be fifty-meter sections of sand that I'll need to walk through. I feel like I've met the right person.

Enjoying riding with most of my gear at camp rather than on my bike, I cycle to Twyfelfontein—the site of petroglyphs, or rock engravings. The walking trail through the engravings is gorgeous—through chunks of red rock, reminiscent of a miniscule Zion National Park. The engravings are of animals, including giraffe, rhino, and one of a lion with paw prints for feet, and were made by cutting the hard patina covering the sandstone. Most are at least 6000-years-old and credited to the ancient San.

From the petroglyphs, I ride another washboard road to Burnt Mountain and the Organ Pipes. Burnt Mountain is a volcanic ridge that appears purple. Across the road, a short path leads into a gorge that houses the organ pipes— an aptly named 100-meter-long stretch of up to four-meter-high brownish-black glistening dolerite columns.

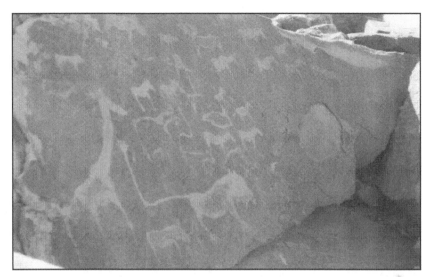

Petroglyphs

I depart Aba Huab in the refreshingly chilly morning air. The scenery of reddish mountains and bouldery rock formations continues to be gorgeous. Some real green is added: trees with green leaves and grass tufts with a greenish rather than brown tint. I cycle primarily east for the first time since the first day of this trip. This gives my right arm a break from getting the dominant sun. As the day goes on, traffic, and the ensuing dust clouds, picks up. My ambitious plan to ride the whole 140 kilometers to Uis in a day starts to feel overambitious. There are some steep hills and the road isn't as good as I hoped from my conversation with the cyclist.

I reach the road to Uis and turn south, back into the land of fences. The road is gravel, and I lose my little remaining hope of making it to Uis today. Then a car of white Namibians stops to offer me water. I have plenty and decline. They give me a can of orange juice and an apple. They tell me I should get to Uis today if possible because there's a nice camp with a swimming pool.

"It's really best to get to Uis," they say, without an explanation.

I wonder if they're trying to tell me not to camp along the way. They also tell me that I have a long downhill coming up—down to the river—but then it's hilly.

I drink the juice and feel inspired. How long is this downhill? Can I suddenly do almost seventy kilometers in five hours after needing six hours of riding time to do the first sixty-eight k? I come upon the small village of Sorris Sorris and am feeling so inspired that I don't stop to ask for a spot to camp.

I almost immediately regret it, asking myself what I'm doing—looking for a farm, I guess. I wonder if the white Namibians were cautioning me against staying in Sorris Sorris, and if so, whether this caution was well-founded or simply prejudice.

The long downhill—probably fifteen kilometers—materializes. But I see the road rising in the distance and a farm off the road on my left. Although it's not yet four p.m., I stop here. I don't have the energy to make it to Uis—and don't like the stress of wondering where I'm going to sleep with so few farms around. The farmers don't speak much English or any German or Sesotho, but they tell me to pick a spot for my tent. The hard ground isn't stakeable, and my tent starts to blow away. I put one pannier in each corner, and they serve as indoor stakes. Two goats jump on my tent. I chase them away. Then puppies jump on it. Two kids—a girl and a boy—grab the puppies. They play with them roughly, using one puppy's legs to strangle the other.

I sit outside my tent on its fly. The girl plays with my hair. The boy tries to cut a foam pad with a table knife. At least they are no longer beating on the puppies. I feel dusty and want to rinse off but am waiting for at least dusk to avoid the audience factor. I'm glad I'm not still riding. Seven-plus hours of cycling is enough for one day.

While I cook dinner, the farmer brings me a big piece of metal to use as a windbreak. It works wonderfully. He must have seen me trying to use the mattress.

I think about the cyclist I met at Aba Huab camp. He said there were no farms along this road. Did he mean no white farms or did he simply forget that there are a few? I wonder how a white family would react if a black traveler showed up and asked to camp on their farm. Somehow I suspect they would not be as welcoming as this black family has been to me. Why is it that I feel more racism from whites than from blacks? Nothing that's directed at me, just feelings that shine through in their words about "those people," whereas I've never felt any reverse discrimination or hostility at all from any blacks. Perhaps this is because some whites resent not being in charge of the country they once conquered, whereas blacks see me as a friendly traveler not as an oppressor. Plus, they generally like Americans—because they know our country provides foreign aid. And even if they're not so fond of our cowboy president, they don't take this out on us. They know what it's like to have a president the majority of the people do not support.

I ride to Uis in the morning. When I arrive at the Brandberg Rest Camp and ask about camping, a woman working at the desk tells me she is giving me a room for the price of camping. I don't know why she does this, but I take it. When I walk in, the air feels so cool that I think it's air-conditioned. It's actually not, but is very comfortable. The room has two comfortable twin beds with night tables, a loveseat, a wardrobe, plenty of space for bike parking and yoga, and a private bathroom. This is the first time that I have a room on the solo portion of this trip, the first time I'll sleep indoors since my last night traveling with Paul, back in Zambia, fifty days ago. And the private bathroom with shower is my first since Chipoka, Malawi, less than two weeks into the trip, and that shower sprayed all over the bathroom.

I've gotten so used to the camping routine that I thought I didn't miss rooms, but this is nice, I think, as I listen to the wind gusting outside. I'm not getting covered in sand or dirt and my tent doesn't look like it's going to get blown over, as it has on a few of the windiest nights.

Uis is a small, quiet town with that deserted feel of a place that has lost its reason for being. A nearby mine has closed. The small grocery store that I was counting on is still open, though, and I treat myself to foods that I simply cannot carry with me in this heat: ice cream, cold juice, and cheese. After eating, I wash my laundry in the sink and put it on a chair outside to dry in the wind and sun. Then I nap.

Although I was feeling worn down when riding, I've generally been reinspired by the scenery of the past few days and am no longer thinking about how nice it would be to get lifts through some stretches. Namibia—and maybe also parts of Botswana—had gotten to be too much about destinations, even if the destination was only a campground or unknown farm. Now the trip has become about the cycling again, too. I'm glad to be off the tar roads.

After dinner, I realize I'm full, bordering on too full for the first time since I can't even remember when. Now that I'm usually carrying enough food for a few days with me on my bike, I'm compelled to eat more when I'm staying in a town and the grocery store is only a short walk away.

Leaving Uis, a local tagalong cyclist is suddenly behind me. I don't think I've had one of them since Zambia. I haven't seen many local cyclists at all since then. I don't like the idea of someone following me onto the less traveled road to the Spitzkoppe, but he turns off before I get to my turn. The road is initially a bit rough but gradually improves, then gets corrugated at times but never as bad as the road from the Petrified Forest. It starts out going through rather bland farmland and then takes me briefly back to the land of the fence.

It's so hilly, including steep granny gear climbs, that it takes me two hours to ride nineteen kilometers. The scenery improves as I climb, and bare reddish, mostly rounded rock mountains, including Spitzkoppe, appear in the distance. Spitzkoppe, 1728-meters-high, is nicknamed the Matterhorn of Africa, due to its similar peak. Unlike the Swiss Alp, it is, however, the remnant of an active volcano.

There's a long, maybe fifteen kilometer, mostly downhill stretch to a dry riverbed. I'm having fun, but then I notice the road starting to rise nastily. A tough fifteen kilometers or so of climbing with steep sections follows. The air is still and the sun feels scorching hot. The swarming flies are awful. Why am I doing this, I wonder. At the moment, it feels more like torture than the culmination of a dream. Wasn't it just yesterday I was loving the cycling?

In the future, with the help of a regular meditation practice, I'll get better at accepting change, at letting things go and at being fully present with whatever is. But right now I want to hold onto the cooler parts of the day and the easier riding, whether it's less steep climbs or fewer flies. And now I am too tired to be fully present with the beauty of the land: presence takes an energy that I don't have and a focusing of the mind that I am not remotely thinking about at this time in my life.

A flicker of motion catches my attention, and I spot a pair of dark brown mid-size antelope when they run away from me. They stop where I can still see them, but I can't identify what kind of antelope they are. As I near the top of the climb, a slight breeze picks up and helps to keep the flies away.

I feel okay at the top, but it has taken a lot of my energy to get here. I'm tired, and my legs have had enough for the day. I'm ready to stop and camp but keep going to get to the still distant campground at Spitzkoppe. I again wonder about the cyclist I met, why he didn't warn me about these hills. Maybe he wasn't the right person to have met after all. He said he is a tour guide in Namibia but maybe I should've asked him when he was last here, on this road. Mentally stuck in the land of unmet expectations—in this case, an easier ride—I'm having trouble appreciating the beautiful, desert mountain scenery.

The road remains hilly but most of the hills are gentler. I start to think that the only reason to get to the top of a hill is to see how bad the next one is. The road becomes corrugated. I'm tired and just want to be there. As much as I love to travel to see new things, sometimes when I'm this tired, all I can think about is how much I want to get to camp, and I don't so much care what new things are on the way to camp. It's also at times like this that if I were traveling with a friend, I'd be more likely to suggest we stop and free camp way off the side of the road. But alone, I'm more likely to keep pushing to get to a campground.

I finally reach the turnoff to the Spitzkoppe and turn onto a flatter but especially washboardy road that seems to go on forever. Is this partially my energy level? I feel like crying. It takes me an hour to cycle eight kilometers of bumps, and I'm still not there yet. Along the way, I see the white butts of what are probably impala running from the road. After another five kilometers, I arrive at camp headquarters. I buy a cold orange juice, a welcome sight, which I immediately glug. Cold juice was not available in Malawi or Zambia. If it was ever on a menu, it was more of a Tang than a genuine juice. There the choices for cold drinks were Coke or beer, or occasionally bottled water.

The reserve around Spitzkoppe is protected as a conservation area by the Ministry of Environment and Tourism, and the local community runs a camp with sites scattered around the mountain's base. I think I'll come back to camp headquarters to shower after getting my camp set up, but I don't realize how far the scattered bush sites are. I ride another two kilometers over a sandy road that's not always bikable until I find an unoccupied site, passing only one occupied one en route. By the time my tent is set up, I don't have enough daylight left to return to camp headquarters, shower, and get back to my camp before dark—and I doubt I'd even be able to find my campsite in the dark. There are no lights here, so I rinse off at my site. I feel isolated enough to

Camping at Spitzkoppe

change outside in the dusk. I make a big pot of pasta and eat under the stars, alone in Africa.

As I walk to the rhino panel in the early morning blue light, flies swarm around me, undeterred by insect repellant. The rock art is so faded that it's not impressive. I enjoy walking rather than biking for a change of pace. I walk to the bushman's paradise panel, which is also unimpressive. I'm glad I went to the Tsodilo Hills.

After showering at park headquarters, I fill my water containers at the outdoor tap. A man comes over and says something in a language I don't understand about my collapsible waterbag. Is he asking for it? A woman I met yesterday comes out of the restaurant to watch me. As I leave, I see the man watching me out of the window. Haven't they ever seen a white person at a water tap before? Especially here? I'm so tired of people watching me. Sometimes I think I should just go back to the U.S. now to get some privacy.

After returning to my site, I write in my journal while sitting under a rock overhang because it's the only shade I can find near my tent. It's so hot even in the shade that I put my hair in a ponytail. It has gotten too long for life in the desert.

After the sun sets from view, I eat a heap of pasta while lying on my tent fly and admiring the pink and purple streaks of clouds stretching across the entire sky from mountain to mountain. A wave of loneliness comes over me. Maybe it's because I suddenly want someone to share the moment with. I again think about going back to the States. But what's to keep me from getting lonely there? And I otherwise feel that I'm not done seeing what I want to see in southern Africa. I realize that today is the first day of the trip that I haven't really talked to anyone. All I've said is "I don't speak your language" to the man who seemed to want my waterbag and "Aach" to numerous flies. Sometimes I think the hardest part of traveling alone is that I'll never have anyone to reminisce with.

The next morning I get up early, thinking maybe I can make it all the way to Swakopmund (160 kilometers) in a day. An ambitious idea, but the last 114 kilometers will be on a tar road with a lot of gradual downhill. Leaving my campsite to a gorgeous pink cloudy sunrise, I stop to pick thorns out of my tires and realize that I should've thought to do this yesterday. I think I hear a bit of air escape, but neither tire goes flat, so I start to ride. When I stop at the camp entrance to get water and throw out garbage, I notice that the front tire has gone soft with a slow leak. The man from yesterday is there. Today he speaks some English.

"Where are you going?" He sounds curious.

I answer Swakopmund, and he tries to give me alternate directions, even drawing a map in the sand. I think he's trying to tell me to go through Henties Bay, which would mean 110 kilometers of gravel, and I'm not up for that today. I thank him, then go on my way, the way I'd planned. After turning off the camp road, I stop to fix my slow leak alone.

I return to the road from Uis but continue heading south. This section is even rougher than the last. A screw is jarred loose from a troublesome spot on one of my front panniers. I replace it, and the replacement is also jarred loose. This screw keeps a spring attached to the pannier but I don't want to lose any more screws on this road, so I tie the spring to the rack with string instead. I move my heavy extra water to my rear rack, unweighting the front a bit. I'm glad I didn't take the gravel road to Henties. Flies swarm at times and the hills are gradual. Some mountains are still in view. I'm again in a drier area: the grass is entirely brown, and there's no greenery at all.

The tar road finally comes into sight. I notice three motor vehicles stopped near the intersection. The front one is a van, giving the illusion that this intersection is a taxi rank, or mini-bus stop. Then I notice the video camera filming me. This happened a couple times earlier in Namibia, but I thought this phenomenon had stopped after I'd left the Etosha area. Argh! Am I a wild animal that it's okay to just film without permission?

After forty-five kilometers of gravel, it's noon. If I can average 20 k/hr for six hours on the tar road, I can still get to Swakopmund today. The pace is doable, but another six hours of cycling sounds like too much. I turn onto the tar road, heading west. A headwind picks up. I don't have a chance of making it and will have to find somewhere to camp. Why do I keep planning these overly ambitious days? Lack of accommodation options and insecurity about being able to find safe places to camp along the way. A car stops ahead of me, and I fear another video camera will pop out. Instead a white Namibian couple asks me about my gear. They want to do a bicycle tour in Damaraland and haven't been able to find racks and panniers anywhere, even in South Africa.

I see a sign for accommodation and camping at a castle and turn in. The dirt road leads to a one-story dark stone building with turrets. This is not Ludwig's Neuschwanstein. Two youngish white men stand outside.

One with short, almost crew-cut blond hair says, "Another cyclist. We had our first cyclist a couple weeks ago. His name was, what was it, oh, it was Bob."

"I haven't met many other cyclists," I say, "and none named Bob."

"We just bought the castle recently. We're renovating it, and it's closed."

Ten minutes ago I didn't know this castle was here, but now I have zero motivation to get back on my bike.

He continues. "The campground is ten kilometers down a gravel road, but you can just camp here. You don't want to ride another ten kilometers, and it's rough. Just set up your tent right here outside this wall."

He introduces himself as Vincent and rambles on, "I'll tell everyone you're camping here."

I start setting up my tent with the smaller side facing into the wind. Vincent returns and tells me I can camp in a room instead. He shows me around. It's dusty but cool inside. There's nothing that distinguishes it as a castle. Maybe the golden thrones are all in storage during the renovation. A few guest rooms look like construction zones, but he gives me the one they're not actively working in.

There's a stripe with a giraffe motif painted across the top of the walls of my barren room. Away from the sun, wind, and flies, I lean my bike against a wall. Two women bring me a mattress and pillows and a tray with a mug of tea and milk and sugar. It's starting to feel like a castle.

Later while I cook dinner in the kitchen, Vincent tells me about Bob. "Probably in his thirties, dark hair. I think he cycled in Malawi and Zambia. He's riding around the world."

"That sounds like my former riding partner, but his name was Paul," I say, looking up from my pot of pasta and wondering about the around-the-world bit. This is the first I've heard of Paul since we split up.

"Paul, that's right. That was his name. Not Bob."

"He biked in some other countries before we met up in Malawi, but I never heard him call himself an around-the-world cyclist," I say.

"He talked with his company and found out that they're not doing so well and can't hire him back now. So, he decided to go on to South America after southern Africa," explains Vincent.

I remember the admiration I saw in Paul's eyes while listening to Rob the Canadian speak about his solo around-the-world trip.

"A very nice guy," Vincent says.

"Yeah, as long as you agree with him," I respond, wondering how this trip would've been different if I had.

chapter nineteen

MISSING

I continue west to Swakopmund. Soon after leaving the castle, I hit the 5,000-kilometer mark for this trip, just over three months since Paul and I left Blantyre. As I ride, mountains rise above railroad tracks to my left, the south, and mining scraps lie to my right. Otherwise, it's a barren landscape, without any trees or grass. When I stop for a cookie break, a car pulls up behind me. Its white occupants ask me what I'm doing, then introduce themselves as reporters from an Afrikaans paper in Windhoek, and ask to interview and photograph me. They ask all the usual questions. Where did you start? Where are you going? Are you alone? Why?

I talk about really getting to know places traveling through them at people speed rather than just passing through and not really seeing them. They promise to email me a copy of the article. Maybe my trip can help promote cycling here.

Swakopmund is a German town on Namibia's west coast. There's something satisfying about reaching an ocean on a bicycle tour, even when it's not the end of the tour. In the U.S., it's traditional for cyclists to dip their rear wheel into whichever ocean they start a cross-country tour at and their front wheel into the other ocean at the end. Although I didn't start this tour at the Indian Ocean on Africa's east coast and I'm not finishing it here on the west coast, I still dip my front wheel into the Atlantic Ocean. I relax on the beach eating a lunch of three-grain bread with tangy mustard cream cheese, crisps (aka potato chips), and yogurt. When some kids come along and ask me for food and to sponsor their soccer team, I decide it's time to walk around town.

Swakopmund is one of the biggest towns I've been in since Lusaka two months ago. Colonial-era buildings, including a historic railway station,

Franciscan hospital, former hotels, churches, an old school, and a bank, highlight the center of town. Half-timbered houses line some of the streets. Street names include Kaiser Wilhelm, Bruecken, Strand, and Schlosser. This town is more German than anything else I've seen in Africa, but the plants are all wrong. Palm trees line the streets. Additionally, the South African chain stores look out of place. I stop in at the tourist office to ask about road conditions and distances to campsites in Namib-Nanklauft Park to the south.

"Those roads can get bad," says a white woman with a thick German accent.

"That's what I've heard, but I'm wondering how they are now."

"I don't know," she shrugs. "The conditions change all the time, depending on use."

"What are the most recent reports you've heard?"

"We don't get reports, but I did hear someone who came through say they aren't too bad now."

"Thanks, that's helpful. I'm cycling." I smile.

"This isn't the country for cycling. The distances to campsites are too great," she says authoritarily.

"I've already been cycling here for three weeks."

"Then you've been lucky," she responds. The stodgy part of Germany has made it here, too.

A couple days later, enjoying the cool coastal air and clouds and the abundance of food that comes with being in a town, I'm still in Swakopmund and camped at Desert Sky Backpackers. I'm getting organized to get back on the road when I realize my passport is not in my moneybelt. I start to panic, then tell myself I must've missed it. I look another five times, but it's still not here. I check all my pockets. It's not in any of them. I thoroughly search my tent and can't find it. I look in panniers I haven't even opened since I had it at the bank this morning. I remember going back to the teller when I realized she hadn't returned it to me, sticking it in a pocket because I felt that everyone was watching, then stopping in the lobby and transferring it securely, or so I thought, to my moneybelt.

It doesn't make sense, but it's not here. Where could it be? I think about all the places I went after the bank—to have photos developed, check email, get my hair cut, buy groceries at two different stores, an art gallery, buy a book, browse through other shops. Today was my day to get caught up on errands before heading into the more remote desert of southern Namibia tomorrow. I'd been feeling good about heading out of town in the morning. Now I wonder whether I will be.

It's after six and all the shops are probably closed, but thinking that I need to do something, I walk back into the center of town. I retrace my steps. The stores are all dark, and my passport does not stare up at me from the pavement. I walk to the police station and ask the officer at the reception desk if anyone has turned in a lost passport today.

"Is it any of these?" he says as he opens a drawer. A few passports lie scattered amidst other items. Norway. The Netherlands. Malawi. Israel.

Wondering if this is an opportunity to change my identity, I ask, "do you have any from the U.S.A.?"

"I don't think so." He rummages around in the drawer and grabs a few others. None are from the U.S., but he nonetheless looks at the photos to confirm that they are not mine. He advises me to check back tomorrow in case someone found it and didn't turn it in yet.

I thank him and slump as I walk out the door. I walk back to the backpackers with thoughts of "what now" racing through my mind. What are the chances of someone turning in a lost U.S. passport? Back at the backpackers, I sit in my tent studying my map and guidebook, thinking about alternate routes to Windhoek if I have to go to the U.S. embassy. I know I should take a direct minibus, but I want to bike through the desert. I wonder if it would really matter if I traveled without a passport for a few days here. I lie awake for hours.

Morning finally comes and I walk back into town and start checking with shops as they start opening. Both grocery stores say no, as do the bookstore and hair salon. I wait for more stores to open at 8:30 and get more no's. Then I walk into the internet cafe.

The woman there looks at me, gets a huge smile on her face, and says, "I'm so happy to see you."

My face mirrors her smile as I say, "You have my passport."

She tells me she found it on the floor after I left and was asking everyone who came in if they knew where I was staying. No one did.

"Thank you so much. I'll tell all the travelers I meet to come to this internet cafe," I gush. My step is lighter as I walk back to Desert Sky to pack up.

In the afternoon I bike to Walvis Bay. I told myself last night that if I were biking to Walvis Bay with my passport today, I wouldn't complain about the notoriously awful wind. It becomes hard to keep this promise. I'm enjoying the scenery, with sand dunes to my left and the Atlantic Ocean to my right. But as I ride along, the wind picks up. It slows me to ten kilometers/hour, on an almost flat tar road. Then it changes direction and starts blasting sand across the road. The sand stings my face and hands. I think about stopping, but there's nowhere to take shelter, so I keep riding. Large trucks coming from the opposite direction carry such a drag of sand with them in their wake that I stop and turn away from them as they pass. After a few kilometers, the wind lets up somewhat. A truck goes by me, blaring his horn. He stops up a slight hill ahead of me. I wonder if he's going to offer me a ride or if something is wrong with his truck. As I get close, he gets out. His angry stance tells me to keep going. As I pedal by, he yells at me—in Afrikaans. I smile and internally laugh at him. He took the time to stop his truck and wait for me to yell at me, then did so in a language I don't understand.

chapter twenty

DESERT CHALLENGE

Leaving Walvis Bay in a heavy coastal mist, my bike is probably as heavy as it has ever been. I'm carrying twelve liters of water and seemingly insane amounts of food, including pasta and sauce mix, granola, powdered soy milk, bread, peanut butter, jam, blueberry muffins, apples, oranges, sunflower seeds, cookies, crisps, raisins, and an avocado. I figure the water will last into a third day and the food will last into the fourth. I've bungeed my front panniers to my rack, in addition to their usual clips, so I don't need to worry too much about losing more screws on rough roads.

I'm headed back into the desert—and the most remote desert region that I plan to ride through. It's 235 kilometers to Solitaire, the first town of any sort. There's a lodge somewhat closer, 150 or so kilometers away, that has water and might let me camp. Before the lodge, there are a couple primitive campgrounds without water in Namib-Naukluft National Park, and possibly a farm with water near the lodge. Once I'm out of Walvis Bay, the road will be unpaved and possibly rugged. It includes a couple mountain passes. This is the ultimate challenge of this trip, sort of like going into the wilderness but on a road.

As I ride out of Walvis Bay, the road is still tarred. My bike computer starts flashing zero as my speed even when I'm riding, then it jumps around to various speeds though mine remains constant. Finally it settles on zero. I hope it just got too much moisture in it and needs to dry out, something that shouldn't take too long once I leave the coastal mist behind. But I wonder what else can go wrong with my bike. And though speed isn't important, it'd be nice to know how far I've gone once I get into the rugged desert.

I enter the park, and the tar road turns to gravel. It climbs gradually through a dirty-colored sandy landscape with some small dunes but mostly flatter stretches of sand with a few distant rocky mountains. After a couple hours, I leave the coastal clouds behind and ride under a blue sky. The air is still cool, though it warms as I ride east. A few small plants appear along the roadside. As I get farther into the park, the road gets rougher and my computer still doesn't work. I feel like I've come far enough that I should be at the Vogelfederberg campsite by now, but it's not within sight. Suddenly my front rack rubs against my tire. With a bad feeling, I stop.

I get off my bike and immediately see that the rack has broken. The upside-down U-shaped piece that holds the two sides together above the wheel is broken on the left side. This is bad, though not as bad as a broken wheel. I remember a conversation I had with my best friend after he arranged to have this rack sent to me in Malawi. I half-jokingly said, "If I break another rack, I think this trip is over." Is it? Did I mean it?

I don't think so, but I am frustrated. I move off the road and try to hose clamp it together. One car blasts by. As I'm working on it, a white farmer stops and offers me a lift to Solitaire, still 180 kilometers away.

"I might be able to fix it," I tell him.

I get the hose clamp on, feel good about this, stand my bike up, and bounce it a few times to simulate riding on a rough road. The rack bounces out of the clamp. The farmer offers to help and wires it together. It holds for an extra bounce but still bounces out. I consider taking the U piece off and riding without it, since both sides seem stable on their own. But I'm concerned that if one side breaks, it could fall into the wheel and cause even more damage. I stare dejectedly at my bike.

Here I am in the desert, where I most want to be riding, and now I can't. Unless I can figure out a makeshift repair. I can't think of anything that would hold the two ends of the broken piece together any more securely than the wire and hose clamp.

"I need to get going. My wife will be expecting me. Do you want a lift?" he asks.

"I'm not sure. Maybe I should go back to Walvis Bay and get it fixed there. Isn't Solitaire very small?"

"Yes, it is, but there's a mechanic there. He'll be able to fix it for you. He'll figure something out."

I'm still tempted to return to Walvis Bay but concerned that starting out from there all over again, with just as much food and water, after getting it fixed may lead to another break.

"Okay," I say, hesitantly.

As we load my bike into the back of his pickup, I feel defeated. I was so up for the desert challenge. And I lost. I was so mentally and physically prepared, well-rested and with plenty of supplies. Yet my bike wasn't up for it. And this is my fault because I never really prepared it for this trip. If I'd planned this ride while living in the States, I would've researched racks for rugged trips and bought new ones—and maybe even bought a new bike. But when I came to Africa with the Peace Corps, I brought this bike with me simply to be able to ride around Lesotho and do some shorter tours during my vacation time. I didn't choose it for a rugged, months-long, self-contained tour, and now this has caught up with me.

Only one kilometer down the road, we pass the Vogelfederberg campsite. I was so close. I wonder if I had made it here today, would I have made it all the way to Solitaire or would my rack have broken tomorrow anyway? I suspect that extra weight caused the break, and my bike would have been lighter tomorrow with less food and water. But would it have been enough lighter to make a difference? How much farther would I have gotten? There's no way to know.

As we drive through the dirty-colored sandy landscape, I start to think that maybe this isn't such a bad area to get a lift through. But then the sand gets redder and the mountains get closer, and I want to be biking. We drive through Kuiseb Canyon, which I'd planned for early on my third day of riding through the park. The road goes up, then down into, and back up out of the rocky canyon. Parts of the route are steep, but I wish I'd been able to try it, especially in the cool, early morning air. Traveling at car speed is disorienting. The scenery comes at me too fast, and I don't have time to absorb the canyon's beauty. We pass through fenced-off farmland and then another canyon. As the road turns southward, we drive by the lodge where I'd planned to ask permission to camp my third night in the park. It all just goes by.

We arrive in Solitaire. The farmer drops me off at a lodge, campsite, and shop and introduces me to Moose, the large, bearded, white owner/manager.

"We'll find a way to fix it in the morning," he assures me.

From camp, I watch the huge red ball that is the sun drop through the sky to the horizon, and I feel I've just passed through an area without getting to know it. I'm disappointed at already being here, and it feels wrong to have missed the desert challenge.

In the morning, Moose tells the white man working in the auto shop that he needs to fix my rack.

"I don't know what I can do about that," he grumps as he takes my bike.

I return to my campsite, figuring I'll be spending the day here. Only an hour-and-a-half later, though, the man brings me my bike and tells me it's fixed. He's drilled holes through both the U-piece and the piece it attaches to, wired them together, and put the hose clamp around both. The repair passes the bounce test. I test ride it around the campsite with my front panniers on, and the rack still holds. I'm not sure how long this fix will hold up, but the only way to find out is to ride it. I'll try to avoid the bumpiest roads and having too much weight on the front of the bike.

I depart Solitaire the next day, with my bike computer working again, on what Moose describes as an "average" road for the area with "some bumps and some hills." Some of the bumps are corrugations, and I cautiously ride over the first ones even more slowly than I usually do. My rack holds. Concerned about putting too much weight on it, I started this ride with only four liters of water, less than the usual six I've been carrying but not finishing when I'm counting on getting to a camp with water that night. Sesriem is only eighty kilometers away, but it's a brutally hot day and the desert air is so dry that I'm no longer sure four liters will be enough.

A red car pulls up, and I think it must be my camping neighbors from Solitaire. I originally met them when we were all at Desert Sky in Swakopmund. Now that we've run into each other a couple times, we've become casual friends. They said this morning they'd be coming this way later today. But it's not them.

"Are you from New Zealand?" asks a white woman.

"No."

"We have bread for some cyclists from New Zealand," she says.

"I haven't seen any other cyclists out here."

I'm thinking about asking if they have any extra water, but she closes her window and they drive away.

Though I love the sparseness of the desert, when the midday sun beats down on me, I suddenly find myself wishing for a tall, shady oak tree, as ridiculous as it might look here. As I ride on, the red sand dunes of Sossusvlei come into view. Almost out of water, I'm relieved to arrive at Sesriem, a lone campground in the desert and the gateway to Sossusvlei. As I pull in, I see two cyclists outside the small camp shop.

"Are you from New Zealand?" I ask.

"Yes," they say, probably figuring I must've heard of them.

"Did you get your bread?"

"Yes." They laugh. "We got to the store here almost out of food. It doesn't have much, so we sent a note with money back to Moose with someone going that way and asked him to have someone coming this way bring us bread."

They were in Solitaire just before me, took a long route here, and spent the last couple of nights camping out in the desert.

"The campsite is fully booked. They're sending people to the overflow area over there." They point to a shadeless, parched, dusty field. "We found some people willing to share their site with us. Maybe you can do the same."

A spot in the dust field costs 180 Namibian dollars ($24 U.S.), the same as a shady site. I can't imagine setting up my tent in the direct sun in this heat when there are other options. Several sites are empty, though booked, and I sit at one for awhile, resting, drinking water, and wondering whether anyone will come to claim it. Later I ride through the camping loop, to see if my friends with the red car have a site, but I don't see them anywhere. I meet some German and Canadian students living in Cape Town who ask about my trip. I ask if they're interested in sharing a site. They are but don't have one either. The camp entrance closes at eight, and people with reservations have to arrive by then. We wait and take over an unoccupied site. We'll split the costs of the site if anyone comes to check, but no one does.

"*Beep. Beep. Beep.*" I'm jolted awake way too soon by my five a.m. watch alarm. It's still dark out. Getting up before the sun always feels wrong to me. I'm tempted to roll over in my tent and go back to sleep, but I've got a long day of desert cycling and hiking planned and want to be on the road as the sun starts to rise. Once I'm up, I'll appreciate the beauty of the early morning light, I know, but getting up and forcing myself to eat breakfast in the dark before my stomach wakes up is tough. I listen to the cacophony of tent zippers, as other campers are also rising early.

The gates providing the only access into the national park area of Sossusvlei open at 5:30 a.m. I ride through shortly afterward. The road is tarred, though with more potholes than pavement in places. A stream of cars flows past me, tourists trying to get to Sossusvlei to see it in the early morning light and to hike before the heat of the day. By six, the early crowd is far away and only an occasional motor vehicle passes me.

I'd been planning to cycle the sixty-five kilometers to Sossusvlei without stopping along the way, but after forty-five, I stop at Dune 45, unsure why I'm

From Atop Dune 45

doing so. My bike leans against a sign and waits for me while I climb the red dune. I follow the trail of footprints along its ridge. The sand here is estimated to be three to five million years old. This is no place to rush. Nature compels me to climb slowly by sinking my feet into the sand.

From the top, at over 150 meters, I look out at white sand plains bordered by red sand dunes merging into blue sky. There's one scraggly tree off to my left, and a couple others off to my right. Below me, a black-and-white bird flies by. I look down on its back. A few bugs scurry around in the sand. The only sign of human life other than my own is the footprints in the sand.

I'm tempted to stay here for a while, sipping water, sinking into the sand, and absorbing the energy and peacefulness of nature's solitude, but I also feel compelled to go on, to see the famous Sossusvlei. After all, it's what brought me here, to this part of Namibia, and my brain just won't allow me to skip it, even if I may have found a better place along the way. It's still twenty kilometers away, then another sixty-five kilometers back to camp. Logic nags at me that I need to get going. I make my way slowly down the dune, glad the sand keeps me from hurrying, back to my bike and the road.

The road cuts through the white sand plains, and I look around at the dunes as I ride. Now that it's nearing midday, people are returning from their morning hikes, and most of the traffic is going in the opposite direction. As usual, my bike keeps me on a different rhythm than the tourists in motor vehicles. I arrive at the Sossusvlei shuttle area, the end of the tar road, in the noon heat. Sossusvlei is four kilometers away along a very sandy track, sand too deep to bike through, too deep even for two wheel drive cars. I park my bike against a tree and take a four-wheel-drive shuttle.

As I'm arriving, two hikers are leaving. Once the shuttle leaves, I'm alone. I'm surprised at the greenery at the base of Sossusvlei and her neighboring dunes. Bushes climbing the bottom of the dunes are a true forest green, a color rarely seen in the desert. Cold winds from the Atlantic Ocean, which is about sixty kilometers away, mix with the desert heat to form early morning fogs, whose moisture supports the plant life. I wander, setting out for an unnamed dune that is deceptively far, hike along its base for a bit, then return to Sossusvlei herself. I'm more immersed in the dunes here than at Dune 45, completely surrounded by them. There's no way in or out except over them. The sun is searingly hot, but somehow this feels right. It is the desert after all.

I think about what I'd heard about Sossusvlei from my Peace Corps friends who were with tour groups. Their groups always came early to see the sunrise over Sossusvlei. Spectacular, they said, but crowded with other tour groups, all on the same schedule. I prefer it this way. Although I would've loved to see a spectacular sunrise, I'll gladly trade it and its crowds for the solitude of the midday heat.

I think back to the *"beep beep beep"* of my five o'clock alarm. Was that really just this morning? It feels so far away in both time and space.

I stop at an intersection that looks different than on my map. The roads go straight and right rather than left and straight. A white man driving a luxury camp vehicle stops.

"Isn't it too hot for you?" he asks. "Do you know it's already 38 degrees and was 45 yesterday?" Celsius. 38 degrees Celsius is about 100 degrees Fahrenheit, and 45 degrees Celsius is more than 110 degrees Fahrenheit.

Actually, I didn't know, or care to know. Numbers are a man-made invention and have no place here in the sparsely populated desert. The heat seeps into and out of my skin.

"It is hot, but it's okay. I'm used to it and have lots of water." Well, maybe I'm not exactly used to it being this hot before noon, but I did start today's ride with eight liters of water and feel prepared.

"Is this the D626 road?" I ask, pointing to the road going right. I can't even ask if it's the road to anything. It doesn't go anywhere except through the desert. There are a couple turnoffs to luxury lodges along it, no towns, and then it simply ends at an intersection rather than in a town.

"Yes."

"What's it like? Is it as sandy as this road?" I look back along the way I've come.

"There's no more sand, but there are a lot of bumps. Where are you planning to stay tonight?" He looks up the road I just asked about.

"I'm going to camp somewhere in the desert. I've heard it's very safe here."

"Do know about the campground up the road?" He looks back at me.

"Do you mean Betta's? That's way too far for today." I'm aiming for Betta's tomorrow night.

"No, there's another one before that. It's called End of the World."

"Where is that?" I ask.

"I think it's near the intersection with the D827 road." Another seventy kilometers.

"That might still be too far for today with these road conditions. I'll see how it goes, though."

A white couple in a car stops at the intersection. I go on, and they stay to talk with the man. They soon catch me.

"Is there anything we can do for you?" they ask.

"No, but thanks for asking."

"That man said he was going to radio ahead and arrange someplace for you to stay tonight."

"Okay, thanks."

The ride gets even tougher, and I think about how appropriately the End of the World campground is named. As I slowly climb a long, corrugated uphill into a headwind, I hear R.E.M. singing "It's the End of the World (as we know it)." And just as they do, I feel fine. I approach a lone tree, watching it like a silo in Kansas that can be seen for miles. My thoughts turn to a genuine lunch break and rest. As soon as I stop and start to pull over into the small shady patch, I'm swarmed by flies. Buzz. They fly at my face. Buzz. They land on my arms. Buzz. They are all over. There must be hundreds of them. I thought flies like sun. What are these doing in the shade? I wonder if it's too hot even for flies here.

I cancel my lunch plans, run back to the road, and hop on my bike, afraid that the swarm will accompany me and I'll be unable to outride it going uphill. Some do stay with me, but not the whole swarm. The wind helps get rid of them.

Small trees dot the landscape. There are frequently bluish mountains in the distance. My thoughts turn to being given a luxury room at the camp, though in many ways I just want to camp out on my own.

Later in the afternoon, the luxury camp man drives by and stops.

"How are you doing?" he asks.

"I'm fine but getting tired. This has been a slow, tough ride. I'm not going to make it to the End of the World today. I'll find somewhere to camp."

"Wait a minute," he says, then radios his camp manager.

"My manager has arranged for you to camp at a ranch about ten kilometers up the road. The ranch is another two kilometers off the road, but you can see it. It's the only one around here."

"Great, thanks. That's very nice of you."

The ten kilometers feels like at least twenty, but he's right. I can easily see the ranch house from the road and turn into its long driveway. As I approach, I see a man working in the yard.

"Hi. I'm the cyclist who was told she could camp here," I say, stating the obvious.

"They said you can stay in this little house," he says, apparently referring to the owners.

He shows me a small building off to the side of the main house. There's a kitchen and bedroom inside.

"You'll have to come outside to get to the bathroom," he says and shows me a bathroom off the porch. "I hope this is okay?"

"Sure, no problem." Maybe he doesn't realize I've been camping and am used to walking outside to get a bathroom, when there's even one to get to.

"Is there anything else?"

"No, thanks a lot. This'll be great."

Though I'm thrilled with the hospitality, I'm just a little disappointed not to be camping out alone. It feels like another challenge of this trip has been unmet. I want to be comfortable alone in the desert overnight, and this seemed like the place to try, with all the reassurances of safety I'd gotten. I put my water bottles in the refrigerator and figure I'll be happy with cold water instead of personal growth tonight.

chapter twenty-one

FREE CAMPING, OR NOISES IN THE NIGHT, PART 2

Leaving the ranch, the road improves and smooth tracks take me through the spaciousness of the desert and its welcoming desolation. I ride through this landscape of red sand sprinkled with bushes or even green trees. Sometimes I climb. Sometimes I descend. The only constants are the sand and the rocky mountains whose land I am riding through. As the day goes on, the road gets sandier and rougher. I walk briefly a few times on sandy sections. Clouds keep it from feeling overwhelmingly hot, but I feel drained when I arrive at Betta's Camp, and my stomach is queasy. I have to sit down to rest and drink two cans of juice before I can muster the energy to set up camp. I think the heat has drained me, despite the clouds. It has been hot enough recently that my candles have melted together, and I'm especially pleased to see a large enough overhang over my picnic table that there's space for my tent in its shade. There's even a light with a switch, so I'll have good light to read by but not shine on my tent when I'm ready to sleep. Out here I take pleasure in the simple things.

I meet a few other campers as I pack up in the morning. They've come from Aus, where I'm headed over the next few days.

"How's the D407 road?" I ask.

"It's okay. Not too bad," they reply.

But it starts out awfully sandy, and I almost wonder if they meant a different road. I think about turning around but don't know if the other road would be any better, and it's longer. I walk several times and involuntarily stop several others, as the sand is just too deep to pedal a loaded mountain bike through. The scenery isn't worth this drudgery. I'm not as close to the mountains as the past couple days, and the sand seems to have lost its reddish sparkle. Even with a tailwind, I think about trying to get a lift—and I know I must be tired. An older, local white man pulls over in a beat up pickup truck.

"Do you want a lift?" he asks.

"I think so," I reply, "This road is just too sandy."

"I'm only going six kilometers, but I'll take you that far if you want."

"Oh," I reply, trying not to sound disappointed. "How's the road up ahead?"

"It gets better. You've come through the worst of it. It's better all the way to Helmringhausen. There's no more sand."

"Okay, then I'll just keep riding. But thanks."

"Are you sure?"

"Yes. I prefer to ride. I was just concerned that if the road stayed so sandy, I'd be walking most of the day."

The road does generally get better, but better is relative. It's still tough riding, with many bumpy sections, some climbing, and some sand, including some deep enough I need to walk. I can only average about ten kilometers per hour in these conditions. Today I'm grateful for clouds and a delightful late afternoon breeze that combine to keep me motivated enough to keep riding.

Fences make free camping prospects look bad, and I'm also concerned about running out of water in this heat. Suddenly as I crest a hill, I look down on my wish come true: a farm close to the road. I stop and look around. It feels empty, but I knock on the door anyway. No one answers. Walking around to see if anyone's out back, I spot an outdoor sink. I can't resist the opportunity and fill my water bottles and wash up a bit. As the cool water splashes on my face and runs down my arms, washing the day's dust and sweat down the drain, I am again reminded of how little it takes to satisfy me out here on the road.

There's a simple rhythm to this life of self-contained bike touring that is soothing to my soul: get up, eat breakfast and review map, pack up camp, ride for several hours with breaks for snacks, lunch, and rest, find place to camp, set up camp, shower if possible, cook and eat dinner, review maps and guidebook, write in journal, sleep, do it all over again and again and again. Notice the absence of modern gadgets from this routine. Computers, cell phones, and televisions with 100 channels but nothing on are simply not part of my day-to-day life out here. With having enough food and water and finding a safe place to camp a typical day's only goals, I am reminded of how simple the essence of life is. The modern rush to get ahead, to accumulate more stuff, bigger houses and cars, tends to take us away from this essence. We are always living in the future or the past, and forgetting that the present is all we ever really have.

Here in the desert, away from so many of the gadgets and conveniences of modern life, I am reminded how simple—and satisfying—life can be if we let it. It isn't more stuff that brings us happiness; it is appreciating what we do have. Here I am grateful that no matter how tough the riding gets, I am surrounded by nature's beauty, even when I have trouble seeing it through my frustration. Here I am grateful that I never run out of food or water, and that my stove never fails me at the end of the day. Here I am grateful for the kindness of strangers. Here I am grateful for this opportunity to be truly free, to live close to the earth, with only what I can carry with me on my bike and what I can find inside me to sustain me.

Now that I have plenty of water, I debate going on and wander around the farm. What would I do if I stay and no one comes home by dark? Would I be bold enough to set up camp near someone's house without permission or would I go on and risk having to camp between a fence and the road? As I ponder, I hear the rumble of a motor vehicle approaching and watch as it turns in. The owners have returned, and so I don't need to decide.

Once I have permission to stay, being able to just stop and camp on a farm is liberating. I'm not confined to having to get to towns and campsites. This farm is surrounded by mountains. As the sun sets, pink clouds settle in. I set up my stove in the yard near a big metal tank and concrete steps that lead up to it. The tank and steps act as two sides of a windblock. The wind is swirling and seems to be coming from every direction, so I sit on a piece of concrete and act as the third side of the windblock. Gazing out at the desert, I think about the juxtaposition of the usefulness and ugliness of this concrete and metal and nature's calming beauty. Having a nice place to camp and dinner is all it takes to make a tough ride worth it.

As I bike along the smooth crushed gravel C13 road under a hot sun, more than forty kilometers into the next day's ride, an SUV pulls over. Inside is the white couple whom I met without introductions on the road the morning I left Sesriem. They tell me their names are Pepe and Mike.

"How have you been? How did that ranch work out?" they ask.

"I'm good, and it was fine. It's been a pretty ride the last few days. I didn't think I'd see you again. Where have you been?" I say as I lean on my handlebars.

"We spent the past few days at a camp. Now we're headed to Luederitz. What about you?"

"Me, too, but it'll be a couple days until I get there."

They go on their way.

About forty-five minutes later, they return.

"We brought you some things," they say as they hand me a 1.5-liter bottle of cold water and some sweet baked goods. There's something about traveling alone in the desert that seems to bring out the goodness in others.

"Thanks, you guys are great," I say. I have plenty of water and don't relish the idea of carrying more extra weight but cold water is always appreciated.

"We'll see each other again when you get to Luederitz," says Pepe.

"That'd be great," I say, "but I think you might be gone by the time I get there."

"Oh no, we'll see each other again," she says as they drive away.

But we never do.

The road gets sandier, and I frequently need to walk along brief stretches. A crosswind sometimes blows me across the road, and I have to walk back to the less sandy side to ride again. I ride through mountains, but they aren't steep. It's mostly cloudy and another mid-afternoon cool breeze comes along, a nice pattern as long as it's not a headwind.

I ride along, thinking that this is going to be the first time on this trip that I'm not going to bathe for two days in a row. I figure I'll either find a farm to camp on or camp way off the side of the road. Instead it's the first time that a campsite I didn't know about comes along at the right time. I see a sign for camping and a guesthouse at Tiras Conservancy in eight kilometers and smile.

When I arrive, I meet an older, white German-Namibian couple. They invite me in for a drink, and we chat while he drinks coffee and I drink a slightly lemony flavored cool drink.

"It looks like Schwarzenegger is going to be the next governor of California," says Peter.

What a great joke, I think. When I lived in Washington, D.C., I got *The Washington Post* delivered and read at least the headlines every day, but here I haven't heard a thing about the upcoming U.S. elections. But Schwarzenegger not only running for governor but also way ahead in the polls? He must be joking.

I ask them about their lives here. They still cattle farm but haven't had much rain in two years. They explain that they own this farm and it's one of four farms that have formed a conservancy together. They keep the tourist business small-scale to keep the place from getting overrun and ruined. They make enough of a living to be able to stay here.

"Where are you headed tomorrow?" he asks.

"Aus."

"It's all downhill. You'll have an easy day."

"Great. I've had plenty of tough days."

The campsite is up a hill across the road, and Peter insists on taking me in his pickup truck. The site is set on the far side of a hill from their house. Cement walls enclose it on three sides, and there's a bit of an overhang for shade. The bathroom is a short walk uphill. There are no other signs of civilization within sight. In the late afternoon light, a gravelly, sandy plain stretches to the craggy Tiras Mountains in the northwest. A hawk flies overhead.

"There's no charge for you to camp here."

"Wow. Thanks."

He drives away but later comes back.

"I want to invite you to dinner with my wife and me," he says.

"That's really nice of you. But I'm a vegetarian, and I don't know if you've got a vegetarian dinner planned."

The shocked look on his face tells me they not only don't have a vegetarian meal planned tonight but also probably never do. This is the first time on this trip that I feel like I've missed an opportunity because I'm a vegetarian. I wish I'd thought to say that I'd love to join them and would be happy to bring my pasta.

In the morning, the pitter patter of rain on the overhang above my tent surprises me. Figuring it won't last long, especially after having just heard that they haven't had much rain in the past two years, I decide to wait it out inside my tent. When I depart a couple hours later, the rain has stopped. It soon begins again, making this my first time riding in rain since Malawi. The small drops of water landing on my skin are almost a welcome break from the usual dry air that seems to suck the moisture out of my skin as I ride. Setting up and breaking camp in the rain can be a drag, as equipment gets wet, but riding in a light rain in the warm desert is not. In Malawi the rain was cold and penetratingly chilly. Here it is a simply a bit of almost warm moisture in a dry land that needs it.

The ride starts out with a long downhill stretch and a tailwind. The road is a fairly smooth mixture of sand and small gravel most of the way, and the early rain keeps the dust down. After an hour, I've gone twenty kilometers. Remembering what Peter said about going "down" to Aus, I have thoughts of doing sixty kilometers in three hours. These are quickly erased as the road starts to climb, and keeps climbing—gently but definitely upward. Though the rain stops, dark clouds remain. They break at times and when they do, it starts to feel humid.

Some motorists pull over.

"There's a cape cobra in the middle of the road up ahead," one says. The cape cobra is one of Africa's most dangerous snakes.

"Okay, thanks," I reply.

"It's ten to fifteen kilometers from here," he says more urgently, perhaps sensing my lack of concern.

"I'll look for it." I don't want to run over a snake, and especially not a cape cobra, but somehow I don't see one in the road as much of a threat. I can easily go around it, if it's even still there, which seems unlikely. I'd be much more concerned if they told me it was at a campground I was going to.

"Do you have enough water?"

I tell them I do, and they go on.

After three hours of climbing, I'm tired of climbing and low on energy, though I've been eating. I'd been hoping to get to camp early to have half a day to relax and catch up in my journal, but this isn't happening. And I've now got a headwind, making what are probably some short downhill stretches feel like I'm going up. I push myself through two more hours. I never see the cape cobra, or any other wildlife. Oryx antelope, bat-eared foxes, black-backed jackals, springbok, rock rabbits, and hares all live here but remain out of my sight—the secret life of the seemingly barren desert. After sixty-three kilometers, there's still no sign of Aus. What was that about sixty easy kilometers? Once again, I'm reminded how hard it is for motorists to judge bicycling conditions. What looks easy in a car frequently is not on a bicycle. After another kilometer, I reach the tar road —and a sign showing that Aus is another five kilometers away.

The campsite in town is drab and located next to the gas station and a small store, but I'm too tired to keep going to the campsite outside of town. I get a glimpse of the steep hill leading out of town, and it'll have to wait for the morning. Plus camping at a store does have its appeal—not having to pack up and carry food. I snack on a chocolate-coated coffee ice cream bar then crisps and juice, and I feel much better.

After adding fresh tomatoes to my pasta dinner, I lie on the ground outside my tent, amidst that slightly oily gas station smell that seems to know no bounds of continents, and write by the light of what looks like a streetlight shining on my site. A mosquito buzzes around, and I hope my jacket and long pants keep me from getting bitten. At the beginning of the trip and into northern Namibia, I was taking dioxycycline as an anti-malarial. After neither seeing nor hearing any mosquitoes for weeks in this dry land, I gave it up, along with the side effect of increased sun sensitivity, which seemed dangerous in the desert sun and heat.

After granola and yogurt for breakfast, I set out for Luederitz, 130 kilometers away. The tar road takes me through the area still known by its German name of Sperrgebiet, meaning "closed area." Diamonds were discovered here in the early 20th century, and the German government subsequently closed the area to anyone except mining companies. Although the mining companies left long ago for more prosperous areas, much of the area remains closed and access is restricted. Thus, prospects for free camping are not good and I've got to get all the way Luederitz.

Dark clouds hover overhead. Pink early morning light filters through them, lighting up a few wild desert horses as I ride by. I cruise for the first two hours and quickly cover fifty-three kilometers. I don't even feel energetic, but I'm going downhill to the coast.

My Namibian nemesis strikes: a strong wind starts blowing. It almost instantly gets so strong that I consider it uncycleable, even with lots of downhill. I pull off the road. As I snack on crisps, I get blasted by a dusty-colored sand, similar to what I encountered leaving Walvis Bay. It stings so badly that I turn my back toward it. I can't see much of the road in either direction, let alone the curving gray rocky mountains beyond the dunes. The wind howls and howls and turns from being mostly a sidewind to a full headwind. I remain stopped for more than twenty minutes, then only manage ten kilometers in my first hour of riding into the wind.

The wind gradually lets up, though it never stops completely, and I'm able to increase my speed to fifteen kilometers per hour over the next few hours. The clouds lighten at times but never completely break. I gradually feel better, but it never again becomes a fun ride. Eight consecutive days of touring cycling is too much and it's never easy to do over 100 kilometers on a loaded mountain bike, but with all of today's downhill, it shouldn't be this tough. But this is Namibia and so along with my low overall energy, the wind makes it tough. The thought of resting tomorrow keeps me going.

As I near and then descend into Luederitz, the sand becomes boulder-strewn. The wind convinces me to stay at a backpackers' lodge in town instead of going to the campsite that's fully exposed to the wind on a promontory outside of town. The lodge doesn't have camping space, and this is the first time I pay to stay in a room since Zambia. It's nice to have a kitchen to cook and keep stuff cold in, and good lights to write and read by at night. But I'm somehow not as comfortable indoors as I usually am in my tent, which has come to feel like home. Being inside a building I feel less in touch with a place than when I'm essentially living outdoors.

Luederitz is a colonial town amidst the desert. As I wander around, I notice lots of people hanging around on the streets. In Malawi, I might have thought this town was almost empty, but now that I'm used to sparsely populated Namibia, it feels like culture shock. I feel watched. I'd adjusted to the solitude of the desert so well that I miss it.

I stop in at an internet cafe and am surprised to see an email from Paul titled "Where are you?" sitting in my inbox. He tells me that he joined some people for a 4x4 trip into the mountains from Swakopmund, their vehicle rolled over, his bike got crushed, and he fractured his back. I never like hearing that someone has been hurt, but he sounds well enough now and sympathy doesn't exactly spring forth. Mostly, I can't help thinking about the irony. People were so worried about our safety biking through Africa. He stopped cycling and got in a motor vehicle crash, and I've been safe cycling. So much for biking being dangerous.

Later I walk to a German church to see stained glass windows in the late-afternoon light. They aren't any fancier than some in Europe, just surprising here in Namibia. One has a German town crest on it. Another catches my attention: the bull in the center is sticking out its tongue.

I can't help overhearing a German conversation the proprietor is having with some German tourists. He tells them Namibia has its road and rail network because of the years the Germans were in charge. He also talks about Luederitz, saying there are between nine and twelve thousand residents. Some work on the boats, or in the fish factories, but unemployment is still at forty percent. AIDS is another problem facing them. It might be as high as sixty percent, though the official statistics say twenty.

"*Das Krankenhaus hier ist sehr schlecht. Ich würde lieber zu Hause liegen und sterben als dorthin zu gehen*," he says. "The hospital here is very bad. I'd rather lie at home and die than be brought there."

In the morning, I take a boat ride and encounter another group of Germans. They are the only other passengers, and the captain asks them if they all speak English since, "*die Dame kein Deutsch spricht.*" The lady does not speak German.

"*Das stimmt nicht*," I correct him.

His surprised look tells me he hasn't met too many Americans who speak German in Namibia. Nonetheless, he gives his introduction in German, and I understand most of it. The boat motors around a couple of islands. As we approach cape fur seals lounging on rocky shores, the scent of their guano wafts our way. Jackass penguins, named for the braying sound they make that is similar to a donkey's braying, inhabit one island. Dolphins swim nearby. None of them seem to mind the chilly wind, or our presence. The crew puts up the sails, and we sail briefly on the return.

Back at the internet cafe, I send a few emails inquiring about multi-day Orange River rafting trips. The Orange River is the border between Namibia and South Africa. I've heard it's beautiful and tranquil, and a few days off the bike but still in nature has a strong appeal. One company has space on a trip that starts nine days from now, which looks good for me. But it feels weird to be thinking about scheduling anything ahead of time. I've gotten so used to not having a schedule or any deadlines. I wonder how late I can book the trip.

After doing a series of yoga poses while focusing on my breath in my room—privacy for yoga is one advantage of a room over a tent—I climb the steps from the courtyard to the main part of the backpackers. While cooking dinner, I meet a German cyclist. He only started cycling in Keetmanshoop, about 300 kilometers away, so we don't have too many notes to compare, but it's still good to meet another cyclist. We're such a rarity here. He's headed into South Africa by public transport and plans to do some cycling there and maybe go into Lesotho.

I go on a 4x4 tour into the Sperrgebiet. Going on a tour is the only legal way in off the tar road. An Afrikaner couple from Pretoria are the only other participants. They come to Namibia on vacation every year. She's been dreaming of getting into the Sperrgebiet and he's been wanting to see Bogenfels, a rock arch featured on some of Namibia's phone cards, for years.

We drive through beautiful sandy desert scenery—some windblown dunes, sometimes lots of small plants, sometimes very rocky. It's fun to be in an area so natural, with a lack of both inhabitants and tourists, and see what this desert is like when it's not overrun by 4x4s and feet. We sprinkle water on lichen, and they open up and change from gray to orange. We stop at a few former mining areas with what are now rundown buildings the desert has started to reclaim. Sand is halfway up the walls of some.

Our lunch stop is at Pomona, a mining ghost town that was abandoned in 1931 when the price of diamonds plummeted overnight and the mine was suddenly closed. Our guide is sick and naps in the car while we explore. I wander the rocky, sandy landscape, looking at how much the sand has taken over some of the buildings and also at the plants. There are lots of small green ones, some with yellow and some with pink flowers. As usual, the wind is my companion.

After having a picnic lunch at the former school, we drive to Bogenfels, or bow rock. This is one of those rare works of nature for which "simply amazing" seems the only apt description. The fifty-five-meter-tall, brown-and-black rock arches up from the shore to a point reaching for the distant blue sky, then curves back down into the sea, where it disappears underwater. The mid-afternoon sun glints off of it and the ocean. A path along the rocky shore takes me downward until I stand almost directly under the arch in such a serene spot

Bogenfels

that I could stay all day. But I want to see more, and so I hike up Bogenfels. This turns out to be more of a neat thing to do than good for views, and I lose the aura of the arch standing atop it. As I stand there in the wind, my clothes puff out so much that I look like a marshmallow person.

Most of my mornings in Luederitz have been calm, but it's breezy the next day, when I get up early to leave. The wind is in my face as I cycle out of town. Making it all the way back to Aus—130 kilometers—in a day starts to feel unlikely. I wonder if I've made a mistake by leaving today, but I go on. I have no desire to stay in Luederitz any longer. I've seen what I came to see and rested. My soul tells me it's time to be back on the road. And I listen.

Now that I'm traveling alone, I'm listening to my intuition again, something I've done most of my life but got out of the habit of doing while traveling with Paul. Rather than denying the feeling of what's right for me and making the logical choice to wait out the wind and stay longer in Luederitz that at least a part of me knows isn't really right for me, I go on, realizing that a day really can make all the difference in the world and that by leaving today, the whole rest of my trip may be very different than if I wait another day or two. We never truly know where life is leading us, and sometimes the logical choices aren't the right ones for our souls. Though I struggle into the wind, I'm at peace with my decision.

Once out of town, I turn with the road and the wind becomes a sidewind. It's brutal at times and seems to get worse as I ride along. Near the turnoff into the Sperrgebiet, I start to get sandblasted. The sand generally stays low and hits my legs, but some hits my face. As I ride, heading east, parts of the road ahead of me look fine and parts I can see the sand blowing across. I see a dune that looks like it's slowly moving in the wind. It is—dunes do slowly move, though imperceptibly to the human eye. The thought that maybe I can ride out this bad stretch keeps me going. Then the wind turns into more of a headwind and slows me down to six or seven kilometers per hour going uphill. It's taking so much energy and is such a struggle to go even that speed that I decide it's not worth it. I do something I've never done on this tour: get off my bike and walk on a tar road. Walking at four kilometers per hour is much easier. Generally, I'd rather be riding, even if it's tougher, but not in this crazy wind, my Namibian nemesis. After I've been walking less than half a kilometer, a pickup truck pulls over.

"Do you want a lift to Aus?" asks the white man driving.

"Yes," I say, almost without hesitation.

The white driver and his black passenger get out and lift my bike into the back of the pickup. The passenger, who had been sitting in the front seat, hops into the back with my bike.

"You don't have to move. I'll sit in back," I say.

He looks puzzled and stays in back. I suppose his boss wouldn't allow me to sit in back. So I sit in front with the white driver.

He tells me that he's working on putting in the new Aus-Luederitz railroad and talks as if he's fairly high up in the project. The line has been out of use for three to four years because it wasn't made strong enough. They're putting in an entire new railbed and tracks, which he expects to take two years. He catches a foreman sleeping in a pickup as we drive by.

"They [blacks] are so lazy. They're given good working farms and the farms are decrepit within a year because they've torn the buildings apart for firewood."

I remain silent and let him keep talking.

"The government had to give them jobs because after independence, terrorists became freedom fighters and reminded the government that they'd fought for them. The pre-independence government wasn't racist but was fighting communism. I was in the same schools with them [blacks] and saw that they are different."

"Did you have any classes with them?" I glance over at him but cannot see the expression on his face as he looks ahead.

"This is as far as I'm going," he pulls over to the side of the road.

As the black man passes my bike out of the back of the truck, I thank him and thank the driver for the lift. But I'm surprised to be let off here since he'd offered me a ride to Aus, and I wonder if I somehow offended him. I notice that he takes a turn down a dirt road after letting me off.

I'm within thirty kilometers of Aus and this feels good. It's windy but soon tapers off to only a breeze. Tufts of grass in the sand surround me with a background of rocky mountains. The sun lights up the landscape so that it sparkles in a way that it couldn't on my ride in to Luederitz under the dark clouds. I stop for a quick lunch break of avocado, cucumber, and cream cheese sandwiches that I made last night to prepare for my projected long ride. Then the wind kicks in again, and I feel frustrated, especially since I still have a lot of climbing to get to Aus. I ride a little, then stop near some desert horses.

A double-cab pickup offers me a lift, and again I accept. This time the black man stays in front with the white man, and I sit in the back seat. They're also working on the railroad. We chat mostly about my trip and what I've been doing in Africa. They offer me a ride farther east to the Fish River Canyon turnoff tomorrow, but I decline. That's new cycling territory that I want to bike through, not zoom through at car speed. Taking a ride back to Aus along a road I'd already biked was one thing, but I don't want this bike trip to turn into a car trip. They drop me off at the Klein Aus Vista campsite, outside of town, around noon. It's so windy that I don't set up my tent until much later in the day.

I sleep without my fly on my tent, so there's less flapping. Yet still the roaring wind wakes me up frequently, and I lie in my sleeping bag, thinking about having to ride into it in the morning.

It's a chilly early morning wind and slow going into it, though not as bad as yesterday. The wind feels so chilly most of the day, I even get goose bumps during a stop in the shade. The wind not only keeps me from feeling hot but also helps keep the flies away.

I can see mountains but am not really in them for most of ride. Then I climb the one steep hill of the day and suddenly I'm on a plateau where the landscape is drier. There aren't any more bright green trees. Everything is again shades of brown, and I know I must be out of the coastal moisture zone. As I bike along, I get into an area that does have some slightly green shrubs.

I'm ready to stop for the day when I arrive in Goageb. It looks desolate from the highway, and not much better once I turn in. People are hanging around the petrol station/bottle store/hotel. I go inside.

"I'd like a room for tonight," I say to the white receptionist.

She looks troubled.

"Are you full?" I ask, though I can't imagine it. There aren't that many people or cars around, and no other bikes. This looks more like a place that doesn't get enough business rather than one that has to turn people away.

But she nods her head and says, "Yes. Are you on a bike?"

"Yes. Is there a safe place I could set up my tent?

She looks relieved. "Yes. I'll show you."

We walk out of the lobby.

"We're renovating," she says, and I suddenly understand that they are closed for renovation rather than full.

She shows me a sunny spot in the yard then says, "Or there's a bed in a house other people are sleeping in. You could sleep there."

I decline, unsure who these "other people" are and not wanting to impose. Later I ask her, "Is your restaurant serving dinner?"

"No, it's closed, but we're going to *braii*. You're welcome to join us."

"Thanks, but I'm a vegetarian." *Braii* is Afrikaans for barbecue, and I don't expect them to have any veggie burgers handy. Again I'm sorry to miss a meal with locals, but I have zero desire to start eating meat. "I have some spaghetti with me. I can cook that. I just thought maybe I should save it for the route to Fish River Canyon. I don't think I'll see many stores along the way."

"Do you eat eggs? How about if I give you some eggs to cook?"

"Yes, that'd be great."

She gives me six eggs, which I scramble in my pot.

"What do I owe you?" I ask in the morning.

"Nothing."

People can say what they want about Africa being primitive, but it sure is wealthy with hospitality.

I turn south off the tar road east onto a gravel road a couple days later. For the first time in Namibia, after almost seven weeks here, I have a tailwind for most of the day. And, despite carrying eight liters of water in case I need to free camp, the day becomes one of my favorite rides in Namibia. I can feel the wind pushing me up the hills. Now that I've left the cooler coastal region, the temperatures are easily getting back into the 30s °C (90s °F), and the breeze feels wonderful. The road parallels a railway line for awhile. As a freight train passes me, it toots and the conductor waves. There's a friendly feeling out here. He probably doesn't see too many people. There are mountains on both sides. It's a pretty ride, made especially enjoyable by the north wind and relatively smooth road. Under these conditions, 100 kilometers isn't too much for a day, and I easily make it to the Canon Roadhouse, where the proprietor gives me a discount on camping, by mid-afternoon.

Groceries are so scarce in this part of Namibia that I've been eating at restaurants whenever they are available at campsites. At the roadhouse, I'm thrilled to see couscous with vegetables and also cheesecake on the menu. Last night I ended up with roast potatoes, potato salad, and green salad—the only vegetarian option the restaurant at a small campsite offered. Both meals are good, seasoned food but not really bicyclist portions. I make up for this at the all-you-can-eat breakfast buffet the next day by eating three plates of food: scrambled eggs, cheese, tomato and cucumber slices, pieces of rolled pancakes, a thick slice of homemade bread with butter and jam, fruit salad with yogurt, muesli with fruit and yogurt. A feast amidst the scarcity of the desert.

It only takes just over an hour to ride to the Hobas campsite at the Fish River Canyon. I choose a site with a shady area for my tent under a tree and a bench to use as a windbreak. After I set up camp, I ride my unloaded bike a bumpy ten kilometers with lots of climbing out to the main viewpoint of the canyon. Again on a different schedule than the tour groups, I'm the only one at the viewpoint. I stare into the depths of the canyon of shades of brown rock stretching to a mostly dry riverbed. It's nowhere near as colorful as the Grand Canyon, but it is big—160 kilometers long, up to twenty-seven kilometers wide, and up to 550 meters deep. I hike three kilometers along the rim to Hikers Point. I could ride my bike around on the road but want the change of pace hiking brings. The view from the point includes a broader section of the canyon. I start my return hike when the buses arrive.

The next day's ride starts out bumpy and with steep hills to climb, but then I pass a warning triangle for a road-scraping machine—a gift from the road gods. Suddenly the road improves. I cruise downhill on freshly scraped roads. Even when it's time to climb again, the road remains smooth and occasionally twists close enough to the canyon for a view. It's one of those rides where everything just comes together: scenery, smooth ride, and even some tailwind. I feel like I could keep riding forever.

I arrive at the Ai Ais Hot Springs Resort, an oasis of manicured green grass in the desert but with little shade. There's a restaurant and a small grocery store, plus the hot springs, rooms, and a camping area. It's geared towards South African tourists but there aren't many here now. I'm happy to see a pay phone for the first time since I left Aus five days ago. The rafting trip I've been considering starts in a couple days. I'm now sure I can make it in time, and I hope it's not too late to register. I call as soon as I check-in for a campsite.

"I'm so glad there's going to be another woman on the trip," says the woman who answers the phone for the rafting company. She tells me that with me there are now thirteen men and two women, plus two male guides.

I spend most of the rest of the afternoon at the indoor hot pools of varying temperatures, ranging from very hot to scalding. A cold pool to balance them out would be nice, but instead I rest in the lounge chairs between dippings and let the evaporating water cool me off. The chloride and sulfur of the water fill the indoor air with their odors.

The rafting camp is about 135 kilometers away, and the trip starts with dinner two days from now. I'm tempted to stay here again tomorrow night, get a real early start, and do it all in one day, especially since there aren't any camps or lodges along the way. I'd like the challenge. But I've finally accepted that a planned 135-kilometer day of mountain biking in the desert is simply too much to be able to count on finishing. If the conditions are good, it's very doable. But if they're not, I risk missing the trip I just paid for. Plus, this is my last opportunity to camp out alone in the desert, something I've been really wanting to do ever since leaving Sossusvlei. I decide to stay and relax here for part of tomorrow, leave in the afternoon, ride for a few hours, and camp out along the way.

As I ride away from Ai-Ais, nearing the end of my time in Namibia, I reflect back on this country I've come to treasure.

Solitude. Sand. Sun. Wind. These are the themes of cycling in the Namibian desert. Time with nature. To think. To be. Alone in Africa. Something I'd come to think was impossible. A place free of what I'd come to consider the hassles of Africa: staring kids—and adults, constant requests for money and sweets, a general lack of privacy, and marriage proposals based on my skin color. Some days I cycle for ten hours and see only that many cars.

Here it's just me and my bike, a team after four months on the road. I keep the pedals going round, and my bike carries all my gear on its racks. Occasionally, the sand on the roads gets so deep, I need to walk and push my bike. Usually, though, we roll along through the living desert. Sometimes small trees dot the landscape. Sometimes there are rocky mountains in the distance.

Something has taken me to this magic place. It's my heart, and the true freedom of allowing it to lead me. Now I go where I want and am happy to be there. I do what I want and am happy to be doing it.

I am at peace with the world. And there's no greater happiness, though there is struggle. Struggle into insane winds, and struggle along sandy roads. Though the conditions are not always what I'd want, I am always right where I want to be.

As the sun lowers toward the horizon, I pull off the road and walk through a dark gray, sandy gravel field. I haven't seen any people or vehicles since I turned onto this road three hours ago. Like on my second night in Namibia, free camping off the side of the road, I am glad to have a dark blue tent and to be out of range of passing headlights. But I'm much more relaxed and not spooked by noises in the night. I'm comfortable alone in this country I've come to love. The Namibian desert encourages me, inspires me to keep going, into South Africa.

The Namibian Desert

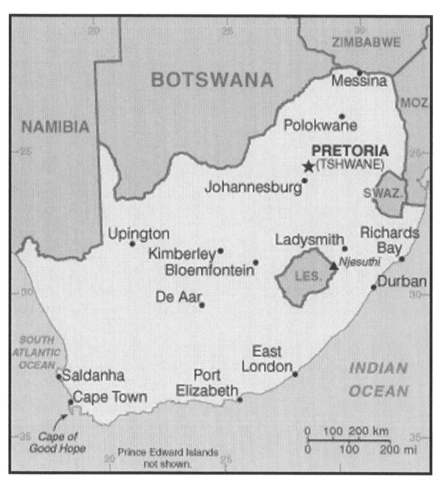

South Africa

chapter twenty-two

Into South Africa

I set off from the rafting camp for the border of the country I hadn't originally included in my tour plan—and the country most Americans think of when I say southern Africa.

South Africa is a country of opposites and contrasts: black and white, first-world development and third-world poverty, apartheid and Nelson Mandela, million-dollar homes and townships of tin shacks without electricity or running water, historical racial tension and current peace, dry barren sections of the interior and lush coastal scenery, mountains and beaches. South Africans themselves are predominantly white Afrikaners or English-speakers, or members of any one of eleven black ethnic groups. The AIDS rate is one of the highest in the world, yet President Mbeki still refuses to admit that HIV causes AIDS. Johannesburg is the rape capital of the world and violent crime is not uncommon, yet this doesn't make the whole country any less safe than many others.

It's a country which, even after living in Lesotho, the country it completely surrounds, is still somewhat of an enigma to me. I lived near it and visited it but don't feel I fully know it. I didn't include South Africa in my original tour proposal because I thought it was too hard to know what areas were safe and didn't want the responsibility of trying to figure this out for a group. But ever since I split up with Paul, whenever I've said to the South Africans I've met that I planned to finish my trip in Namibia, they've replied, "Why not continue into South Africa?" They've all assured me that at least the western part of the country and the Garden Route, along the southeast coast, are generally safe enough. So here I am, continuing my journey more than four months into a planned three-month trip. It's late October now. Back in the States, the Yankees have just lost the World Series to the wild card expansion

Florida Marlins, heralding the onset of a long winter. But here it's mid-spring, probably too late already to see the wildflowers this region is famous for, but maybe I'll catch a glimpse of a few. Like after winters in the States, I long for the fullness of the colors of a spring wildflower season.

I cross into South Africa at its main border post with Namibia, along the Orange River. I've heard lines can get long, so I'm relieved to find none when I arrive. I'm dismayed, though, to see a sign for "Springbok 117 km." This is farther than I expected. I've already come fourteen kilometers, and a 131-kilometer day sounds daunting.

It seems only fitting that the road rises and rises ahead of me. South Africa will be the last country I'll continuously bike into on this trip. Just as I've risen to meet the challenges of this trip so far, now I must rise to a different kind of challenge: being a white traveler in a land where white travelers are much more likely to be targeted for crime than any of the others I've cycled through, and where crime is much more likely to be violent. Yet not riding in South Africa would in a way be like not riding at all in the States. I rode in the States despite violent inner-city housing projects and gangs. I just didn't ride in the projects. Likewise, here I won't bike in the townships. Yet in the U.S., I never worried about crime in rural areas, and here I feel compelled not to venture down just any deserted backroad alone, unsure what—or whom—I may find.

Here, camping off the side of the road is definitely not an option. There's too much chance of running into someone out looking for trouble under the cover of darkness. If there happens to be a farmhouse within sight of the road, it could be an option. But farms here frequently go on for kilometers and kilometers, with the farmhouse kilometers down a dirt road, not conveniently placed for a cyclist to ask for permission to camp.

Heading south on the N7, the main tar road to Cape Town, I climb through hills that look like piles of dirt and rocks. Then there's a stretch of road construction, with rocks across the road, closing one lane. But there's enough space for my bicycle tires between the rocks, and I ride in this closed lane. After the construction, the hills become dotted with small grass-green plants, and I smile when I see small buttercup-yellow flowers along the roadside.

Now that I'm in South Africa, I can't help thinking about the Peace Corps volunteers I know who were targeted as whites and robbed here. Katie and Will had their backpacks grabbed off them at knifepoint in the Johannesburg taxi rank. Tom had his wallet stolen in the Bloemfontein taxi rank. He asked one witness why no one helped him when so many people were around.

She said, "He [the thief] needed it [your money] more than you do." I've also heard about South Africans witnessing carjackings without making any effort to help the victim, afraid that they too will get attacked. It is this inaction that concerns me as much as the crimes themselves. Carjackers don't generally care about bicycles, and I don't plan to go into any taxi ranks. But these tales serve as a reminder that skin color still matters here, and that I need to be alert and cautious.

Skin color means so little to me that years later, I won't even remember the color of everyone I meet only briefly here in South Africa. I'll remember them for their words or actions, but the colors will all blend together in my mind. Because the patterns of earlier in the trip no longer hold and there's no denying that race is important to many here, I identify everyone whose color I do still remember by it for the remainder of my story, and I leave those whose color I've forgotten colorless.

As I near Steinkopf, I'm surprised to see bicycle caution signs along the highway. Somehow these signs reassure me that I do belong here. I stop at the Steinkopf information office. The friendly white woman here gives me a good map of the Northern Cape, as this part of South Africa is known, and information about campsites. I'm disappointed, though not surprised, that there's no campsite here, and I go on. I'm tired on the hills. One hundred-and-thirty-one kilometers is just too far on a mountain bike. Finally, I reach Springbok, stop at a gas station mini-mart and eat ice cream on my way to the caravan park, as campgrounds here are known.

After a shower and pasta dinner, I'm so exhausted and unmotivated to set up my tent that I decide to sleep out in the open without it. I got used to sleeping under the sky on the rafting trip, but I never thought I'd spend a night in South Africa like this. I was so unsure of my safety here when planning this trip that I left South Africa out of my plans. Now I'm sleeping without even the security of a tent. I feel safe around my fellow campers, though I haven't met them.

In town the next morning, I run errands. The white woman at the tourist office is surprised to see a woman cycling alone, but she tells me about other cyclists who've come through the area. I head to an internet cafe and a grocery store. Now that I'm in South Africa, services are more frequent, and I no longer need to carry food and water for days. I'll usually be camping in or near towns. When I'm not, I'll be going through a town at some point during the day. Clouds inspire me to buy chocolate for today's ride. I never even thought about carrying it with me in Namibia. The desert heat would have turned it to chocolate sauce.

The clouds keep the temperature comfortable but are dark enough that they add a dreary overtone to the landscape. Almost fifty kilometers into the ride, I look down and see my front rack break again—in the same place on the other side. I stop and struggle to get a hose clamp around the break and the front fork as I hold my bike upright. I finally get the clamp fastened and start riding. One piece of the rack pulls out of the clamp almost immediately. I try again, thinking that maybe the clamp wasn't tight enough. But it slips again. I try once more, adding a bungee cord. It still doesn't hold. I lean my bike against a guardrail. I'm ready to accept a lift and wish someone would stop and offer me one, but no one does. I'm sick of broken racks.

I analyze the problem: the hose clamp is slipping. I ask myself how can I get it to stop slipping. The thought of duct tape springs into my mind, and I tape the clamp in place. As I nervously start riding again, the rack leans a bit but stays centered enough that it doesn't hit the tire. As I ride through patches of light rain, I gradually relax. The rack holds even as I ride off the tar road onto a dirt road that leads to the Verbe Caravan Park in Kamieskroon.

I arrive to find a chain across the entrance but no closed sign. I look around, wondering what to do. No one is here, not even a worker. It looks well-kept, not rundown or permanently closed and deserted. I notice a woman walking by.

"Is the park open?" I ask her.

"Yes."

"I don't see anyone here. Is it safe for me to camp alone?"

"Yes, because it's right next to the police station."

She points out the shop down the road where I need to register, and I ride there.

"My daughter normally runs the park but she's on the farm now," says the white man at the shop.

"Is it safe for me to stay alone?" I like second opinions.

"Yes, I'll walk back with you to unlock the ablutions."

Though I go with him, I'm still not convinced I'm ready to camp here alone. I'd envisioned other campers around, like in Springbok.

"You can sleep in the kitchen in case it rains," he says.

"That'd be great," I say, looking at the gray clouds hovering above us.

"We've never had anything stolen, but you can't be too careful."

I wonder if perhaps they've also never had a woman camp here alone. It starts raining lightly almost as soon as I get my bike inside. The kitchen is a small, windowless building with a stove, sink, fridge, table and chairs, and a linoleum floor. I spend a cozy evening away from the wind and rain.

As I open the door in the morning, I'm surprised to see and feel a heavy mist that settles onto my skin. The ground is wet from overnight rain. What a change from the Namibian desert. This change in weather allows for a lazy early morning spent relaxing. I no longer feel a desire to ride some kilometers in the cool early morning air. Now, waiting for the mist to clear is more appealing. I'm not naturally an early bird anyway; I simply prefer not to do the bulk of my riding in the burning midday sun, when it is burning.

Knowing I won't see a bike shop for days, I stop at the gas station in town and ask the black woman there if they have a mechanic.

She shakes her head no.

"I'm having a problem with my bike rack. Do you know anyone with a drill and some wire?"

Again she shakes her head no.

"Thanks anyway. Have a good day."

She turns away.

I depart, wondering why she was so unfriendly. Did I somehow offend her or is she just an unhelpful person? Then I realize maybe she doesn't speak English. In southern Namibia and on earlier trips to South Africa, I got so used to interacting with only people who spoke English that I didn't even think about it just now. It's possible she doesn't, though she certainly could've said something in another language.

As the mist burns off, the day becomes sunny. There's greenery on the hills and sometimes mountains in sight. One small tree has round yellow flowers, and some small pink flowering bushes add to the spring colors. My legs are still sore from the long ride into Springbok at first but then they get warmed up and feel better. My rack is holding up okay. I stop and lean my bike against a guardrail just after starting a four-kilometer downhill and take a picnic break at what is probably my prettiest lunch stop of the whole trip. Magenta flowers are surrounded by small shrubs of various shades of green, and blue-green mountains stretch into the pastel blue sky. I eat bread with jam and linger to enjoy this stunning scenery.

I ride into Garies, planning to set up camp in the caravan park and then try to get my rack fixed. Other campers, all blacks whose camps look semipermanent, tell me that no one who works at the park is around. Not wanting to leave my things completely unattended, I change my plan and ride to the gas station, which has a garage. I explain to the white mechanic how the other side of my rack broke in Namibia and was fixed with a drill and some wire, and ask him to do the same on the newly broken side. He agrees to help after he finishes up another repair. He starts to drill but stops and keeps going inside the workshop. I'm concerned that he drilled too big a hole and made the U fragile.

"This piece isn't going to work for you anymore," he says.

I look around at the heaps of metal junk and old tires outside the garage and envision my trip ending here, in Garies, South Africa. Blantyre to Garies doesn't have quite the same ring as Cairo to Cape Town, popular endpoints for long African cycling journeys, or at least for dreamed journeys.

"I'm making you a new one out of this bar." He holds up a rusty iron bar, much thicker than my broken piece.

This is something I love about Africans. They make things work and find ways to fix things. There is always a way.

He bends the bar into a U shape, then welds flat plates to each end to give the tire enough clearance. He drills holes through the flat plates and bolts them to my rack with machine bolts. I think my rack is now sturdier than it has been since it first broke in Namibia. As I'm getting ready to leave and putting my front panniers back on my bike, I hear a woman's voice behind me.

"Do you want to stay with me tonight?"

I turn toward the voice and see a white woman with short gray, curly hair looking at me. Who are you? I think.

"Well, do you have a place to stay?" she asks.

"I'm planning to camp in the caravan park," I reply, though I'm not sure I mean it.

"Come stay with me. My husband is a police officer in town. We like to host visitors." She looks directly at me.

"Is there something wrong with the park?" I'm still not sure about this invitation.

"Yes, it's not a good place. Will you stay with us?"

I hesitate. South Africans are known for their hospitality, but this invitation comes out of nowhere. Not even any small talk has preceded it. I'm sure I've never met her, and she's inviting me to stay in her house. I hear my mom's voice saying, "Never go home with strangers." But I also hear another voice saying, "What if there really is something wrong with the park? You got a bad vibe there on your way into town. You might be a lot safer inside a police officer's house."

"Okay," I say, "and my name's Heather."

The woman introduces herself as Bronwyn and tells me she lives only a few blocks away. She drives slowly so that I can follow her on my bike through what could be a middle-class neighborhood of one-story houses in the U.S. At her house, I meet her husband, potbellied Inspector Vernon with crew-cut brown hair. He tells me that he's working the nightshift but Bronwyn will make me dinner.

"You're welcome to stay in our house as long as you want, and you're not to pay us a dime," he says.

After we chat, he convinces me to stay and rest here tomorrow and even insists that they'll do my laundry with theirs. I feel saved from the caravan park. The timing of my rack breaking seems to have made things work out. I'm reminded of my first night on the road with Paul, when his broken bike led to the invitation to stay at the road camp in Malawi. Again a problem has turned into an opportunity to get to know people and a culture.

Bronwyn makes me rice with canned veggies and potatoes for dinner. White South Africans tend to eat a lot of meat, and cooking vegetarian can be a challenge for them. This meal is neither hearty nor satisfying, but I don't think she knew what to make for me. I feel ungrateful for thinking this, but food is my fuel.

"What would you have done if you'd been in the caravan park tonight?" she asks as we eat sitting at the kitchen table.

"I don't know. Maybe I wouldn't have had any problems. What's wrong with it?" I pick up a piece of bread.

"Hooligans go there late at night. But Vernon always goes by when he's on duty. He would have found you anyway and brought you here."

"Do you have kids?" I ask, trying to lighten the conversation.

"We have a son and a daughter. Our daughter hates her father."

"Why?" I ask, thinking attempt failed.

"Do you want some ketchup?"

I guess she doesn't want to tell me why, and the potatoes are so bland that I accept her offer of ketchup.

Bronwyn keeps asking me what I would have done if I'd been in the caravan park tonight, and I get tired of this. I wonder why she's doing it. Maybe she has an early stage of dementia. She reminds me of my grandmother, who frequently asks the same question three times in a five-minute conversation. Or maybe she thinks that I'm not grateful enough, that I should be profusely thanking her for saving me from the caravan park.

"How do you like living in Garies?" I ask.

"I don't like it, no way, no how. I want to get out of here." She frowns.

"What don't you like?"

"There are too many hooligans here. I'm scared whenever he works the nightshift. I don't want to stay, no way, no how." Her eyes dart around.

I wonder if her fear for me is really fear for herself. She feels so unsafe here, even locked in her own house, that I couldn't possibly have been safe in a tent at the caravan park.

She tells me to sleep as late as I want in the morning and cook my own eggs for breakfast. Later, when I'm in my room getting ready for bed, she knocks on my door. She motions me out into the carpeted hall and turns off the light. She opens the front door and tells me to listen. I hear voices in the street speaking Afrikaans. After a few minutes, she closes the door.

"See, you heard them," she says.

"Yes, but I didn't understand them." They didn't sound threatening.

"They were speaking Afrikaans but you heard they were here and throwing stones," she replies definitely, ending the conversation.

I didn't hear any stone-throwing and wonder if she is paranoid. Maybe she felt a need to show me Garies' bad side after telling me how much she doesn't like it.

At eight a.m., there's a knock on my door. Bronwyn comes in, then Vernon. He offers me tea and brings it to me in bed.

"You are queen in my house," he says.

This is kind of creepy. I think his wife should be the queen in his house. Maybe I shouldn't have agreed to stay an extra day.

After I wake up, I go into the kitchen to make breakfast. When I go to the stove, Bronwyn tells me to have muesli, which she later calls "goat food." I was counting on eggs, but it's her house, so I have muesli. I'm getting the impression that this isn't exactly make-yourself-at-home hospitality.

I continue to get mixed messages from Bronwyn. She complains that I didn't close the ketchup bottle last night. She tells me the stove works, and I wonder if this is her way of saying she wants me to cook. I don't feel so welcome. This isn't turning out to be a relaxing rest day.

After lunch we sit in comfy faded tan living room chairs.

"You can ask me anything," says Vernon.

"How did your life change when apartheid ended?" I ask, not thinking about what it meant to be a policeman, generally known for their repression during the struggle.

During the 1940s and 1950s, the already repressive, ruling white National Party began enacting the laws that together came to be known as apartheid. These laws included requiring blacks to have passes to enter the white cities, setting up puppet authorities to govern blacks in designated ethnically distinct homelands, denying blacks and coloreds voting rights, classifying every South African at birth as "white, Native, or colored," and making any opposition to apartheid a criminal offense. The African National Congress (ANC) protested. During one campaign in the early 50s, eight thousand volunteers broke various apartheid laws and were jailed.

In the mid-50s, at a mass meeting of three thousand black, white, and colored delegates, the Freedom Charter, which came to define ANC policy, was adopted. It stated: "The people shall govern; all national groups shall have equal rights; the people shall share the nation's wealth; the land shall be shared by those who work it; all shall be equal before the law; all shall enjoy equal human rights; there shall be work and security for all; the doors of learning and culture shall be opened; there shall be houses, security, and comfort; and, there shall be peace and friendship." This on a continent that is frequently considered unsophisticated, eight years before the U.S. Civil Rights Act passed into law.

In March of 1960, demonstrators protested the pass laws at police stations. Most dispersed peacefully, but those at the Sharpeville police station, south of Johannesburg, refused to leave. Fighting ensued and the police opened fire. Sixty-nine blacks were killed in what became known as the Sharpeville Massacre, and the struggle against apartheid ramped up several notches as it took a violent turn.

As 1960 progressed, demonstrations included stay-aways from work and public pass burnings. The government declared a state of emergency and the United Nations Security Council responded by passing a resolution calling for it to abandon apartheid. The government instead banned the ANC, making it illegal to be a member, and passed additional repressive laws.

Nelson Mandela declared, "The time comes in the life of any nation when there remain only two choices: submit or fight. That time has now come to South Africa. We shall not submit."

Mandela spearheaded an arm of the ANC dedicated to economic and symbolic acts of sabotage. He and nine other ANC leaders were arrested, found guilty of treason, and given life sentences. As the white government stifled the opposition, the police became an instrument of repression. They enforced bannings, detained prisoners without trials, and made house arrests. Deaths of political prisoners became common.

In 1976, in what became known as the Soweto Uprising, black youths in Soweto protested the imposition of Afrikaans as the medium of instruction in their schools. The police opened fire and killed a thirteen-year-old boy. Protests spread across the country, and 575 people were killed over the course of several months.

For some, being a policeman during apartheid perhaps wasn't so much about public service as it was about defense of the country's status quo from the internal threat of the ANC's demands for equality. Yet I don't think to ask Vernon how old he is or how long he's been a policeman, but my best guess is that it's the only career he's ever known and that he began working in the 1960s or maybe early 1970s. And thus no matter what his intentions were when he joined the police force, defense of apartheid was a cornerstone of his job for most of his career.

"I was a killing machine during the war," he says.

I don't know how to respond to this. I asked how his life changed but now I realize maybe I didn't really want the answer.

I can't reconcile my first impression of him as a friendly, open man who welcomed me into his home with his description of himself as a killing machine. Is this what apartheid did to good people? Or was he more than a cog in the machine? What were and are his beliefs? I'm afraid to ask.

Suddenly I feel awkward about staying here, in the house of a self-described killer. I don't feel at all threatened personally. It was surely only blacks whom he killed and that is in his past. But I feel an inherent contradiction in the idea that my supposed safe haven from the hooligans of the caravan park is a killing machine. I suppose this is the way they used to think here. Not everyone, not even nearly all the whites. But the ones who believed in apartheid, believed in their superiority by virtue of their skin color.

"I want to get a life with my wife and kids back," he continues, with tears in the corners of his eyes. "I know a lot of policemen who went to psychologists through the government programs, but then they are marked and never get promoted again."

I suddenly feel the full impact of apartheid as so much more than the suppression of human rights. I feel the specifics of how it affected individual lives rather than the generalities of how it repressed blacks and coloreds and divided the land and its people. Some of my Peace Corps friends used to say they could feel the tension in the air when they crossed the border from Lesotho to South Africa. Here I feel the tension in one life, and this has a much greater impact on me. I wonder how Vernon's life would be different if he hadn't been called on by his commanding officers to kill blacks in the name of white superiority, if he'd been able to have a more mundane policeman's career pursuing thieves or simply directing traffic. I wonder if Bronwyn would be happier if she and Vernon had met and married in a South Africa that embraced diversity rather than segregation at any cost. I wonder if Vernon's daughter wouldn't hate him in a South Africa with a different past.

"The police got screwed by both sides," Vernon says. "And the police don't have amnesty."

He's referring to the post-apartheid government program forgiving people who confess to their apartheid-related crimes.

I have no more questions for him, at least not any I have the guts to ask, and the conversation shifts to my projected route through South Africa. He asks where I'm heading tomorrow.

"I think Vanrhynsdorp. It's a really long ride, and I'll have to get an early start, but it looks like it's the next town with a caravan park. Do you know if that caravan park is okay?"

"Yes, it's fine."

"Or I could just do a short day and stay in the hotel in Bitterfontein. I'd rather camp, though. I'm used to being outdoors all the time."

"That hotel is closed. You can camp at the police station in Nuwerus."

"How far is that?"

"About eighty-five kilometers."

"That'd be great. Are you sure they'll let me camp there?"

"Yes, definitely, just tell them I sent you."

In the morning, Bronwyn cooks fried eggs for me and offers me muesli, bread, and a banana. Suddenly, now that I'm leaving, she's again the picture of hospitality. I sign their guest book and ask if there's anything I can send them from the U.S. to thank them.

"Just a note telling us that you got back safely. I'd really like to hear from you." Vernon's hospitable side shines through.

He gives me a hug and asks for a kiss. I give him a quick kiss on the cheek.

"You made my day," he exclaims. His slightly creepy side shines through.

Bronwyn also gives me a hug and a kiss, but refuses to be in the photo I ask to take of them.

chapter twenty-three

TO CAPE TOWN

I ride back through Garies to the highway, conscious that my new front rack piece isn't centered over my wheel, though it seems fairly sturdy. The sun already feels hot at eight a.m. All day I ride through dirt-brown hills dotted with greenery. Looking back at one stop, I can see mountains, but there are never any within view while riding.

I'm glad to be out of that house of tension and awkwardness. I keep hearing Bronwyn's voice saying "no way, no how," and thinking about how cranky she was, then feeling bad for not thinking better of one of my hosts. She is the one who invited me into their home. And I still can't reconcile Vernon's description of himself as a "killing machine" with his sensitive, caring side. Another South African enigma.

A headwind picks up and I'm glad to arrive in Nuwerus. I follow signs for the police station and arrive at a fenced-in compound with a security gate and barbed wire along the top of the fence. There are wire cages around the windows. Welcome to South Africa, I think, where not just anybody can walk into a police station. What exactly are they afraid of? Probably riots. The fear must be a remnant of apartheid. Vernon told me crime is now very low in this area.

In 1977, Steve Biko became the forty-sixth political prisoner to die in jail. By this time, new opposition organizations had been created, and they organized a series of boycotts and strikes throughout the 1980s. The police regularly beat and shot unarmed blacks. Businesses started complaining that apartheid wasn't working anymore. Britain condemned the apartheid government, and the U.S. Congress passed the Anti-Apartheid Act, which promoted disinvestment. Ninety U.S. companies closed down their South African operations.

I ring the bell on the gate.

"Yes?" says a voice through an intercom.

"I'm cycling, and Inspector Vernon from Garies said I could camp here tonight."

Buzz. The latch on the gate clicks open. "Someone will be right out," says the voice.

An officer emerges. "We can't let you camp here because we don't really know who you are."

Perhaps they think I'll just go away, but I don't have any other options. "What would you suggest?" I ask.

"There's a hotel in Bitterfontein, fifteen kilometers away," he says.

"That's the direction I came from. I was told it's closed, and it looked that way." I continue, "I'm going towards Vanrhynsdorp. But there's no way I can make it by dark at this point, and I don't think it's safe for me to be riding after dark."

He nods in agreement but doesn't say anything.

"I might have been able to get an earlier start and get there in one really long day, but now it's too late. Inspector Vernon promised you'd let me stay here if I told you he sent me."

"The captain said there's no way we can let anyone camp here. The only way you can stay is if we put you in a cell."

Spending the night in a South African jail cell would put me in the company of Nelson Mandela, perhaps not such a bad place to be.

In the late 1980s, the Premier Pieter Wilem Botha offered to release Mandela if he renounced violence.

Mandela replied, "I am surprised by the conditions the government wants to impose on me. I am not a violent man. It was only when all other forms of resistance were no longer open to us that we turned to armed struggle. Let Botha show that he is different to Malan, Strijdom, and Verwoerd [his predecessors at the helm of white South Africa]. Let him renounce violence. I cherish my own freedom dearly but I care even more for yours."

I've heard of touring cyclists sleeping in jail cells, and it's probably a better option than the side of the road, but I'm not ready to give up on camping here.

"May I speak with him myself?"

"I'll ask." He disappears into the building then returns only a few minutes later.

"I've arranged to have a bed put into a room for you. You can stay, but it's at your own risk."

At my own risk? What a change from Zambia and Botswana, where the police tended to tell me how safe I was camping at their stations.

My room adjoins a small courtroom and looks to be the judge's chambers. In addition to the bed two men bring in, the room includes a basic wooden table and chair, and a small bathroom with only a sink and toilet.

I quickly light my camping stove outside, then bring it inside to cook because I somehow suspect the police would prefer I remain invisible to passersby. I spend the evening journaling in my room and thinking about South Africa.

Mandela was released by Botha's replacement Frederik Wilem De Klerk in 1990. He agreed to suspend the armed struggle in exchange for the government repealing repressive laws and releasing political prisoners. Nonetheless, De Klerk maintained that majority rule wasn't suitable for South Africa because it would lead to the domination of minorities.

Negotiations began, interspersed with mass strikes and violence. In April of 1993, a right-wing gunman assassinated Chris Hani, a popular ANC leader. Fears of civil war dominated the nation. Mandela appealed for calm, holding the nation together, while De Klerk did little. Mandela then called for the setting of an election date. When April 27, 1994 was proposed by the white government, he announced, "the countdown to democracy has begun." Right-wingers continued to protest and threaten civil war, but the election took place peacefully, and millions of South Africans voted for the first time in their lives.

The ANC won a decisive majority and inherited a whole new set of challenges. In a country of thirty-eight million, an estimated six million were unemployed, nine million destitute, ten million had no access to running water, and twenty million didn't have electricity. Sixty percent of adult blacks were illiterate, and fewer than fifteen percent of black children under fourteen years of age went to school.

As I ride away from the police station and continue south the next day, the landscape becomes drier. Brown hills are dotted with grayish-green plants until the plants take over and the hills themselves look grayish-green. Pink flat-topped mountains appear in front of me. As I'm getting into Vanrhynsdorp, a car pulls up next to me.

I hear "Hi, Heather." It's a Dutch couple I met on the rafting trip. Though we weren't close on the trip, it's good to see familiar faces. We buy cool drinks and stand by the side of the road, chatting about our travels since then.

As I continue south through hilly terrain, the traffic gets heavier and I miss the peace of the Namibian desert. At least I have a tailwind here, and momentum from the downhills helps carry me up the next hills. I enter a more populated area, with frequent green lawns and crops growing down in the valleys and sometimes also along the roadside. I see pine trees, which are not native to South Africa, for the first time since Malawi. And unlike the sparse trees of the Namibian desert, the trees at a campsite by a dam in Clanwilliam are lush with full green leaves. Real shade.

The early-morning light angles onto the dam water, a spot to savor. But the air is full of that it's-going-to-be-a-hot-day oppressiveness and there's lots of climbing leaving Clanwilliam, so I don't linger. Clouds move in and keep the temperature comfortable. As I ride through more green, hilly, populated farmland, a headwind hits me. I don't have much energy. Traffic gets on my nerves. I'm just not enjoying the ride today, resisting what is, rather than accepting it as part of the adventure. Trucks grind up the climbs, and I'm enveloped in the stench of diesel fumes. Lots of people honk to say hello, but I don't appreciate it. On the gravel roads of Namibia where I sometimes saw

South African Countryside Along the N7

fewer than fifteen cars a day, it was nice to know there was a friendly person around. But here so many people honk that it's noise pollution.

A white man with a hostile stance gets out of his car at a pullout and motions for me to pull over. Still riding, I ask him why.

"I'm a traffic officer."

"It's hard to tell," I say, stopping. His car is unmarked and he's not wearing a uniform.

"South African law requires bicyclists to pull off the road to allow trucks to pass."

I've never heard this and have trouble believing it, but I admittedly didn't research traffic laws. I don't want to get into a legal debate, so I say, "I've had no problem with trucks. They've been very deferential to me."

"Two trucks back there crashed," he motions back the way I've come from.

"What does this have to do with me?"

"The truck in front was slowing down because you were in the road, and the truck behind hit him."

"If the truck behind hit him, then that driver shouldn't be driving. He wasn't paying enough attention to traffic and should be prepared to stop," my bicycle advocacy background chips in. I can't argue South African law, but I can argue cyclists' rights and traffic safety with anyone.

Sometimes I miss my bike advocacy career. I miss the excitement of working for something I so truly believe in, of seeing bills passed that will improve conditions for cyclists and knowing I helped get them passed, of seeing bike facilities built and programs that I fought for implemented. But I don't miss the fighting and the adversity—and all the people who don't return phone calls. And I especially don't miss working in an office, which is so deadening and disconnecting, whereas cycling and camping is so enlivening and connecting. In some ways, I can't imagine ever going back to working in an office. Yet I am considering it. A friend of a friend has suggested that I meet with someone he knows at the Bicycle Empowerment Network in Cape Town to discuss potential job opportunities with them when I'm there.

"It's for your own safety." His whole body seethes as he gets back in his car and drives away.

I wonder if he really is a traffic cop. Maybe I should have asked to see his badge. Or maybe it's best that I didn't ask in case he, too, was once a killing machine.

After a descent, I turn off the N7 highway at the Citrusdal exit and ride on quiet tar roads through gently rolling farmland to The Baths, a laidback mineral spa resort with a campground. The Cedarberg Mountains are off to my left, the east. These gentle hills are probably the flattest road I've been on since Sossusvlei.

I cook a veggie stir-fry pack for dinner. It's a nice change from my usual pasta dinners. Just like the Reese's ad, I dip a chocolate bar into a jar of peanut butter for dessert.

I spend a rest day at the Baths. My legs and mind both need this break. This is my first genuine rest day since Solitaire just over a month ago. I've had lots of non-biking days (Luederitz and rafting) but was always doing other things. Garies was too mentally draining to be considered a genuine rest day, although it was a no-exercise day.

I relax in the spring-fed hot pool in the early morning, while the air is still cool. Then I return to my campsite, which is right on a stream with a small waterfall. It's relaxing to listen to the water as I read and write, but the traffic makes the experience less idyllic than it sounds and a less-relaxing spot than I'd hoped for. All the Baths campsites are right on the entrance road.

I soak in the hot pool again after dinner and meet a bunch of elderly white folks. One seventy-year-old Afrikaner man who used to hitchhike around South Africa is interested in my trip. His accent is difficult to understand, but he tells me that the Baths is celebrating its one-hundredth birthday today and they are having a party tonight. Maybe this is why there was so much traffic on the entrance road.

Back on the N7, I climb a seven-kilometer pass with a light breeze. The already-bright sun beats down from a cloudless sky, and I need to squint to look down into the verdant valley on my left. The wall of rock out of which the road was carved is on my right. A shoulder makes the traffic less bothersome, but a new problem arises on the descent: swarms of gnats. When I speed downhill, I ride into the gnats. Sort of like anything can be a weapon, anything can hurt if it hits you hard enough, and the impact of these tiny gnats stings my face and arms so much that I have to slow down.

I ride into drier terrain. Wheat fields are prominent through the gently rolling countryside. Mountains linger in the distance off to both the east and west. I appreciate the roadside trees allowing for breaks in the shade.

I arrive in Piketberg during the tourist office's lunch break. I get a cold soda and sit in the shade. A woman comes along and asks me where I'm going.

"Cape Town, but I think I'm going to stay here tonight," I reply.

"There's a campsite up the mountain. The one in town isn't safe for a woman alone," she offers.

"I don't think I'm up for riding up the mountain this afternoon," I say, thinking about how unappealing climbing a mountain in the mid-afternoon sun sounds.

"You should get a room at the Manor. It's just up the street, and it's the cheapest place in town."

I thank her but wait for the office to open. The black woman there confirms that there are the two campsites, saying the one up the mountain is twenty kilometers away.

"Is the one in town safe? It didn't look like anyone was there when I rode by."

"Yes, it's safe. The gate is locked at night, and they haven't had any complaints."

She calls the caretaker. When she gets off the phone, she looks at me with an expression of surprise.

"He doesn't think it's safe for you to stay there tonight. They have ten men staying there and no women."

"What would you recommend?"

"The Manor has the cheapest rooms, but Christina's is almost as cheap, and it's self-catering, so you could cook rather than eat at a restaurant."

"Do they both have ground floor rooms?"

"The Manor's rooms are all on the second floor, but Christina's are on the ground floor."

This cinches my decision. I prefer not to carry my loaded bike up stairs.

I'm the only one staying at Christina's, and so I have the house to myself: kitchen, TV room, bathroom, and my choice of bedrooms. It's a clean, comfortable place. The owner and her workers, all black and whom I meet only briefly, are friendly. I think I made the right choice. After settling in, I walk through town. Though it's a mostly black town, I get amazingly little attention without my bike, and this is a nice change. Planning to make steamed veggies with cheese for dinner, I buy cold food and drinks and put them in the refrigerator, a luxury of sorts when I'm used to camping.

When I depart just after seven the next morning, the sun already feels hot but the air still holds an overnight chill. I turn west off the N7 onto the road to Veldrift, which takes me closer to the coast. As I climb, I ride under gray clouds. The day suddenly seems drearier and cooler. I get chilly on a couple downhills but welcome this after yesterday's heat. There are brown fields on my left, to the south, and hills or small mountains in the background on my right. As I ride along, they fade into the distance. The landscape becomes one of mostly brown farmland with some green and an occasional house. Purple flowers spring up along the roadside and the road flattens out. I arrive in Veldrift feeling good and decide to go on to Vredenberg. On a hot day, I might've stopped but instead I just ride through and take the turn south. The wind picks up. It's mostly a frustratingly slow headwind. I almost regret going on but know I've only got about ten kilometers to go. I ride through Vredenberg, then stop at a pay phone.

I stand looking at the yellow phone with a phone card in my hand and thinking about Peter and Friedline, a white couple whom I met in Luederitz, for probably a full five minutes before picking it up to make the call. Although they insisted I should call and come stay with them whenever I arrived, I hesitate, wondering whether they really, really meant it. I remember them telling me that they did, but I also think about Vernon and Bronwyn and the stress of that visit and wonder if I really want to call. Finally I pick up the phone and dial. It rings several times, and I think they must not be home. Then Friedline answers.

"Hi, it's Heather, the cyclist from Luederitz," I say.

There's a moment's hesitation and I wonder if I've made a mistake by calling.

"Where are you?" she asks.

"I'm here in Vredenberg."

"Oh, we'll come collect you. We were just talking about you last night."

"I can bike. I just need directions."

"No, it's complicated and the road is rough. We'll come collect you."

As I wait, I try to conjure up their faces, which have gotten a little fuzzy in my mind with all the people I've met since them. But ten minutes later, a truck pulls up and I know it is them: Friedline with her dark brown, curled hair brushed off her face, and Peter with his thinning, light brown hair and a slight resemblance to a friendly Jack Nicholson.

"We're so happy you're here," she says, smiling. "You can spend tomorrow resting at our place."

"I hope you like dogs," she continues after we get into the truck. "We have a bunch."

"Sure, I love them," I reply.

"When was it that we met? How long has it taken you to cycle here?"

"Well, it must have been mid-October that I was in Luederitz, so that would make it right around three weeks ago, and I did take a few days off for a rafting trip."

"That's great. You've made great time. It took us a couple days to drive back, and I guess we've been back for a few weeks now. We went to Namibia after our younger son's wedding in early October."

As we approach their one-story house, the yard full of purple wildflowers grabs my attention. Purple is my favorite color, and I know I've come to the right place. It's a spacious, open, airy house with huge living room windows and sliding glass doors that look out to the not-too-distant ocean. A feeling of serenity washes over me. There's not a drop of tension here. And certainly no fear of hooligans.

As we go inside, a couple of Rhodesian Ridgebacks greet me. Another, larger one—perhaps eighty kilograms—and a Jack Russell are napping. I think about my parents' two big dogs, a black lab mix and a golden retriever, as I pet the ridgebacks.

"How long have you lived here?" I ask.

"We bought the property eleven years ago. It had been subdivided for development. We built the house ourselves," says Peter.

"We added a cottage house for Peter's father when we realized that he wasn't happy living alone in the Transvaal. He was locking his door at four o'clock in the afternoon because he was afraid. We finished the house for him before we finished our own," adds Friedline.

"Now our younger son, Friedrich, and his wife, Gedda, live in the cottage house. They're coming over to say hello in a few minutes," she continues.

The younger couple pops in with a burst of energy, the glow of newlyweds, and their two basset hounds, and join us in the living room. Later the older son, young Peter, and his girlfriend come over and bring their dogs. They live down the street and have another two Rhodesian Ridgebacks. All eight dogs frequently spend the days with Friedline while the others are at work.

They are a military family. Both Peters, Friedrich, and Gedda are in the Air Force, and Friedline used to be before she retired. Friedrich and Gedda are about to move to the Transvaal. He's transferring because he wants to get promoted from major to colonel and needs experience working in a different region. They ask lots of questions about my trip, and I ask them about biking into Cape Town. I don't want to accidentally end up in any townships.

"Don't worry," says Peter. "You can just take the R27 all the way into the city. It doesn't go through any bad areas."

Apartheid is over, but the remnants live on. Ten years ago, in 1993, the white American student Amy Biehl was completing a Fulbright project developing voter registration programs in Cape Town when she drove three black colleagues to the Guguletu Township. A mob of black youths attacked the car and dragged her out. Defending her as a "comrade"—a friend of the black struggle—her colleagues yelled at her attackers to stop. They didn't listen. As they threw a brick at her head, then beat and stabbed her, they chanted, "One settler [white person], one bullet." Amy's colleagues took her to a police station, where she died. One of her attackers later testified that he believed it was okay to kill whites because this was the only way blacks would get land back from them.

Mandela governed with the theme of reconciliation, and South Africa has moved past the civil unrest that surrounded the time of Amy Biehl's death. But a peaceful election and transition to a democratic government didn't erase its violent past and the belief that violence, even murder, is sometimes a necessary, or at least acceptable, means to an end. There are still a few, a very few, places in the country where it is simply not safe for whites to walk down the street. These places are some of the townships, which I want to make sure I don't inadvertently end up in, and downtown Johannesburg. The risk today isn't so much getting beaten to death by an angry mob as getting violently robbed—and possibly killed in the process—by a brazen criminal. Randomly biking through Cape Town's townships alone, or even with a group, would cross the line from adventure to extreme risk, a line I choose not to cross, at least not knowingly.

Peter gets out a map and shows me my projected route. He also gives me advice on a back way out of Vredenberg that will keep me off the highway for longer. They offer to let me use their computer for email. I send messages to my best friend and parents, telling them I'm staying with some nice folks and eight dogs. I haven't told them how staying with Vernon and Bronwyn turned out, so it shouldn't worry them that I'm staying with people. I also get a message that a Peace Corps friend, the grandmother of our group, has had a stroke but is recovering.

We all have dinner together: pasta salad, cooked veggies, and tomato-and-cheese toasties (grilled sandwiches), and they also have meat. There's plenty of food, and I don't refuse their offers for seconds. Food cooked with love is so much more nourishing than that cooked with resentment or fear. Everyone here is so friendly, asking me about my trip and telling me about the recent wedding. I feel much more comfortable than I did with Vernon and Bronwyn. This feels more like true hospitality. Maybe just because these are warmer, more open people. I meet their kids, and they cook me meals without grudges. Everyone has their demons and their secrets or issues, but whatever theirs are, I couldn't guess, and their kids certainly don't hate them. I feel great, more upbeat than I've felt in awhile—suddenly revitalized.

I spend the next day relaxing with them. We have tea with biscuits early, then Sunday brunch, do a bit of shopping, then hang around. In the afternoon, we go to the undeveloped beach down the road to look for whales who frequent the shorelines at this time of year. We stand scanning the horizon, with a gentle ocean breeze brushing against our bare arms, and listen to the waves lapping the shore but don't see any whales. Young Peter and his friends are hanging out, so we stop to say hello. Most of their conversation is in Afrikaans, so I'm mostly a bystander, but I don't mind. I'm still somehow absorbing the culture.

Peter drives me into Vredenberg in the morning, and I ride from there feeling strong. Following his map to the town of Langeboon is an adventure, as the reality of the roads isn't as clear as it looks on his map. From there, the terrain is hilly out to West Coast National Park. Once I enter the park, there's less traffic, and more flowers as I go along. I'm now in what's known as the fynbos vegetation zone, one of six floral kingdoms in the world. The plants are mainly evergreen with either hard leaves reminiscent of aloes, or with fine needle-like leaves. Initially, small yellow flowers are dominant, then more pink ones but also some white and purple ones to add variety, proteas among them.

The road through the park takes me west and then north around a lagoon. As I ride north, the ocean is on my left and the lagoon is on my right. I stop at an overlook and get a brief glimpse of a couple whales, which look like splashes in the distance. I'd love to camp in the park, but tent camping isn't allowed. Officially, there are too many snakes, though I haven't seen any. I turn around, leaving the park, and head for Yzerfontein. As I approach the caravan park, I'm dismayed to see a "No tents" sign. I tentatively walk into the office.

"Is there a place for tent camping here?" I ask.

"Sure, we have a cyclist area. Do you want to be in that or have a site with electricity?"

"The cyclist area will be great."

Or so I think. It turns out to be a dreary spot by barbed wire in an otherwise nice park. But I am grateful that I'm not again looking for an alternative to a caravan park, or wondering where I'm going to spend the night.

The next day I ride into Cape Town. At fifty kilometers out, Table Mountain, with its signature flat top, comes into view. The landscape is still rural for another twenty or so kilometers—mostly small green bushes, sometimes flowers, sometimes an ocean view. Then I reach the suburbs, with lots of middle-class to upscale developments and characterless strip shopping malls that could be anywhere in the developed world. Like Peter and Friedline said, there aren't any bad-looking areas.

The R27 surprises me by merging with the N2, the main highway into Cape Town from the north. Unsure where to get off, I stay on it for two exits, with speeding traffic zooming by. I ride through town to Ashanti Backpackers, the only backpackers' hostel in central Cape Town that allows camping. Though it has been such a long journey to get here, my arrival is anti-climactic. Cape Town is the beginning or end of many cyclists' African journeys, but for me, it's a stop along the way, a chance to rest, enjoy a beautiful city I've been to a couple times, and take advantage of big city services. Yet Cape Town symbolizes a successful journey through a land I never thought I'd bike through alone. The thought of ending my trip here and calling it a success crosses my mind. But I still want to see the famous Garden Route. I've heard too much about its beauty not to go when I'm so close and have the time.

When I arrive at Ashanti, I don't even have the energy to go shopping for food, so I get pizza in the smoky bar. I'm exhausted, much more so than I expected to be after only two days since my rest day with Peter and Friedline's family. Maybe because it has been so windy. Maybe because my stomach's bothering me. Maybe I'm just depleted from my long journey so far. I'm so much stronger cycling now than I was at the beginning of this trip back in Malawi. But on some deeper level, I think my body is also ready for a real rest, more than a day or two off the bike. My reserves are gone, yet I'm not ready for my adventure to end.

I spend six days in Cape Town, an eclectic mix of a city that encompasses the northern end of a peninsula that stretches southward into the Atlantic

Ocean. Cape Town is truly dominated by Table Mountain, reaching 1087 meters into the sky. It is a landmark not only for those of us on the ground, but also for seafarers—and how early settlers knew that they were definitely approaching Cape Town and not some other city.

The city center lies just north of the mountain and is a mix of government ministries, museums, shops geared towards both tourists and locals, street markets, backpackers' hostels, hotels, restaurants, internet cafes, and travel agencies offering all sorts of African tours—from two hours in a local township to five weeks on a truck through several countries. Ashanti, where I'm staying, is in a neighborhood known as Gardens, adjacent to the city center. The townships are primarily to the east and southeast of the center. Upscale neighborhoods and suburbs are more generally to the west, stretching out to the ocean. North of the city center lies what is now known as the Waterfront, but that I think of as mostly a sterile, glossy, insular tourist trap of shops. I suppose highly visible security guards help some people feel safe, but it feels so fake to me. Shopping at the Waterfront is not what seeing Africa is about, and I avoid it entirely on this trip. Robben Island, where Mandela was imprisoned for years and now a World Heritage Site where former prisoners work as guides, lies twelve kilometers offshore to the north.

As President, Mandela prioritized reconstruction and development. In addition to averting civil war, his successes included providing over a million homes with running water and electricity within a few years. Yet some who didn't directly benefit still complained about the slow pace of government action. And violence continued to plague the country, with police reporting an average of fifty-two murders a day and one car theft every nine minutes. Mandela left office in 1999, and his Deputy Thabo Mbeki was elected South Africa's second black President.

I run my errands in the Gardens and downtown. I've been having trouble with my tent zipper and I go into a branch of the store that I bought my tent at in Bloemfontein, near Lesotho.

"Can I help you?" asks a cheery, white salesman probably in his twenties.

"Yes, thanks. I have one of your tents. The zipper frequently isn't catching and won't fully zip. I think the tent is still under warranty. Is this something that's covered?

"When did you get it and what kind of tent is it?"

"August of last year. It's a two-man, like that one, except it's blue," I say, pointing to one of their two tents on display.

"Our tents have special self-sealing zippers, so you can't have trouble with the zippers. They'll always work. And if you only got your tent last year, it would have one of these special zippers."

"Well, I did, but it isn't always zipping. I have been camping a lot, so maybe it has gotten more use than expected and is worn out."

"No, it would still be working. That's how our zippers are designed. Let me show you." He walks over to one of the display tents and zips and unzips it several times. But all this shows me is that they don't have a tent with a broken zipper on display.

I tell him mine's not working like that and ask if I can get my tent replaced under warranty, and he replies that they only do warranty replacements by mail and they take several weeks.

"That doesn't work for me. I'm only in town for less than a week, and I need a tent for this trip," I say, trying to hide my frustration. I want him to try to help me, not see me as an angry customer to get rid of, but I'm feeling mired in the bureaucracy of a chain store's systems and not seeing any of the we-can-make-it-work attitude that I love about Africa.

"You could buy a new tent."

"That's not what I want to do. Do you know of anywhere in town that repairs or replaces zippers?" I ask.

"Yes, there's a luggage store that does." He writes down the name and address for me.

I have the luggage store replace my tent zipper. And concerned about wear on my bike, I have a bike shop replace my chain and rear cog cluster and lube the hubs. I buy new tires and get advice on a route out of town from the shop's owner, Shane. He recommends retracing my wheeltracks to leave going north then turning east. I go to a movie and a yoga class, get caught up on email, and talk with my parents and best friend.

I meet with my friend's contacts, Paul and Andrew, about a potential bike job here and quickly determine from our conservation that they don't have a job to offer me—perhaps shorter-term volunteer opportunities after my tour is over, but not a full-time job. Paul mentions that he's applying for a job with a New York City alternative transportation group. I know about this job opening because a friend emailed me about it in case I was interested, and I think about how ironic it would be if they had two applicants currently in

South Africa for a local NYC job. But I can't imagine going back to an office job in the States anytime soon and don't apply. For me, it's either stay here or apply for jobs leading bike tours in the States next year. If I go back, I want to be on the road.

In some ways, I could spend a month in Cape Town, exploring neighborhoods, enjoying its beauty, relaxing in its conveniences, but my legs are getting restless and tell me it's time to move on, to be back on the road. And this time, I listen to my body.

Sculpture originally titled "Sad Angel Spirit," a tribute to the artist's family members lost to both war and AIDS, at Kirstenbosch Botanical Garden in Cape Town

chapter twenty-four

The Holidays in South Africa

Leaving Cape Town, I'm aware the year-end holidays are approaching. I don't have any special plans. I'll just be wherever my bike takes me, perhaps with some help from a bus by New Year's. I'm not sure how long I'll spend getting to and along the Garden Route or whether I'll bike through northeastern South Africa into Swaziland afterwards. I want to see Kruger National Park—South Africa's best known and biggest wildlife park—and Swaziland, then learn to scuba dive in Mozambique before returning to the States. I still don't have a ticket back, but I've started to think that after the Garden Route might be the time to get one. Especially now that it doesn't look like a bike job is going to materialize for me in South Africa, and I don't otherwise have much desire to stay in Africa long-term for now. I'm starting to feel that I'll be done here soon. It'll be time to see family and friends in the States, whom I now have come to believe will never come visit me here.

I have my first flat tire since leaving Spitzkoppe almost two months ago. I stop by the side of the two-lane tar road to fix it, remove my punctured tube, and start to pump up my new tube. My pump breaks as the pumping piece pulls all the way out. It looks like it should screw back in but doesn't. I fiddle with it for a while and just can't get it. I think about trying to get a lift back to Hermanus, where I stayed last night and know there's a bike shop, to buy a new one. I wish some passing vehicle would stop and offer me one, but no one does. Suddenly I look around and realize there are houses within sight, not right along the road but within sight.

I can see the turnoff to DeKelders, where I was thinking about stopping to look for whales. That must be where the houses are. I wonder if I can find someone with a pump that I can borrow to pump up my tire and at least get

Bicycle Scarecrow Along the Way from Cape Town to DeKelders

rolling again. I walk my bike the kilometer-and-a-half or so into DeKelders. I see a sign for a guesthouse and ring the bell. A black woman answers the door.

"Hi. My bicycle pump has broken. Do you by any chance have one I could borrow for just a few minutes?"

"I'm sorry. I don't have one," she says apologetically.

"Do you know anyone around here who does?"

"I don't know, but there's a coffee shop on the ocean. Maybe he'll know. Just go down this street and turn right at the end."

The coffee shop is easy to spot. Cars line both sides of the neighborhood street. A set of wooden stairs leads past a garage up to a casual outdoor seating area overlooking the ocean.

"Excuse me," I say to the busy-looking white man who seems to be in charge, as a waitress with a tray of coffees bustles by. "My bike pump broke, and I was told you might know who has one I could use."

"Sure, I have one. It's just down in the garage. I'll get it for you in a minute. Where's your bike?"

"It's just down the stairs. I'll wait for you there." The coffee shop is crowded, and I don't want to get in the way of his customers.

"There's a bicycle shop in Gansbaai, so you'll be able to get a new one there," he says, handing me the pump.

Gansbaai is only a few kilometers away. How fortuitous that my pump broke here, both where I could borrow one and near a bike shop. I wonder if it is simply a coincidence or if I was meant to come here.

After fixing my tire, I look up and realize two whales are so close to the shore they'd been blocked from my view by the cliff. I follow some other people out on a trail through the fynbos to the cliffs. I sit there awhile, enveloped in the ocean's salty air, and watch six whales. Sometimes they just float around or totally immerse themselves underwater. The ocean looks darker where they submerge. Other times they lobtail—wave their tails above the water—and the calves jump completely out of the water and land with an audible splash. When I return to the cafe, the man offers me a free drink. I sit on the deck, drinking juice, and gazing at the sea and the mountains.

I cycle into Gansbaai in the lingering daylight, follow the tent and caravan signs to the water, and ring the office bell. An older white man answers.

"Where are you from?"

"I'm from the U.S.A. and cycling from Malawi."

"Come here," he yells to someone inside.

His wife and adult daughter come to the door. He asks again, because he wants them to hear my answer.

"Wow. I'd join you if it weren't for my husband," says the daughter. I later learn she meant she'd join me in a car.

"You should sleep in a bed," says the wife. "And we don't want anyone to bother you. We're giving you a chalet for the night as our guest."

The chalet consists of a large room attached to a trailer. It has a large picture window and a glass sliding door with views of the kelpy ocean. The trailer looks like it's the main bedroom, but it's so dreary with only small windows and worn furnishings, I sleep in the main room, warmed by the hospitality of strangers.

After cycling past farmhouses and amber fields, then along the ocean, I arrive at Cape Agulhas—the southernmost spot in Africa, where the Indian and Atlantic Oceans meet. They look like one big ocean, shades of turquoise in the sun. Black rocks separate the oceans from the land, where a plaque marks the spot. I'd had visions of photographing my bike with one wheel in the Indian Ocean and the other wheel in the Atlantic, but now that I'm here I see that this just isn't going to happen. There's no beach, just wet, slippery, uneven black rocks, unsuitable for walking even an unloaded bike over. But even so, just arriving here, at the very end of the African continent, is somehow too significant to just turn around and leave right away. And so I linger, sitting on different rocks and enjoying the ocean view, taking photos, snacking, wandering, and talking with tourists who ask about my trip.

"Have you ridden all the way from northern Africa?" asks one.

"No, there's no good way through all the way from the north. There's too much instability in the central African countries. I've just ridden from Malawi, via Zambia, Botswana, and Namibia," I reply.

"How far is that?"

"Almost 8,000 kilometers."

"8,000 kilometers on a bicycle!" He turns to his wife, "Honey, did you hear that? She has ridden 8,000 kilometers on that bicycle." He turns back to me. "How long did that take?"

"About five months, with lots of days off along the way."

"Are you alone?"

"I am now. I started out with a riding partner. That didn't work out, so we split up in southern Zambia."

"You're brave."

"I never intended to be." I shrug. "I didn't plan this trip alone and probably never would've started it alone. It just turned out this way. I was following my dreams and this is where they took me."

"Good luck and stay safe." They get back in their car and drive away.

For most of this trip, I never expected to travel for this long. Somewhere along the way, I'm unsure where, it became my epic journey. There are some things in life that seem to have an energy of their own, and this trip is now one of them. Although I sometimes think about stopping and the end is now in sight, it's as if I can't make the decision to stop. I'm just too much in travel mode and there's still so much I want to see that the only choice I can really make is to keep going.

"I'm headed to Arniston tomorrow," I say a few hours later to the caretaker as I check into Struisbaai Caravan Park. "What's the gravel road like?"

"I advise people to go around on the tar road, even though it's longer," she says.

"I've heard that the gravel roads here tend to be very bumpy, and also that they might not be safe for a woman cycling alone."

"That's all true."

This is a drag. I feel confined and restricted. I want to get away from the constant motor vehicle traffic on the tar roads that I've felt since leaving Cape Town, but I feel I can't safely do so.

In the evening, alone in the wind, I cook pasta and hope it's safe for me here alone overnight if no other campers show up. It's a pretty spot on the Indian Ocean, with a white sand beach, and I wish I could just appreciate it without any concerns. But somehow I don't feel as safe here in South Africa as I did in Namibia. I don't know how much of this is based simply on South Africa's reputation. It's certainly not based on anything I've heard about this particular area. The community looks well-enough off, with several B&Bs, so it's probably safe. I tell myself I'm probably not the first woman who has ever camped here alone, but I don't really know if this is true. I sleep with my pocketknife handy, though I'm unsure whether I could ever really use it as a weapon.

After an uneventful night, a mostly flat ride on the tar road through more amber fields takes me inland and then back to the shores of the Indian Ocean at Arniston. I check into the South of Africa Backpackers' Resort. I have my own room, which I'm disappointed to see looks like a basic chain hotel room in the U.S. but without a private bathroom. The idea of the luxury that goes with a resort seemed appealing for a Thanksgiving rest day tomorrow, but now that I'm here I'm not so sure. A sterile chain hotel is not exactly someplace I normally think about spending a holiday.

I escape the sterility by exploring the area. I cycle into town looking for a grocery store but find only a mini-mart and a couple fish restaurants. I walk through an area of white-washed fishermen's cottages, and I can feel their residents' eyes on me. I follow a sign to a large cave I'd read about and arrive at the trailhead to find out I'm too late to go today; the cave is accessible only at low tide. I want to send Thanksgiving emails but there's no internet in town. Nothing seems to be going right.

It has only been a week since I left Cape Town, but it feels like a long time since I was there. I haven't had the same energy I had earlier in the trip. Sometimes I wonder if I'm sick or if I've just depleted all my reserves. Or is it just that I'm not as inspired by South Africa as Namibia?

Gray clouds and a light drizzle greet me when I look out the window on Thanksgiving morning. I do yoga in my spacious room, then head downstairs to the all-you-can-eat breakfast buffet, which includes eggs, beans, mushrooms, cheese, toast, fruit salad, juice, and tea. Though I'm used to traveling and eating alone, there's an odd feeling to having a big Thanksgiving meal alone. The tradeoff for all this independence and freedom to do my own thing that I've come to love is the occasional pang of loneliness, and that hits now. I think about my Peace Corps friends with whom I spent the last couple Thanksgivings in Lesotho. Several stayed in Africa to travel after we finished our service and a couple extended and are still in Lesotho, but as far as I know, I'm the only one still traveling in Africa.

Later in the day, I go for a swim in the pool then a sauna. It doesn't exactly feel like Thanksgiving any more. But I call my parents, get their answering machine, and leave them a message. They'd mentioned getting invited to my cousin's, and I wonder if they went there, but I don't have his number with me.

Dad calls me back early the next morning, still late Thanksgiving night in the U.S.

"We went to our new New York house," he says, "We thought it would be nice to spend Thanksgiving there. We love being right on a lake."

It's good to hear his voice before I go on, unreachable again. He fills me in on the family news. My mom isn't feeling well so she went to bed while he stayed up to call. One of my cousins is quitting her job to start her own consulting business.

"And how's your trip going?" he asks.

"Good," I say. "I was just at the southern tip of Africa a couple days ago, and now I'm headed north through eastern South Africa. This area is much more developed, so I'll probably be able to email more regularly."

"That'd be great. You know Mom worries."

Yes, I do, I say, knowing that wishing she wouldn't won't change anything—and wondering whether she's the only one who worries.

Bontebok

I ride away from the Swellendam Backpackers along the purple-flowering jacaranda-lined neighborhood street for a day trip to Bontebok National Park. Once in the park, I cycle part of a scenic loop and see a few bontebok—dark brown and white antelope. The gravel roads of the park are a welcome break from the fast traffic on the tar roads. After a picnic lunch, I hike the aloe hill loop trail without seeing another person. Then I jump in the Breede River and swim in my bike clothes. Cooled off and refreshed, I lay on the grassy riverbank with mountains looming in view. I feel that I've finally found the South Africa I came to see. People are camping here, and I wish I were amongst them. Leaving the park, I see four mid-sized grayish-brown antelope with white cotton-ball tails on a hill off the side of the road. When they see me coming, they run with cantering hooves farther away.

On my way out, I stop at the visitors' center to ask about them.

"Those were gray rheebuck," says the man working there. "But they're shy. I'm surprised you saw them."

"Sometimes it helps to be on a quiet bike."

I arrive at Attawkas Cottage in Oudtshoorn planning to camp. The white owner, Katot, shows me the grassy camping area, which includes a shower heated by paraffin.

"My middle son wants to bike around Africa, and I want you to meet my wife," he suddenly says. "Let's go inside."

"How long are you staying?" his wife, Ilse, asks.

"Two nights."

"Do you want a room for the price of camping? No one has booked it."

"Sure, if you're sure."

"Definitely, today is Wednesday, and it's booked for the weekend. You can have it until then."

They make a space for my bike under the stairs, show me the room, and offer me tea, which I gratefully accept after having cycled in the rain. Again I'm struck by the hospitality of South Africans. This feels more like coming home than to a campground.

A couple of Australians are hanging around waiting for their tent to dry, and we all sit on wooden stools at the kitchen counter.

"Did you go to the Cango Caves?" I ask the Aussies. The limestone caves, thirty-two kilometers from town, are among South Africa's most popular attractions.

"Yes, we went yesterday."

"What did you think?"

"They were alright, but they'd been vandalized a lot."

I frown. I'm planning to bike out to them tomorrow and don't want to be disappointed.

After the Aussies leave, Ilse invites me to join her family for a light lunch—potato salad with sundried tomatoes, bread, boiled eggs, cheese, and avocado. They all ask lots of questions about my trip, and we chat easily, as if we're old friends catching up. I walk into town to an internet cafe. When I return, Ilse tells me she brought me a couple library books by Ann Mustoe, a British woman who has cycled around the world twice. I'm not enthralled by the writing, but so few women do long bicycle tours alone that I'm interested in reading about the experiences of those who do and find myself flipping through them.

"I think I'm going to ride out to the caves tomorrow, but the Australians said they'd been vandalized. Do you think they're still worth seeing?" I ask.

"There has been some vandalism. This is South Africa. But it's not that bad. And definitely do the adventure tour if you go."

"I'm this close. I think I'll go."

"We want to hear more about your trip. I'm making you dinner tonight. Spaghetti with a spinach and feta sauce."

"Wow. That's great. But are you sure? You already made me lunch."

"I know. But I want to. And my other son will be home for dinner. You have to meet him, too."

I feel genuinely welcome with them.

The next day, I ride out to the caves through gently rolling, grassy hillsides and pass a few ostrich farms. This area calls itself the ostrich capital of the world, and several farms offer visitors tours. Some even offer ostrich rides, but I bypass them all.

At the cave, I hesitantly buy a ticket for the adventure tour. I'm not sure I really like the idea of squeezing through small spaces underground. The first part of the tour takes us into large chambers. Van Zyl's Hall is ninety meters long by fifty meters wide by fourteen to eighteen meters high. Many of the stalactites and stalagmites have met in completed columns. Despite my comfort in the large chambers, doubts about the second part of the tour linger in my mind. But once we begin, I feel better. Ducking, then crawling, through the first small passageway, I focus on what I am doing—going forward—and

Stalactites and Stalagmites Meeting in the Cango Caves

never feel that the walls are too tight. Climbing and pulling myself up the aptly named chimney—a three-and-a-half meter shaft only forty-five centimeters wide—is a bit difficult: the walls are slippery and the handholds are tough to find. But knowing that thousands of people have done this before me helps give me confidence, and adrenalin takes over. Crawling into, then sliding out of the postbox—a twenty-seven-centimeter-high slot—is fun. When the ninety-minute tour ends, I'm pumped. I'd do it again if there wasn't a wait.

Although Thanksgiving is not an African holiday, it has also heralded the approaching December holiday season here. I leave Oudtshoorn for the Garden Route—the more expensive part of the country—the day the South African school holidays begin.

The holidays mean more travelers, both South Africans and Europeans, and prices go up. Camping at caravan parks, with the price per site the same for a group of eight with two autos as for a solo cyclist, becomes ridiculously expensive. I start camping at backpackers instead, but I don't always fit in. So many of them are into finding the coolest bars, whereas I'm into getting to bed early so I can get up and enjoy cycling in the coolest part of the day. When I was eighteen and on my first independent trip traveling through Germany with a good friend, I loved meeting the other people staying at the hostels with us and even kept in touch with an Australian woman for a while. But then I was more on the beaten path, traveling by train and seeing what so many others were seeing. Here I'm more on my own path, and I'm not sure I like the transition back to the land of more travelers, where it's easier but also so much less rewarding.

The lush Garden Route may be the most beautiful area of South Africa, with its forests and streams and string of towns right on the warm Indian Ocean. But it has been said, perhaps unfairly, perhaps not, that the Garden Route isn't the real Africa. It is unquestionably geographically part of the continent, and also unquestionably the most Westernized part. Rather than a place to get to know traditional African culture, the Garden Route is more of a playground, with, in addition to its natural beauty, animal parks and all sorts of adventure activities, including paragliding and bungee jumping. It is thus a very different kind of traveling, and traveling here can easily become more about seeing the sights than about getting to know the land and its people.

Cycling along the Garden Route, I get in the habit of staying places for two or three nights and exploring the towns or areas for a day or two. I go to the post office tree in Mossel Bay—where sailors used to leave postcards for other ships to bring back to their families in Europe—on a steam train ride from George, and mountain biking in both Knysna and Harkerville. I have good days and bad days. But the true adventure is gone, and the highs are no longer as high and the lows no longer as low, now that I know where I'll be sleeping at night and that there'll be well-stocked grocery stores and restaurants nearby every night. The roads are never too rough or too sandy. There's so much more here, but also so much less. So much more stuff and development,

Along the Garden Route

but so much less connection. I no longer feel the kindness of strangers. No one stops to ask if I have enough water—very reasonable since it's plentiful. No one invites me into their home or invites me to dinner. It's not that the people aren't friendly; they are. I think it's more that cyclists aren't so unusual here and perhaps people somehow sense that my experiences here aren't so unusual either. I felt so much more connected riding through sparser land than I do here amidst so many more people. Here I am just another tourist, or just another cyclist, or perhaps even just another American, though we are still a bit rare here, especially since 9/11. Or maybe I'm just tired, and it is getting to be time to go home, or at least back to the States. In many ways, Africa feels like home. But my only home here is my tent.

At the Island Vibe Backpackers in Jeffreys Bay, I sit in my tent and watch the ocean's waves rolling in towards the shore below, and I consider staying for Christmas. But there's nothing else to keep me here—it's largely a surfing town and I don't surf—so I decide to go on to Port Elizabeth, where I'll end the continuous cycling portion of my journey.

The area between Port Elizabeth and Durban, farther northeast along the coast, includes the former homeland known as the Transkei, historically home of some of South Africa's most violent ethnic strife and one of the areas where it's just too hard to figure out where I'd probably be safe and where I wouldn't. And so, a little more than six months after setting out from Blantyre with Paul, I spend Christmas Eve cycling into Port Elizabeth. I hope I'm not making a mistake by planning to spend Christmas in a city rather than in nature.

The old road to Port Elizabeth, which I choose over the newer but busier N2, leaves Jeffreys Bay staying closer to the coast. Once I leave the developed area of J Bay, I cycle past short green plants—still fynbos, I think—on both sides of the road. Views of the ocean off to my right come and go. There's more traffic than I expect on this old road, but at least it's quieter than the N2. A tailwind suddenly picks up. I feel good about this ride and wonder if maybe I should've waited and made it a Christmas ride but then I might not have had a tailwind. The road crosses the N2, goes by a river, then starts climbing—one last pass of the trip. It takes me through some mountains, becomes gently rolling, then starts climbing again as it stays inland. I see only a few people all along the route, but they give friendly waves, and this adds to my feeling good about this being my last ride. Flattening out, the road takes me through farmlands then to the outskirts of the city.

The wind picks up as I get closer to, then go through, the city. It's still mostly a tailwind and pushes me along. I stop to eat a sandwich along the side of the road, and it's hard to stay stopped, as the wind tries to push me forward. As I go on, the wind makes it hard to stop at traffic lights. I turn towards a backpackers—and more into the wind. As I ride along the harbor, I wonder if I should dip my front wheel into the Indian Ocean here, at the end of my trip. The wind is so strong I have to stop a couple times. So much for an easy end to my ride, I think. A mega gust of wind batters me, and I know I can't ride through it. As I pull into two adjacent empty parking places and grab my brakes, the wind proves to be stronger than they are and blows me into the curb. I start to tip over and catch my bike. But the wind is too strong and my bike is too heavy, and the momentum of my falling bike and the wind push me over. I fall onto the sidewalk. What an unceremonious ending to the trip. I stand up, looking around and glad no one seems to have noticed. I try to wait out the wind, but it gets worse. I spot a sign to the backpackers at the next intersection. When there's a bit of a lull, I cycle to the intersection, turn right, and am stopped by the wind, a fierce headwind that is impossible to cycle into. So I walk two blocks, adding to the unceremonious end to my trip. Then I turn right again and cycle the last half block to the backpackers, so at least I ride the very end.

"Have been you biking in this wind? It's almost gale force," asks the young white man working at Kings Beach Backpackers.

"Yes, I didn't know it was going to get this strong."

"It wasn't forecast."

"Well, it was a great tailwind for awhile, but then I had to turn into it to get here."

"So, where are you headed on that bike?"

"Here. I'm done." There's something about verbalizing the end of my trip that makes it more real, and suddenly I realize that I really am done. But I also realize that he's waiting for more of an answer and so I continue, "I've been cycling around southern Africa for the past six months, but I'm going to get the Baz Bus from here because I don't want to ride through the Transkei."

"That's probably a good idea."

"Could I get a camping spot with a windbreak?"

"Sure, I'll show you. And my name's David."

He shows me the camping area in the grassy backyard and suggests a corner next to a cement wall and a small building. After I set up my tent, he returns with a mattress, sheet, and pillow.

"I want you to be comfortable."

"Wow. Thanks."

It does make my tent comfy. I wonder if this is a Christmas special, or a cyclist special.

On Christmas morning, I set out for a bike ride along the coast. With dark clouds dominating the sky, I ride along the ocean going south from the city. There's pleasantly little traffic and some other cyclists out riding. A sign for Cape Recife inspires me to turn off the main road, though I don't know where it will take me. An open gate leads to a quiet road through a nature reserve. Fynbos grows in the sand on both sides of the road. There are sporadic ocean views as the road winds closer to, then farther from, the shore, ending at a small lighthouse. I try the door, but it's locked. A car is parked, but I don't see any people. I sit on a wall by a gate, listening to the sea, enjoying the peace and solitude, looking at the ocean and the sand, and thinking about the end of my trip.

The end of a long bicycle journey is frequently anti-climactic, as the trip is never really about the end but rather about the journey. The endpoint itself is sometimes almost arbitrary, determined at least partially by transport options. This trip was never about getting to Port Elizabeth; it was about seeing and getting to know more of southern Africa. And so getting to Port Elizabeth brings me almost as much sadness as joy. Sadness that I don't feel safe to just keep biking all the way to Swaziland from here, but joy that I've come this far, so much farther than I'd originally planned. Sadness that the end of my travels is near, but joy that I've been able to live my dream for the past six months. Sadness that I'll be giving up the rhythm of day-to-day bike touring, which has brought me so much joy. And along with all this sadness and joy is a deep gratitude to all the wonderful people I've met along the way and all the warmth and connection I've felt.

I think back to boarding the ferry in Kazangula, Zambia without Paul and going into Botswana alone, figuring that I'd see how it went. At the time I needed to at least give biking alone a shot to keep my dream from dying. At the time I resented Paul for no longer wanting to do the trip we agreed on and for being so critical. But now that all seems so far away to have almost been a different trip. I needed Paul to have a riding partner to start this trip with, but even more I needed to be rid of him to travel at my own pace, to feel truly safe alone in Africa, to shed the Peace Corps culture of fear—those two years of being told things weren't safe, and to grow in a way that only solo travel allows. I needed to be on my own for this trip to become epic, to learn true independence and the freedom of traveling with no schedule, and because it was the only way to erase any doubts about whether I could indeed do it on my own.

Since I'm still thinking about biking from north of Durban to Swaziland, I'm not even sure how "over" this trip really is, but Port Elizabeth will always be an ending of sorts. I ride back to the backpackers, simply thinking that it doesn't feel like Christmas biking in shorts and short sleeves. Though this is my third Christmas in southern Africa, a part of me still feels that Christmas should be cold and ideally snowy.

In the afternoon I join my fellow travelers for a Christmas feast at the backpackers. There are about fifteen of us, making for a comfortable crowd. Just like Christmases back in the States, there's so much food, it's easy to be a vegetarian, even a very hungry cycling one. I devour butternut squash, roast potatoes, canned veggies with melted cheese, rice, pasta salad, and green salad. Then we have cake, ice cream, and fruit cocktail for dessert. I'm glad I'm at a backpackers that made such a Christmas feast, rather than alone at a caravan park for the holiday.

After eating, I call my parents, then play Trivial Pursuit with some of the other folks. Rain keeps me from a planned late-afternoon walk on the beach, but eventually I go out in the evening anyway, figuring I may never be on the Indian Ocean for Christmas again. So I walk the few blocks to the beach, take off my Tevas, and wade into the ocean. Cool waves splash on my shins as my feet submerge below the graying surface. No one else is around, and it's somehow spooky, alone in a South African city after dark. I return to the backpackers and hang my wet hat and jacket over my bike, which rests inside in a hallway. I spend the rest of the evening relaxing in a comfy chair, reading my guidebook and writing.

I take my bike on the Baz Bus—a backpackers' bus that takes both bicycles and surfboards—and a shuttle to Hogsback, in the mountains. I love the fresh mountain air and lakes and waterfalls, but insanely steep hills everywhere always seem to inspire me to cut planned long rides short. After a few days,

Hogsback

I'm ready to move on and bus to Cintsa, back on the coast, renowned for its beaches and apparently also, unbeknownst to me, a New Year's Eve hotspot. I try to register at Buccaneers Backpackers' Lodge.

"Don't you have a reservation?" scowls the black receptionist.

"No, sorry, I've been traveling for six months and haven't generally needed them."

She frowns at me. I'm not sure whether she doesn't believe me or just doesn't care. To her, I am not an adventurous bicyclist but rather an irresponsible backpacker. Now that I'm traveling by bus, my trip has changed—not merely in my primary form of transportation but also in people's perceptions of me.

I'm about to tell her that if she really doesn't have space for one more tent, I'll go check out the place down the road when she says, "We can squeeze you in, but you won't have a platform for your tent."

Naturally, I agree. I don't think my tent would know what to do if it was set up on a platform. I find my appointed spot, in a small clearing amongst dusty bushes with a few other tents. A couple tents have their doors open, and I can see their occupants inside, either sleeping or passed out. This place definitely has that party sort of aura, and I wonder if I've made a mistake by coming here and should've stayed in Hogsback.

The next day is New Year's Eve. I go for a fifty-kilometer bike ride and appreciate the gentler hills, then I walk along the beach. I figure I'll skip the party that night but eventually I wander over. I almost immediately see a couple whom I met in Hogsback. I hang out with them for a while and end up staying through the midnight countdown and singing of Auld Lang Syne. As I walk back to my tent, I surprise myself by realizing that the party was fun. I've gotten so used to traveling on my own, where going out at night generally wasn't an option, that I'd forgotten it could be fun.

chapter twenty-five

IS IT SAFE?

Durban reminds me more of New York City than any other African city I've visited. The city center area is full of street vendors set up selling things—anything from crafts to food—people going about their business, and regular shops. It bustles with life, traffic noise, and chattering voices in an assortment of languages I don't always recognize. Tourists and touristy things are much less visible than in NYC, but there's otherwise a similar, though less rushed, feeling. Here I'm shopping for a plane ticket back to the States, getting photos developed, and deciding whether to bike again from Ballito, north of here, or continue taking the bus. I stop in at two bike shops.

"Ride north or inland, though that's hilly," says a white man at the first, "but not south." Durban is on the coast, so riding east is not an option.

"I'm planning to go north but unsure about going all the way to Swaziland," I say.

"It's safe all the way," he says, "I know a couple guys who have done it."

It's great to hear this reassurance, affirming the emails I'd gotten from the backpackers I had contacted. Yet I notice that he says "a couple guys." Perhaps he's less familiar with some of the black African cultures than I am. A couple of guys having done something here doesn't make it safe for a woman alone. But it also doesn't make it unsafe, and it seems I am almost back to where I was in Namibia, trailblazing a path that women alone haven't taken, trying to determine which advice is relevant to my situation, and knowing that the only way to truly know if I will be safe is to do it. I'm not looking for any guarantees, but rather trying to determine whether the risk is too great.

I emailed a few backpackers in Zululand and Swaziland. Of the three I heard back from, one said this area is safe and people who tell me it's not are paranoid. Another recommended not riding because of open spaces, long distances, and that there has been some robbery. The third recommended busing to avoid the heat. While it might seem this is a 2-1 vote against my riding, I am heartened by the lack of mention of violence. Heat, open spaces, and long distances I can handle. It is the mention of robbery that makes me wary, though, and hence my continued research.

"I'm not so sure about northern Zululand [the area closer to Swaziland]," says a white man at the second bike shop. "People might see an opportunity to get your bike."

I remain silent, wanting to see if he has any more to say, trying to evaluate how real the prospects of robbery are.

"But you'll probably be okay."

I must not look reassured as he continues, "I wonder about taking a more inland route, though." He pulls out a map and starts pointing to alternative routes.

"So it's the N2 you're concerned about?" I ask.

"Yeah, there are some areas where there aren't many people around, and I wouldn't want you to run into the wrong ones." He looks up from the map to me.

"The inland route looks a lot longer, and I really want to see St. Lucia. Do you think it's safe that far, or is that already northern Zululand?" I peer at his map.

"It's north of St. Lucia that I'm not sure about. The N2 gets a lot more deserted up there. There are always trucks going all the way to Swaziland, though." Deserted here doesn't mean the same thing it did in Namibia, I quickly realize.

"Thanks for all your advice." This clinches my decision to ride at least to St. Lucia and to continue considering riding all the way to Swazi depending on what else I hear.

The Baz Bus is supposed to pick me up at my Durban backpackers between 7:30 and 8:30 a.m., but it doesn't arrive until 9:30. A little less than an hour later, the driver drops me off south of Ballito. By the time I start cycling, it feels late to be starting a ninety-kilometer ride in the summer. But my only other option is staying in Ballito tonight and this doesn't have any appeal. My ride begins along the ocean, and my legs are happy to be touring again after the past two weeks of traveling more by bus. My bike is again heavier—laden with all of my gear rather than just the water, snacks, and tools I bring on day rides—but it feels right. This is simply how I'm supposed to be traveling. It's not about material comfort and ease, it's about adventure, and most importantly, about what comforts and eases my soul. And this is it: being out in the world and traveling under my own power, rather than enclosed in a motor vehicle.

The R102 road takes me a bit inland, still paralleling the coast but away from any ocean breezes. The temperature easily creeps over 30 degrees Celsius—almost 90° Fahrenheit. An Indian truck driver stops.

"Where are you going?" he asks.

"Swaziland."

"Do you want a lift?"

"No, thanks." It's easy to turn him down. Despite the heat, I have absolutely no desire to take a lift.

Riding more in the heat of the day after a later-than-planned start, the scorching heat drains me and thus also my water bottles, as I feel a continuous need to sip their now-warm, almost hot water. Three liters no longer feels like enough for the day, even knowing I'll get to a backpackers for the night. My map tells me that there aren't any more towns until Gingindlovu, where I'm headed. I think about rationing my water. But suddenly, about an hour later, I spy a roadside store up ahead. As I near, I realize it's not actually on the highway but on a parallel village road. I wheel my bike across dried grass and mud to the store, and suddenly I am fully back in black Africa. The store is a modest building covered with paint that has been fading and chipping for years. It fits perfectly into the less developed part of the continent—and of South Africa. The customers loitering outside, the few shopping inside, and the workers are all black.

As I stand inside, I notice that my arms are soaked with sweat. There's no juice for sale here, so I buy two cold sodas, savoring the rush of cool air as I remove them from the refrigerated display and glad to have found any cold liquid. I sip them standing outside by my bike, in the shade of the store. The other people hanging around are friendly but don't seem to speak much English other than greetings. Then another black man comes along.

"Where are you going?" he asks.

"Swaziland," I say, "though I think I'm going to take the bus from St. Lucia."

He translates his question into Zulu for the others. One woman looks shocked by my answer. I wonder what she'd think if she knew how far I'd come, but he doesn't ask this.

"You're brave," he says

"Why do you say that?" Somehow hearing that I'm brave from a black here in South Africa is very different from hearing it from a fellow traveler. Or from a white South African. I can't write this off as either simple admiration or potential prejudice. It could just be the cultural women-don't-do-those-things-here, but it didn't sound like it, and so I ask, "Has something happened here?"

"I don't want to scare you." He looks away. Just like the cyclist Paul and I met our first day on the road when we were lost, this man does not want to, will not, culturally almost cannot, give me bad news or tell me something he thinks I don't really want to hear.

I know this conversation is over, and suddenly I feel an urgent need to get back on the road, like this stop was a mistake. Although I felt welcome a minute ago and don't feel at all threatened by anyone here, I now somehow don't belong in their world here. I am safe at their store, but am I truly safe in their world here? At least relatively?

Safety is never guaranteed. Even safety at home is an illusion. Kids get assaulted at home. People fall down stairs at home. People die in their sleep at home. Cars crash. Hurricanes come ashore. Freeway bridges collapse. Violent crime isn't exactly uncommon is the U.S. But where is the invisible line between relative safety and high risk? It's a lot less clear here.

I return my empty glass soda bottles to the clerk inside and wheel my bike back to the tar road. I wonder if I should rethink this part of the trip. It no longer feels good, and I could buy another bus ticket in Gingindlovu rather than waiting to St. Lucia. At least I leave the shop feeling much better about my water supply and cooled off.

Arriving in Gingindlovu, which means "swallower of the elephant" in Zulu, I turn onto a smooth, packed dirt road to Inyezane Backpackers. It takes me through rolling green hillsides, but I'm tired and thus happy to see their huge handwritten sign at the turnoff. Inyezane, which means "the place where magical things happen," is set amid sugar cane fields. I register for a camping spot. As I start to set up my tent, the French woman who runs the place comes over.

"I wasn't thinking properly," she says, "You can stay in a dorm for the price of camping. Twenty more people won't suddenly show up tonight."

She shows me to a traditional mud-dung building. Like the others here, it's round. Some have rectangular extensions off one side. All are painted with murals, both inside and outside. Mine has six beds, but I'm the only occupant. The bed covers are also painted, and there's animal décor that somehow strikes me as hippy-ish. I bring my bike inside and unpack and hang my tent up to dry. Despite today's heat, my tent is still wet from being packed with morning dew as I prepared for the potentially early bus this morning. After the New Year's crowds south of Durban and the city itself, it's wonderful to finally be somewhere quiet. I'm immediately comfortable here.

When I wake up in the morning, I don't want to leave, so I don't. I spend the day absorbing the quiet, writing, and doing a bit of yoga. I deal with the store man's comments by not dealing with them. I am now in a place that feels safe—and so I push them away. Until I'm getting ready to ride the next morning, and they come back to me. I wonder what he would've said if he culturally could have been completely open with me.

"I've heard mixed things about how safe it is from here to Swaziland," I say to the woman who runs Inyezane. "I'm not sure I'm going to bike the whole way."

"It's safe," she replies.

"All the way to Swaziland?"

"Yes, and Zululand is generally safe for tourists. When there is violence, it's between tribes, not directed at foreigners. But lots of white South Africans are paranoid and will tell you it's not safe."

Leaving Inyezane, I turn inland to Eshowe, only a short thirty-kilometer ride away, and known for its Zulu Museum and culture. As I climb the tar road through the shimmering green hillsides, I relax. There's a totally different feeling here than at that store. I don't know how much of this is the reassurance I've gotten and how much is being well-rested, but I simply just feel better about riding again.

Two days later, after fixing a broken rack and then making only my second wrong turn of the entire trip earlier in the day, I am weary as I turn onto the tree-lined N2 tar road outside Empangeni. The sun is high in the midday sky, and it's another sweltering day with temperatures easily in the 30s Celsius—nearing and possibly passing 100 degrees Fahrenheit. Although the N2 is a main highway, it feels deserted here. I'm looking for a spot to take a lunch break. Instinct tells me "this isn't it" as I notice a couple black guys walking along the side of the road. I remind myself that it's not unusual for people to walk along the side of the road in Africa. It's frequently their only transportation, but something about these two bugs me. When I was lost earlier, the police recommended this road as safer than my originally planned route. Being here on their advice is reassuring. I don't know that I'm not very far from a township.

I glance back at the guys once and am not surprised that they are still walking along back there. They're both slender, wearing T-shirts and long pants, and probably in their late teens or early twenties. I'm cycling slowly climbing a slight hill, and my energy is low.

Something causes me to glance back again. They're right behind me and running after me. I will later wonder if I had an air of vulnerability around me, or if I crossed that invisible line. I accelerate, but it's too late. It's almost unreal. After all this time of being safe, suddenly I am not. One of them lunges at me and grabs my shirt. He drags me off my bike and it falls over. I stare at it with a combination of presence and disbelief. He pulls me to the ground and jumps around me. I sit facing the two of them with my bike lying between us. The taller one starts to pick it up.

Less than two weeks ago, Joan Didion wrote of her husband's death, "Life changes in the instant." And in this instant, my newfound freedom is gone—and my story has a different ending than the one I'd already written.

Instinct kicks in. No matter what you might think you know you'd do when attacked, you never really know until it happens. There are too many nuances to almost any situation. I simply react rather than think about what to do. Thinking takes time, and time changes a situation. These guys aren't waiting for me to think about how to react. I start to get up, lean towards my bike, flail at them and shout, "Just let me keep my journals." And this is when I realize what is most important to me. So much of my other stuff is essentially just stuff, perhaps essential for this journey but nonetheless replaceable, but my journals are not. I blurt it out in English without thinking. I probably should've tried Sesotho. Even if they didn't understand, hearing me speak an African language might have made them hesitate. It likely would've at least surprised them to hear a white person yell at them in what is considered one of South Africa's black languages. But again, I am not thinking and my reaction comes in English.

They don't visibly understand my English words and instead react to my action of reaching towards my bike by slashing at my arm with a piece of metal that looks like a tool handle. It's not sharp, but anything can be a weapon if it's used violently. Would all this be happening if I were black? It's hard to say, there are so few black travelers here, and no bicycle tourists whom I have seen. Would it be happening if I were a man? The unfortunate reality, which I must admit, is that it is less likely. As my arm is stabbed, I fall backward. Pain emanates from my arm. But I instinctively reach again. Where does this need to resist come from? I think it is a subtle, or perhaps not so subtle, need to show my attackers that I am not a weak woman, not someone simply to be pushed aside. No matter what they may get away with today, the message I want to send on behalf of the women of Africa is that it's not okay to push us around or violently attack us and it is not our place simply to take it passively. For more than two-and-a-half years now I've understood that to many, my reactions have represented white Americans whether I've wanted them to or not. Today I hope that my actions represent the strength of women everywhere. Resistance isn't so much about me as about what kind of world I believe in.

He slashes at me again and demands, "Bag." I remember that I'm wearing a green and black waistpack, as I have been this entire trip. He grabs at it, and I'm surprised that he snatches it away from me without my feeling a thing. I thought it was still buckled securely to my waist, but it must have come loose when I fell. The other one picks up my bike and they dash off into the roadside woods together.

Instinct pulls me to my feet. I am vaguely aware that my arm is bleeding, but adrenalin masks the pain. After I stand up, my first thought is, "It really happened. What now?" "Run after them" briefly flashes across my mind, but this is where logic kicks in and I know that would be foolish.

My biggest fear for the trip has come true, after I'd been reassured by months of safety. But although I'd feared this in an abstract sort of way of knowing it was possible, I never once thought about what to do if it actually happened. And now my only option is to be present with this situation that a part of me never believed that I would ever really be in. There is no contingency plan.

There's not a sound in the air, neither bird nor vehicle nor human. As my new reality and aloneness on the side of the highway settle in, my thoughts turn to the plane ticket in my moneybelt, hidden under my clothes. After traveling without a ticket for almost seven months, I bought it last week—for the middle of next month. I wonder if I can change it to tomorrow. I could keep traveling without my bike, but needing to replace all my gear feels daunting. After more than two-and-a-half years of not being ready to return to the States, suddenly I'm ready. Right now. Where's the transporter? I just want to be somewhere else, anywhere else. And again I am reminded that

I am a privileged American. I can choose to leave not only the scene of the crime or the town but also the entire country and continent. I have options that most Africans simply do not.

My wallet is still in my back pocket, and most of my money and passport are with my plane ticket in my moneybelt. The thieves could come back if they realize they didn't get it. I feel extremely vulnerable standing here, and I realize that I need to get out of here. The world around me comes back into focus. I'd been seeing only the thieves then their absence, the space they disappeared into. Now I look around. There's a big truck stopped way up the road. It wasn't there when I was cycling. Did the driver witness the attack and have enough concern to stop but not the courage to get out and try to help? Did he think the thieves had a gun and not want to get shot?

As I debate whether to walk up the road to the truck and ask for help, I see a white pickup truck approaching. I flag it down. Considering South Africans' reputation for not helping strangers in crime situations, I'm amazed that it slows, pulls over, and stops. As soon as I tell them what happened, the passenger, a young, agile black man probably in his early twenties, runs off into the woods and disappears out of sight.

The Indian driver, an older man with short, graying black hair and maybe in his fifties, says, "He is trying to get your bike and things back."

"That would be wonderful." Wow, I think.

Another pickup stops. The first driver asks the second if he has a cell phone. He does and phones for an ambulance. I stand holding my arm above my head and pressing on the largest wound to stop the bleeding.

"The people here," he starts to say, shaking his head. "I'm so upset that this happened."

"I talked to a bunch of people and the consensus was that this was a safe enough area," I say.

"I'm not sure I'd say that about Natal. But this should not have happened. What is wrong with our country?"

The passenger who chased after my assailants returns with my bike and most of my panniers still attached to it. I am shocked to see my bike again and stare at it. He runs back into the woods and returns with my one missing pannier. I thank him profusely.

"Is it okay if I give you something?" I ask.

He nods affirmatively, and I pull a 50-rand bill out of my pocket and hand it to him. It's worth less than ten U.S. dollars, but money goes a lot farther here and it is an appropriate gesture of appreciation.

He smiles and bows. He doesn't speak much English, and I don't think to ask the driver to translate, so I will never know exactly how he got my things back. I suspect the thieves abandoned them when they saw someone giving chase. They probably didn't have any idea how heavy my bike was and how difficult it would be to drag through the woods. It might have been easier to escape if they'd ridden it. But as it is, they escape with my waistpack.

I think about the camera and film in it. The camera itself is insured, but the film with my most recent photos is irreplaceable. I'm grateful that I sent a bunch of photos back to the States from Durban last week, but I also think of the ones of Hogsback and Inyezane on the just finished roll in my now-gone waistpack.

The first driver is in a hurry and asks the second if he can wait with me. He agrees. Frustrated that an ambulance has not shown up yet, he soon calls again and screams into the phone when it seems he is not being understood. He complains about people answering the South African equivalent of 911 not being able to understand either English or Afrikaans.

"Sit down," he tells me, motioning to the back of his pickup.

"I'm okay," I say.

"No, sit down," he insists.

I look down at myself and am shocked to see that I'm covered in blood. It blends into my purple shirt and purple-blue shorts very well but doesn't blend into my white skin at all. I sit down.

Neither the police nor an ambulance shows up, and the driver grows impatient.

"I don't have all day to wait. I'll take you to Richards Bay myself. I have a friend there."

"Why don't you just take me to the police in Empangeni? It's closer, and we're probably in their jurisdiction." Richards Bay is thirty kilometers away.

"No, my friend will help you. It's better to go to her."

During the drive to Richards Bay, the adrenalin begins to dissipate and I become aware of a throbbing pain in my arm.

"Hang on," says the driver.

I think he's worried that I may pass out, but I never feel like I'm going to. I'm more concerned about getting stuck out in Richards Bay after he drops me off. It's not on the route of the Baz Bus and the only way out by road is back past near where I was just attacked.

We arrive at the computer store where his friend, a white woman with curly blonde hair, works. She agrees to take me to the clinic and the police. The driver unloads my bike and gear from the back of his pickup and puts them inside the store.

The clinic is right around the corner in the same shopping center, but I hesitate. I am a bloody mess, but I think my wounds could probably heal themselves. I can hear Peace Corps saying, "Don't go to local clinics unless it's a life-threatening emergency." But this is South Africa, not Lesotho. South Africa had one of the best health care systems in the world during apartheid—for whites only. The standards may have slipped some since the end of apartheid, but Peace Corps/Lesotho frequently sent volunteers to South Africa for medical treatment. But would this clinic meet Peace Corps standards?

I walk in, not sure I won't walk right back out again, depending on what I find. Looking around, though, I feel comfortable, at least as comfortable as I ever do in doctors' offices. People sit waiting in chairs on both sides of a large reception desk in a sparkly, clean lobby. This looks like a first-world clinic, not a developing-world clinic. We tell the receptionist what happened. She says they'll treat me under the friend's insurance, since she's in their system.

"But, I have insurance," I say.

"Oh, it takes too long for the system to approve a new patient. We'll just use hers."

Even after all my time in Africa, this still sounds strange to me, but the friend is nodding in agreement.

A nurse soon calls us into a very sterile-looking examining room, and she helps me wash my wounds.

A doctor comes in and asks, "Can you move all your fingers?"

As I wiggle them for him, I realize I hadn't thought to check.

Examining my wounds, he says, "Two of these need stitches."

The pain in my arm and hours without food are making me a bit faint, and it's difficult to focus my thoughts, but I make the association, "Stitches. Needles. Southern Africa. AIDS. I should just let myself bleed." I'm afraid I don't have the stamina to argue, so I'm relieved when he produces an unopened, sterile suture kit.

After a local anesthesia is applied, I watch the needle I can't feel entering and exiting my arm. As he's stitching, another wound reopens and it won't stop bleeding, so it gets stitched too. The doctor writes me a prescription for some painkillers, which he says they can fill at their pharmacy here, and he asks if there's anything else. I wash the blood off my legs.

At the police station, a pudgy black officer tells us we should've gone to Empangeni but he'll take the report and fax it to them. It's a slow process. His English is limited, and I need to keep simplifying my description whenever he looks at me quizzically. Finally, we're just about finished.

"Contact phone number?" he asks.

The only one I can give him is my parents' in the States, but I'm hesitant because they don't yet know about the attack, and I know a call from the South African police would terrify them.

"You can tell them now. I'll call for you."

I don't really feel like telling them right now, but I give him their number in the U.S. He looks confused. I explain how to make an international call to him: first dial South Africa's international dialing code, 09, then the U.S. country code, 1, then the number in the States. He tries this. The call doesn't go through.

"This is the wrong number," he insists.

But it isn't. I've called the States many times from South Africa's pay phones. He asks his colleagues for help. None of them can get the call to go through. I lose the faint hope I had of getting my camera back. How can police who can't even make phone calls solve crimes? I'm witnessing South Africa's reportedly ineffectual police force firsthand.

The police officer asks me to sign a report.

Gripping a pen sounds painful. "I'll try," I say.

He gives me a disbelieving stoic look, "Can't you write?"

I wonder if we should have come here first, before the clinic. Would walking in covered with blood rather than a bandaged arm have produced a more sympathetic reaction? I manage to sign the report with a signature that doesn't look like my own, but I need to pry my fingers away from the pen to let go of it with a jolt of pain. I get a copy of the police report, and we return to the store.

No more offers of help are forthcoming, and I know I'm on my own from here. I ask for a recommendation for a nearby hotel. I struggle to get ready. I have trouble re-attaching my one free pannier to my bike, as I find out it's difficult to either pull or leverage with my right arm. I put on my helmet and have to buckle it with my left hand.

I wheel my bike out the door and begin the ride to the hotel. The first time I need to slow down, I instinctively grab both brake levers. Pain radiates through my right arm, making braking unbearable. The reality of my tour being over begins to sink in. If I can't use both brakes, I can't ride distances. Thoughts of possibly touring in Swaziland evaporate. The searing pain in my arm cannot match the emotional pain in my heart.

"What happened to you?" asks the black hotel receptionist, as I walk in awkwardly, both opening the door and pushing my bike with my unbandaged left arm and perhaps grimacing in pain.

I tell her.

"That's not surprising. I'd never ride a bike around here. People here get robbed all the time."

I'm so glad the driver brought me to welcoming Richards Bay. I'm only looking for a hotel room, not sympathy, but a bit of sensitivity would've been nice. But she is in the reality of her world of living in an unsafe area, where danger is perhaps taken for granted. My world of having been safe traveling for almost seven months and in southern Africa for more than two-and-a-half years now simply doesn't mesh with her world. In her world, I am crazy, and she can't sympathize with what she cannot comprehend, what she is unwilling to try to comprehend.

"Could I get a ground floor room?" I ask

"They haven't been cleaned yet. We had a big group here last night. I'll give you a first floor room."

"Is there an elevator?"

"No."

"I'll wait until a ground floor room is clean then. I can't carry my bike up stairs now." It is very difficult to admit being unable to do something, especially something I have done many times on other trips.

"You can leave your bike in the luggage room."

"I'd really like to keep it with me." It was just stolen; it's definitely staying locked in my room with me tonight.

"Then you'll have to carry it up the stairs."

"My arm is in a lot of pain. I'd really like a ground floor room. When will one be clean?"

"I don't know. And I can't have you waiting around. It might be awhile. I can only give you a first floor room."

I give up, take my room key, and wheel my bike over to the stairs. I stand staring at the steps, taking a moment to fully comprehend the need to get my bike and gear up them to apparent safety. There's no way I have the strength to lift my loaded bike at this moment, so I painfully remove each pannier, pausing after each one to let the throbbing in my arm subside. I leave them at the base of the stairs while I carry my bike up. I make two more trips, carrying two panniers in my left hand each time. Once all my gear is in my sterile hotel room with me, I collapse onto the bed, feeling as if I've used my last bit of energy and strength. The air-conditioned air seeps into my skin and cools it. As I lie on the bed, I am struck by the realization that this is when traveling alone sucks: when you're hurt and there's no one to take care of you. If I don't go out and get myself some food, I don't eat. And not only am I very hungry but I also don't want to take the painkillers on an empty stomach.

I shower and wash my hair one-handed, then put on some clean—or at least not bloody—clothes and walk to a nearby grocery store. Doing these things, I realize that I can and I no longer want a transporter to take me back to the States, away from Richards Bay perhaps, but not back to the States. I can't leave Africa now. I have to bike again here. Not tomorrow or probably not the next day, and not here in Richards Bay or Empangeni, but here in Africa, even South Africa. The thieves may have gotten away with my camera, but I won't let them take away my courage, too. I won't give them that much control of my life.

chapter twenty-six

My Journey is Over

Tomorrow I will call the backpackers that I was on my way to today and get a ride there. I will bus to St. Lucia then Swaziland. Cycling in a nature preserve in Swaziland, I will want to focus on the zebras and antelope, but every bump in the dirt roads will send vibrations to my wounds. I will stop frequently for breaks from the pain, but I will not initially be tempted to return to the tar roads. At Sondzela Backpackers inside the nature preserve, people will frequently ask me what happened to my bandaged arm. As I tell them again and again, I will lose hope for South Africa.

I'd felt the warmth of the country. And, now, I've also felt its wrath. And the challenge for its future, in this post-apartheid world. Will the warmth and hospitality of its people and the warmth of its countryside, and the magical place where two oceans meet become South Africa's legacy? Or will the evil specters of crime and AIDS crush all that is good here and leave South Africa a beaten land? Can the land of Mandela and Tutu that persevered through decades of oppression to become a shining example of acceptance in theory, with a constitution that embraces gay rights and recognizes eleven official languages, become a shining example of acceptance in reality? This is its challenge.

How much time does it take to overcome ingrained racial hatred? It has been forty years since the U.S. passed our Civil Rights Act, and we are certainly not free from racial tension. It has only been ten years since the official end of apartheid in South Africa. Not enough time for heartfelt belief systems to truly shift. But more than enough time for frustration to build. Frustration at the stark inequalities in the average socioeconomic levels of blacks and whites. Frustration about the lack of running water and electricity and the poor schools that still plague many black areas. Frustration about the lack of opportunities that drives many to crime.

This land, this region, has become my home. At the beginning of this trip when people asked me where home was, I answered "Lesotho." Somewhere along the way, my answer changed to "my tent." Never the U.S.—a place I'll go back to, a place that was once home and will be again, but doesn't feel like it now. And now, like my adopted home, I too must heal.

As planned, I will learn to scuba dive in Mozambique then return to South Africa for a safari in Kruger National Park. I will bike again in South Africa before I will step onto the plane in Johannesburg that will take me back to the States almost eight months after Elias asked to meet Paul on the plane to Blantyre. I will not let fear cut my trip short. But my bicycle journey will already be over.

epilogue
FIVE YEARS LATER

The question I get most often these days from people who know the story of my trip is "how did you heal?" The only answer that feels true to me, though I know it is not satisfying to some, is that I simply went on and never considered not healing an option. I believe that in every moment, we have a choice. And in a way, I made the same decision after the attack, though I didn't realize it then, that I made after splitting with Paul: to go on and see how it goes, not to let adversity stop me from living the life I want to lead, and to overcome challenges rather than succumbing to them.

So although it was emotionally difficult to get back on my bike, and braking was still physically painful, I did it. Likewise about traveling by bus with my bike and gear and only one arm strong enough to carry things. And learning to scuba dive and discovering that I didn't have the strength to pull myself back up over the side of the boat and needing to ask for help. I did these things because I chose to go on leading the life I wanted to lead, at least as much as I could with the circumstances I faced.

In doing so, I did not blame Africa for the attack. I recognized that one bad thing happened to me in three years there, and that worse could have happened if I'd stayed in the States the whole time. If I could turn back time and not do this trip knowing how it ends, I wouldn't. I wouldn't give up having met all the people I met, seeing all the places I saw, feeling all the connection I felt. I wouldn't give up having experienced the rhythm of life on the road without a schedule and the taste of true freedom that solo bike travel gave me. I wouldn't give up having followed my dream.

APPENDIX
Metric Conversions

1 kilometer = 0.62 mile
2 kilometers = 1.24 miles
3 kilometers = 1.86 miles
4 kilometers = 2.48 miles
5 kilometers = 3.10 miles
6 kilometers = 3.72 miles
7 kilometers = 4.34 miles
8 kilometers = 4.96 miles
9 kilometers = 5.58 miles
10 kilometers = 6.20 miles
20 kilometers = 12.4 miles
30 kilometers = 18.6 miles
40 kilometers = 24.8 miles
50 kilometers = 31.0 miles
60 kilometers = 37.2 miles
70 kilometers = 43.4 miles
80 kilometers = 49.6 miles
90 kilometers = 55.8 miles
100 kilometers = 62.0 miles
140 kilometers = 86.8 miles
2100 kilometers = 1302 miles
5000 kilometers = 3100 miles
8000 kilometers = 4960 miles

1 meter = 3.28 feet
5 meters = 16.4 feet
10 meters = 32.8 feet
20 meters = 65.6 feet
50 meters = 164 feet
100 meters = 328 feet
500 meters = 1640 feet
1200 meters = 3936 feet
1800 meters = 5904 feet
3000 meters = 9840 feet

1 centimeter = 0.39 inches

1 kilogram = 2.1 pounds

1 liter = 0.26 U.S. gallons
6 liters = 1.56 U.S. gallons

GRATITUDE

My friend Jennifer Krassy Peiler invited me on the NYC Five Boro Bike Tour back when we were in high school. Her parents, Margaret and Joseph Krassy, brought us to the Central Jersey Bike Club rides that got me interested in long day rides.

The leaders of a couple of the first multi-day bike tours I ever went on, Jim Creighton on the Maine Coast and Ken Blum from Seattle to San Francisco, inspired me to keep touring.

My high school expository writing teacher Mr. Joe Sepede made writing fun—and funny. In his memory, only a few of the "leeches that infest the pond of prose" can be found in this book. May he rest in peace.

My writing teacher Ana Maria Spagna taught me the craft of writing memoir and offered invaluable insights and encouragement and always stayed positive. My classmates who became friends Laura Berning, Reggie LeVerrier, Carole Ann Moleti, and Thelma Zirkelbach cared enough to keep reading long after class was over and offered many suggestions and much support.

Dorothy Castille, Rich Olken, and Wally Werner read the complete manuscript and provided feedback and encouragement.

Lise Marinelli, Kristyn Friske, and the folks at Windy City Publishers believed in my story. Dawn Wiebe turned my manuscript into this beautiful book.

My parents, Karen and Tucker Andersen, provided the writing space.

Numerous other friends, family, and sometimes even strangers offered support.

My riding partner whom I've been calling Paul made this trip possible.

All the Africans and fellow travelers I met along the way made my story what it is.

Sometimes the most eloquent thing to say is simply thank you. Thank you all.

For Heather Andersen, bicycling is a lifestyle. It's recreation, transportation, vacation, and sometimes work. A traveler at heart, she has cycled on six continents and in all fifty states. She's led three tours across the U.S. and biked over 100,000 lifetime miles. Before starting her African journey, she served as a Peace Corps volunteer in the tiny country of Lesotho.

www.bicyclingheather.com